Add

THE STRUGGLE
FOR
NEW CHINA

THE STRUGGLE
FOR
NEW CHINA

SOONG CHING LING

FOREIGN LANGUAGES PRESS
PEKING 1953

First Edition . . . . October, 1952
Second Printing . . . . . . September, 1953

Printed in the People's Republic of China

To
The Korean People's Army
and
The Chinese People's Volunteers

Valiant Protectors of the
People's Cause

PUBLISHER'S NOTE

This volume is a collection, in five parts, of the articles, speeches and statements of Soong Ching Ling (Mme. Sun Yat-sen) made between July 1927 and July 1952.

Part One consists of eleven articles and statements written by Soong Ching Ling to condemn the betrayal of the revolution by the Kuomintang in 1927. All except one appeared in the period between July and September 1927.

To understand this period it is necessary to know its historical background.

In 1924, the Kuomintang had been reorganized into a popular revolutionary alliance. This reorganization was carried out under the personal guidance of Sun Yat-sen, leader and founder of that party. Influenced by the October Socialist Revolution in Russia, Sun Yat-sen, at the suggestion of the Chinese Communist Party, changed the line he had pursued in the Chinese revolution since 1911. He laid down an anti-imperialist, anti-feudal revolutionary program and the "three great policies" of alliance with the Soviet Union, cooperation with the Chinese Communist Party and advancing the interests of the workers and peasants. The Kuomintang, under his leadership, was then reorganized into a party of a mass character, an alliance of the workers, the peasants, the petty-bourgeoisie and the bourgeoisie.

Thanks to these reforms, the Kuomintang acquired new vitality. Together with the Chinese Communist Party it fought the First Revolutionary War of 1924-27, smashed the power of the warlords south of the Yangtze River and brought about a nationwide revolutionary upsurge. But, just at this time, the right wing of the Kuomintang, headed by Chiang Kai-shek, openly turned against the revolutionary principles of Sun Yat-sen and surrendered to imperialism and feudalism. Beginning with the slaughter of workers in Shanghai on April 12, 1927, Chiang Kai-shek launched large-scale attacks and bloody massacres against the Chinese Communists and the revolutionary people. On July 15, 1927, the Kuomintang in Wuhan similarly betrayed the revolution. Thenceforward, as Chairman Mao Tse-tung has stated in *On Coalition Government,* "Civil war took the place of unity, dictatorship took the place of democracy, and a dark China took the place of a bright China."

On the eve of the open betrayal by the "left wing" of Kuomintang in Wuhan the author issued her *Statement in Protest against the Violation of Sun Yat-sen's Revolutionary Principles and Policies,* in which she strongly denounced those who had betrayed Sun Yat-sen. With firm belief in the cause of the revolution, she broke with the renegades, and, in August, 1927, visited Sun Yat-sen's great and trusted revolutionary friend—the Soviet Union. Previous to her visit, she published her *Statement Before Leaving for Moscow*. During her Soviet tour she published a series of statements and articles including: *Greetings to Soviet Women; For Smena, Official Organ of the Communist Youth; Statement Issued in Moscow; Statement Issued Through Tass; Statement Issued Through Leningrad Pravda; Women and Revolution;* and *Youth and Revolution,* in which she expressed her unfailing loyalty to the three great policies of Sun Yat-sen.

After the invasion of Northeast China by Japanese imperialism on September 18, 1931 the author issued, in Shanghai, an article entitled *The Kuomintang Is No Longer a Political Power,* in which she made a ruthless exposure of the true character of Chiang Kai-shek's Kuomintang regime and the various shameless activities it conducted at that time of national crisis. Here she expressed her firm belief that the revolution would advance in the right direction and attain final victory.

Part Two consists of four statements, all written in protest against the Kuomintang's fascist reign of terror and in defence of the rights of the people.

After 1927, the reactionary Chiang Kai-shek regime carried on a large-scale civil war against the Communists. At the same time, it massacred revolutionary workers, peasants and intellectuals in the cities and villages throughout the country. Its slogan was: "Rather kill a hundred persons by mistake than let one suspect escape". To strengthen his reactionary rule, Chiang Kai-shek painstakingly imitated the fascists in Europe. In November, 1929, he established a secret service later known as the Bureau of Investigation and Statistics of the Central Committee of the Kuomintang. In March, 1932, another secret service agency was set up, later known as the Bureau of Investigation and Statistics of the Military Affairs Commission. These two secret services employed large numbers of traitors, gangsters, bandits, army racketeers and renegades, and unscrupulously destroyed the freedom and rights of the people. The people's patriotic democratic movement was subjected to severe suppression. According to a report published in a Shanghai newspaper at the time, no fewer than 140,000 Communist Party members and progressives were arbitrarily put to death in the three-month period of August-October, 1930, alone.

During these black days the author took up as her main task the struggle to safeguard human rights and to free revolutionaries who had been imprisoned. Together with Lu Hsun, Yang Chuan and others, she sponsored the China League for Civil Rights. The League not only gave direct help to revolutionaries in Chiang Kai-shek's prisons by providing them with legal defence or securing their release, but also dealt severe blows to Chiang Kai-shek's reactionary reign of terror. During this period the author published the following articles and statements: *The Tasks of the China League for Civil Rights; Address to the Press at a Meeting of the China League for Civil Rights;* and *To the Chinese People—A Call to Rally for the*

Protection of Imprisoned Revolutionaries. In these articles the author exposed the criminal brutality of Chiang Kai-shek's secret service agencies and pointed out the importance of giving aid to their victims. In the article *A Denunciation of the Persecution of German Progressives and the Jewish People* the author, in behalf of the League, protested against the terrorist rule of the Hitlerite gangsters in Germany.

Part Three comprises eight statements and articles which expressed the author's views on the political situation arising out of Japan's invasion of China in 1931, and reflects the efforts she made, in this situation, to promote the unity of the Chinese people in resisting Japanese aggression.

After the Japanese invaded the Northeast in the Shenyang (Mukden) Incident of September 18, 1931, the Chiang Kai-shek government persisted in carrying on its civil war against the Communist Party and against the people while carrying on a non-resistance policy in the face of the aggressive acts of the Japanese imperialists. After 1933, it abandoned Jehol Province and accepted the unreasonable demand of the Japanese invaders which converted North China into a "special area", which gave rise to an unprecedented national crisis. At the time of the September 18 "Incident", the Communist Party of China was the first to call for armed resistance to the Japanese invaders.

In January 1933, the Chinese Workers' and Peasants' Red Army declared its willingness to stop fighting with all other troops throughout the country on the condition that Japanese aggression be resisted and democracy safeguarded. However, Chiang Kai-shek's attacks on the Red Army, as well as on the revolutionary people of China, became ever more brutal.

The Japanese imperialist invasion and the traitorous policy of the Chiang Kai-shek government aroused the opposition of the Chinese people throughout the country and caused a split within the Kuomintang itself. The patriotic, democratic movement of the people arose on a nation-wide scale. In January, 1932, the Kuomintang 19th Route Army led by Chen Mingshu, Chiang Kuang-nai, Tsai Ting-kai and others, defied Chiang Kai-shek's orders and valiantly resisted the attack of the invading Japanese army on Shanghai. In November 1933, the 19th Route Army was forced to move to Fukien Province, and its leaders, in conjunction with Li Chi-shen and others, formed a people's government in opposition to Chiang Kai-shek. After signing an armistice agreement with the Chinese Red Army which was led by the Communist Party, they entered into an anti-Japanese alliance with it. In May 1933, Feng Yu-hsiang, Fang Chen-wu and others in cooperation with the Communists, organized the Anti-Japanese People's Allied Army in Chahar Province, and launched their famous resistance struggle against Japanese aggression in Northern Chahar.

The demand of the people of China for national unity in resisting Japanese aggression reached a climax in 1935. This was due to the new Japanese menace to North China which arose in that year and also to the fact that the Communist Party had formally put forward a proposal for establishing an anti-Japanese national united front. Following the "December Ninth" Movement of 1935, ushered in by great student demonstrations in Peking, the Communist Party, in spite of the brutal oppression of the Chiang Kai-shek government, led the entire people in unfolding a wide-spread "National Salvation Movement". In December, 1936, influenced by the proposal of the Communist Party calling for resistance to Japanese aggression, the Kuomintang's Northeastern Army under Chang Hsueh-liang and its Northwestern Army under Yang Hu-cheng staged the "Sian Incident" and detained Chiang Kai-shek, compelling him to accept the demand that the civil war be stopped and Japanese aggression resisted.

During this period, the author fought for the realization of the anti-Japanese national united front and for the democratic rights of the people. She also led the work of the Shanghai Preparatory Committee for the Far Eastern Conference of the World Committee against Imperialist War. In her article *Workers of China, Unite!* the author pointed out that "the Chiang Kai-shek Government cannot unite China, cannot lead the national revolutionary war of the armed people against imperialism, cannot give land to the peasants", that only when the workers, peasants, students and the Volunteers already fighting Japan in Northeast China were united could China be liberated. *Against Imperialist War* was a statement issued by the author in her capacity as the Chairman of the Far Eastern Committee of the World Committee Against Imperialist War. *China's Freedom and the Fight against War* was a speech she delivered at that meeting in denunciation of the war plots of the imperialists. In it, she also elaborated the progressive character of the people's war of liberation, pointing out that "reactionary force can be met only by revolutionary force" and that, not-withstanding the weakness of the armed force of the Chinese people, "armies are not the only decisive factor, ideas also have a role to play". As a consequence, she pointed out, the Chinese People's War of Resistance to Japanese Aggression would certainly be won.

In her *Statement Upon the Assassination of Yang Chuan* and *Statement Issued Upon the Arrest of the 'Seven Gentlemen',* the author again sharply denounced the criminal activities of Chiang Kai-shek's secret service organizations in infringing upon the people's rights. In February 1937, the author delivered her speech *'Follow the Will of Sun Yat-sen'* at the Third Plenary Session of the Central Committee of the Kuo-mintang in Nanking at which she, together with Feng Yu-hsiang and Ho Hsiang-ning, proposed to restore the three great policies of Sun Yat-sen: that is, alliance with the Soviet Union, cooperation with the Communist Party and advancing the interests of the workers and peasants.

In *Confucianism and Modern China,* the author criticized Chiang Kai-shek's reactionary ideology of reviving ancient traditions, and suggested that Chiang Kai-shek's "New Life Movement" be replaced by a movement to better the people's livelihood. In *China Unconquerable* she demanded that the Kuomintang unite with all anti-Japanese forces, pointing out that the economic and social structure of Japan could not sustain a war of long duration against the Chinese people and that the idea that "China is too weak to resist Japan" was therefore incorrect.

Part Four comprises twelve articles and statements which, with the exception of the last two, were published during the War of Resistance to Japanese Aggression.

During the War of Resistance, the Kuomintang reactionaries pursued a criminal policy of passive resistance to Japan and active opposition to the Communist Party and the people. Chiang Kai-shek massed his troops to blockade the Shensi-Kansu-Ningsia Border Region and other Liberated Areas and repeatedly attacked the Eighth Route and New Fourth Armies, which were reorganized from the Chinese Workers' and Peasants' Red Army and are now called the People's Liberation Army. In the areas under Kuomintang rule, Chiang Kai-shek suppressed patriotic democratic movements and deprived the people of their freedom and civil rights.

As a result, the battlefields in the Liberated Areas became the main battlefields in the War of Resistance. Before March, 1944, the invading Japanese army deployed 64 per cent of its total force on the battlefields in the Liberated Areas, while only 36 per cent were used on the battlefields in Kuomintang-held areas. Because of the strenuous efforts made by the Chinese Communist Party together with the Eighth Route and New Fourth Armies during the War of Resistance, because of the people's struggle for continued resistance to Japan and against surrender, because of their persistence in unity and their opposition to splitting, because of their continued struggle for progress and against retrogression, and because of the aid rendered by the victory of the international anti-fascist forces led by the Soviet Union, the War of Resistance to Japanese Aggression ended in ultimate victory.

The author was an active supporter and propagandist for the Chinese People's War of Resistance to Japanese Aggression. In *On the Reconciliation,* published in November, 1937, she took a stand of active support for the Anti-Japanese National United Front. In her *Letter to the British Labor Party Delegates Conducting a Survey of Japanese Aggression in China,* she pointed out that the aggressive war which the Japanese imperialists were waging in China was a menace to the capitalist countries, particularly Great Britain. In *Two 'Octobers',* she expressed her hope that a new democratic republic would be established during the War of Resistance to Japanese Aggression.

In June 1938, the author sponsored the organization of the China Defence League (which was renamed the China Welfare Fund after 1942 and the China Welfare Institute after 1950), and devoted herself to wartime medical work and child-welfare work. In her articles and statements published between 1939 and 1944: *An Appeal for Aid to Partisan Fighters; When China Wins; China Needs More Democracy; The Chinese Women's Fight for Freedom; Open Letter to Friends of China Abroad;* and *A Message to American Workers,* she gave an authentic picture of China's War of Resistance to Japanese Aggression, voiced the will of the Chinese people and exposed the conspiracy of the Kuomintang reactionaries to undermine unity in the War of Resistance.

These articles and statements served as a great motive force in promoting the work of the China

Defence League which was led by the author herself. Through the League, many foreign friends of China donated large quantities of medical supplies to aid the Eighth Route and New Fourth Armies which were carrying on an extremely difficult struggle behind the enemy lines. Moreover, many foreign friends organized medical teams and, through the intermediacy of the China Defence League, themselves went to the anti-Japanese bases established by the Eighth Route and New Fourth Armies to participate in war-time medical work. The International Peace Hospital set up by Dr. Norman Bethune of Canada was an example of the work carried out by such medical teams.

After the surrender of Japan in 1945, Chiang Kai-shek, supported by a new aggressor, American imperialism, continued his anti-Communist and anti-popular civil war. The author published in 1946 her *Statement Urging Coalition Government* and *An Appeal to the American People to Stop their Government from Militarily Aiding the Kuomintang.* In this paper, she defined her attitude towards the anti-Communist plot of American imperialism and Chiang Kai-shek. In her *Message to the World Federation of Democratic Youth* in 1948, she called for opposition to another world war, and expressed her confidence in the defence of world peace.

Part Five consists of twenty-seven articles, speeches and statements, all published after 1949.

From 1947 to 1949, the Chinese Communist Party and the Chinese People's Liberation Army, supported by the people all over the country, finally overthrew the criminal rule of Chiang Kai-shek's Kuomintang.

Under the leadership of the Chinese Communist Party, the Chinese People's Political Consultative Conference composed of delegates representing the Communist Party, various democratic parties, people's organizations, the different areas, the People's Liberation Army, various national minorities, the overseas Chinese and other patriotic and democratic elements was held in September 1949. The conference adopted the Common Program of the Chinese People's Political Consultative Conference and elected the Central People's Government of the People's Republic of China. The establishment of the people's democratic state power in China began a great historical period for the Chinese people.

At the Chinese People's Political Consultative Conference the author was elected Vice-Chairman of the Central People's Government. Following its establishment the Central People's Government led the people of the whole country in carrying out the gigantic work of economic and cultural reform and reconstruction, the land reform and the suppression of counter-revolutionary activity. Sun Yat-sen's ideal, a new China—independent, free and democratic, became a reality at last—26 years after his death. Long enslaved by imperialism and feudalism, the Chinese people for the first time saw a boundless, bright future before their Motherland.

In June 1950, American imperialism launched a war of aggression against the Democratic People's Republic of Korea. This war presented a serious menace to China's borders and to world peace. The Chinese people started a campaign to resist American aggres-

sion, aid Korea, protect their homes and safeguard their
country, organizing volunteers to aid Korea on the
battlefield. This just action of the Chinese people has
struck a heavy blow at the American aggressors and
helped powerfully to guarantee the peace of the world.

In 1951, because of the contributions the author
had made, over a long period, to the cause of world
peace, she was awarded the International Stalin Prize
for the Promotion of Peace Among Nations.

During 1949-1952, the author not only took part
in the work of the government but also entered on new
activities for the people's welfare in the movement to
defend peace. She visited many cities and rural districts of new China, and published more articles in this
period than in any other. Her writings in praise of
the new China include: *A Monumental Period; Speech
at the People's Political Consultative Conference;
China's Children in the Liberation Struggle; Shanghai's
New Day Has Dawned; New China's First Year; A
Message from New China; New China Forges Ahead;
The Inspiration of the Chinese People;* and *China's
Great Mass Movements.*

Her other articles were devoted to the defence of
world peace. Among these were: *On Sino-Soviet
Friendship; Speech Made at the Inaugural Conference
of the Sino-Soviet Friendship Association; A Salute to
Stalin on the Occasion of the Celebration of the 32nd
Anniversary of the October Revolution; Speech to the
Asian Women's Conference; For Stalin's Birthday; The
Difference Between Soviet and American Foreign
Policies; China Signs for World Peace; Friendship Is*

CONTENTS

PREFACE i

PART I

THE STRUGGLE AGAINST COUNTER-REVOLUTION

PART II

THE STRUGGLE FOR CIVIL LIBERTIES

PART III

THE STRUGGLE FOR INTERNAL UNITY AND AGAINST IMPERIALIST WARS

PART IV

THE STRUGGLE TO PRESERVE UNITY AND TO DEFEAT FASCISM

PART V

THE LIBERATION AND PEOPLE'S GOVERNMENT

4

PREFACE

The Chinese Revolution has been a long, arduous and complicated struggle for which much has been sacrificed. It has criss-crossed the lives of all, weaving back and forth, up and down our land.

The victory of the Chinese Revolution is one of the most momentous events in history, ranking in importance with the great October Socialist Revolution. Together they have developed many valuable lessons in the fight for national independence and world security. Together they have shaped the world of the future, that time when the thought of man exploiting man will be relegated to the history books and the atom bomb will be displayed in museum cases along with the club and the cannon.

The Chinese Revolution has been unique in many respects and the more that is written about it, the more benefit can be derived from its experience. General Chen Yi and other friends have advised me that I could make a contribution in this respect if I published the speeches, articles and statements I have issued since 1927, since they consider these writings reflect the revolutionary tide throughout the years, the halts and advances and the final bursting through of people's power to victory. This volume, therefore, represents a partial collection of what I have spoken and written as a participant in China's emancipation struggle.

This is a partial collection because a complete one is not possible. Some of the manuscripts were lost in the escape and flight from Kowloon to Chungking in December, 1941, when the Japanese militarists invaded Kowloon and Hongkong. Thus, when the time came to collect the items for this book, there were few basic materials to which I could refer, with the exception of those pieces which I have written since the liberation of Shanghai. The search I have been conducting for the lost materials has not been fully successful. Consequently, this book can only be a partial collection.

The reader will notice that a great deal of my public writings from July 1927 to May 1949 were directed to foreign audiences. Part of these were issued while I was visiting the Soviet Union. These were expressions of gratitude for the inspiration and help which the Chinese revolutionary masses received from the Soviet people and a vow to continue the struggle until full victory was achieved. The other part, in the main, were directed to the American and British peoples and issued while I was in China through the English language newspapers and other media available here and abroad. Of course, it has always been important, and it still is today, to keep these two great peoples informed of the situation in China and how the fight here affected their own struggle for security and well-being. But another important reason why I had to use this recourse once I was in my country was that my stand on the side of the Chinese people closed practically all facilities which would allow the broad masses to receive any message I had to deliver. The press and radio were in the complete control of the reactionaries.

They either suppressed my statements or they would distort and take my ideas out of context.

While there were some Chinese publications available from time to time, and I made use of these when necessary or as the circumstances would permit, when it was urgent that my opinion carry as far as possible, I had to resort to foreign publications and media. Such actions on my part sometimes forced the controlled press to pick up my statements. At other times, this public airing enabled the people to hear through their own channels.

I wish to make it clear that the fact foreign publications and news services printed my declarations did not mean that in their entirety they were sympathetic to the Chinese Revolution, or that they treated what I had to say with impunity. There were certainly those publications abroad that looked upon our cooperation as part of the joint struggle, in the true sense of internationalism. But the great majority of foreign publications were representatives of imperialism, therefore on occasions they refused to print my messages, or only did so when it served their own purposes or their need for a "sensation" or a "news scoop".

The only other possibility I had of being heard, especially in the middle 1930's, was through the English language publications issued in China which were operated by foreign friends of the Chinese people. These friends assumed the same revolutionary risks as their Chinese comrades. I will always be thankful for their contribution during that most difficult and dangerous period.

Now, with the people in power, the situation has completely changed. All those who stand on the side of the revolution and want to speak out in one voice with the people have available to them the most widespread facilities in our own language and in many others besides. Now the truth can reach the eyes and ears of the masses without limit. It was with this thought that I prepared this compilation, hoping also that it would be useful to students in their research of this period in the Chinese people's struggle.

As I worked on this volume, the struggle entered a new stage. The imperialist aggressors, led by the banker-generals of the United States, intensified their bid for world domination. They arrived at the point of outright physical attempt to invade lands and destroy populations. They struck at our neighbors, the Korean people, and in doing so threatened the victories achieved both by the Koreans and the Chinese people. This we could not let go unanswered. Therefore, today our Chinese Volunteer formations are fighting shoulder to shoulder with the Korean People's Army. They represent the vanguard of the final struggle against imperialism. For that reason I have dedicated this book to those heroes of all the peoples who want peace and peaceful construction.

Soong Ching Ling

Shanghai, June 1951

PART I

THE STRUGGLE AGAINST
COUNTER-REVOLUTION

STATEMENT ISSUED IN PROTEST AGAINST THE VIOLATION OF SUN YAT-SEN'S REVOLUTIONARY PRINCIPLES AND POLICIES

Hankow

July 14, 1927

I feel that it is necessary at this time to explain as a member of the Central Executive Committee of the Kuomintang, that we have reached a point where definition is necessary, and where some members of the party executive are so defining the principles and policies of Sun Yat-sen, that they seem to me to do violence to Sun's ideas and ideals. Feeling thus, I must disassociate myself from active participation in the carrying out of these new policies of the party.

Today we face a crisis and we must probe searchingly into fundamental questions for fundamental answers. We must answer the questions of the nature of revolution in general, of the Chinese revolution in particular, whether it is to be a political or a social revolution, and what changes are involved.

In the last analysis, all revolution must be social revolution, based upon fundamental changes in society; otherwise it is not a revolution, but merely a change of government.

To guide us in the Chinese revolution, Sun Yat-sen has given us his Three Principles and his Three Policies.

It is the Third Principle, that of the livelihood of the people, that is at stake at the present time, the Principle that answers the questions of fundamental social changes in China.

This Third Principle was felt by Sun to be basic in our revolution. In this Principle we find his analysis of social values and the place of the laboring and peasant classes defined. These classes become the basis of our strength in our struggle to overthrow imperialism and cancel the unequal treaties that enslave us, and effectively unify the country. These are the new pillars for the building up of a new, free China. Without their support, the Kuomintang, as a revolutionary party, becomes weak, chaotic and illogical in its social platform; without their support, political issues are vague. If we adopt any policy that weakens these supports, we shake the very foundation of our Party, betray the masses and are falsely loyal to Sun Yat-sen.

Today there is much talk of policy. Sun defined Three Policies, which he decided were the only means by which his Three Principles could be carried out. But today it is being said that policies must be changed to fit the needs of the time. There is some truth in this statement, but change of policy should never be carried to the point where it becomes a reversal, so that a revolutionary party ceases to be revolutionary and becomes merely an organ, operating under the banner of revolution, but actually working in support of the very social structure which the party was founded to alter.

At the moment, we face critical issues. Theoretical and practical differences have arisen between various elements of the party. Drastic solutions are suggested. It is because I feel that the carrying out of some of these suggested solutions would destroy the strength of the party and delay the success of the revolution, that I must speak. These solutions seem to me a part of a policy which would alienate and suppress the classes upon which our strength largely depends and for which the revolution must be fought. Such a policy, I feel, is doomed to failure.

This new policy is proposed as a corrective to mistakes that have been made. But the corrective seems to me more serious than the mistakes.

It is time now for honesty and courage. There have been mistakes, but the fact that some of us are unwilling to face is that we are at least as responsible for many of these mistakes as those whom we would now hold completely at fault. If we look back honestly at the past months in Wuhan, examine our words and decisions unflinchingly, we cannot evade this responsibility. Speeches and statements are recorded in the history of the Party. But now we would shirk the responsibility and shift it to other shoulders.

Yes, there have been mistakes, but we must face the fact that they are not only others' mistakes; they are our own as well. We have helped to make them; we must correct them. Moreover, for revolutionary mistakes, revolutionary solutions must be found. We must not betray the people. We have built up in them a great hope. They have placed in us a great faith. To that faith we owe our final allegiance.

Sun Yat-sen came from the people. He told me a great deal about his early days. He came from the peasantry. His father was a farmer and the people in his district were farmers.

Sun was poor. Not until he was fifteen years old did he have shoes for his feet, and he lived in a hilly region where it is not easy to be a barefoot boy. His family, until he and his brother were grown, lived almost from hand to mouth, in a hut. As a child he ate the cheapest food—not rice, for rice was too dear. His main nourishment was sweet potatoes.

Many times Sun has told me that it was in those early days, as a poor son of a poor peasant family, that he became a revolutionary. He was determined that the lot of the Chinese peasant should not continue to be so wretched, that little boys in China should have shoes to wear and rice to eat. For this ideal he gave forty years of his life.

Yet today the lot of the Chinese peasant is even more wretched than in those days when Sun Yat-sen was driven by his great sense of human wrongs into a life of revolution. And today men, who profess to follow his banner, talk of classes and think in terms of a "revolution" that would virtually disregard the sufferings of those millions of poverty-stricken peasants of China.

Today also we hear condemnation of the peasant and labor movement as a recent, alien product. This is false. Twenty, thirty years ago, Sun was thinking and speaking in terms of a revolution that would change the status of the Chinese peasant. In his early twenties he wrote to Li Hung-chang, petitioning for social and economic reforms. In 1911, he wrote an article on the agrarian question in China, printed in Geneva, in

"The Socialist", in which he said that the basis of social and economic transformations in China is an agrarian revolution. All his life this was one of the big goals he had in mind. Everything he planned he saw as means to the betterment of the life of the Chinese masses.

In 1915, when we were in Japan, he urged Liao Chung-kai to study more deeply into the peasant and labor problems.

It is only in the past few years, after four decades of struggle, that these plans for a revolution of the people have begun to bear fruit. I remember clearly the first All-Kwangtung Peasants' Conference, in Canton, in July 1924. Then for the first time, we saw the people of China, who must be her new strength, coming to participate in the revolution. From all the districts of Kwangtung the peasants came, many of them walking miles and miles, barefooted, to Canton. They were ragged, tattered. Some carried baskets and poles. I was deeply moved.

Sun Yat-sen was also. When we reached home, he said to me: "This is the beginning of the success of the revolution", and he told me again the part the oppressed people of China must play in their own salvation.

All these years, his purpose was clear. But today we talk of recent foreign influence. Was Sun Yat-sen, the leader who was voicing the agrarian revolution for China when Russia was still under the heel of the Czar, was he the tool of foreign scheming?

Sun Yat-sen's policies are clear. If leaders of the Party do not carry them out consistently, then they are no longer Sun's true followers, and the Party is no longer a revolutionary party, but merely a tool in the hands of this or that militarist. It will have ceased to be a living force working for the future welfare of the Chinese people, but will have become a machine, the agent of oppression, a parasite battening on the present enslaving system.

We face a serious crisis. But it is more of a crisis for us as individuals than for China as a country. Whether the present Kuomintang at this moment rises to the height of its ideals and courageously finds a revolutionary corrective for its mistakes, or whether it slumps into the shamefulness of reaction and compromise, the Three Principles of Sun Yat-sen will conquer in the end. Revolution in China is inevitable.

At the moment, I feel that we are turning aside from Sun Yat-sen's policy of leading and strengthening the people. Therefore, I must withdraw until wiser policies prevail.

There is no despair in my heart for the revolution. My disheartenment is only for the path into which some of those who had been leading the revolution have strayed.

But although there are members of the party who are straying from the path Sun charted for the revolution of China, millions of people in China who have already come under the banner of the Party will continue on this path to the final goal. This means that I shall not keep faith alone. I am certain that all true members of the Kuomintang will take this revolutionary path.

STATEMENT BEFORE LEAVING FOR MOSCOW

Shanghai

August 22, 1927

If China is to survive as an independent country in the modern struggle of nations, her semi-feudal conditions of life must be fundamentally changed and a modern state created to replace the mediaeval system which has existed for more than a thousand years. This task must needs be done by the method of revolution, if only because the alternative method of gradualness postulates a period of time which is denied the nation by both the cancerous force of Chinese militarism eating from inside and foreign imperialism ravaging from outside.

To forge a fit instrument of revolution, Sun Yat-sen reorganized the Kuomintang on a revolutionary basis in the winter of 1924, and reinforced the Three People's Principles by formulating the Three Great Policies of action. The first of these policies calls for the inclusion and support of the nation's workers and peasants in the work of the revolution. These two massive elements of the national population—one carrying on and sustaining the life of organized society and the other producing food on which man lives—represent nearly 90 per cent of the nation. And, in view of their numerical strength and the fact that the masses ought to be the chief beneficiaries of the revolution, they must be drawn into it if there is to be life and reality in the movement.

The second of the policies laid down by Sun recognizes the necessity of cooperation between the Kuomintang and members of the Chinese Communist Party during the period of revolutionary struggle with Chinese militarism and foreign imperialism. The Chinese Communist Party is indubitably the most dynamic of all internal revolutionary forces in China; and its influence over the masses and power of propaganda enabled the Kuomintang to control its military elements and subordinate them to the civil authorities.

The third of Sun Yat-sen's policies deals with the profoundly important question of the connection of the Soviet Union with the Kuomintang. The connection is sometimes justified on the ground that the Soviet Union has no unequal treaties with China. This, however, was a minor consideration in Sun's view of the matter. In formulating the third policy, he was moved by larger reasons. Just as he regarded the Chinese Communist Party as the most active revolutionary force in China, so he envisaged the Soviet Union as the most powerful revolutionary force in the world; and he believed that a right correlation by the Kuomintang of these two outstanding revolutionary forces would signally assist the revolution to realize national independence for China. Sun was not afraid or ashamed to avow this revolutionary thesis, since he knew that the revolutionary role played by France, in the person of Lafayette, in the American revolution was repeated in many a chapter in the history of freedom.

It was a statesmanlike application of these three policies of Sun and the correlation of the forces deriving from them that enabled the Kuomintang power to put an end to ten years of disorder and confusion in Canton, and to create and finance revolutionary armies that conquered their way to the historic line of the Yangtze and—after shattering the main force of the Fengtien army* in Honan—penetrated to the bank of the Yellow River. Besides its striking administrative work at Canton and the great military achievement of the Northern Expedition, the Kuomintang scored memorable successes in a field in which China has always known defeat and humiliation. It raised the international status of China to a point never attained before, compelling the representatives of great powers to meet the foreign minister of Nationalist China as an equal in council, and causing men in high as well as in the scattered places of the earth to heed his statements on Nationalist aims and aspirations. In those days—it is but three months since—the Kuomintang may have been hated and even feared, but none dared to despise it.

Today it is otherwise. The famous name of the Nationalist Government is now sunk to the level of other semi-feudal remnants in the North; and those who have been entrusted by the revolution with leadership are allowing the new militarist clique in the Yangtze to capture and utilize the Kuomintang; and they themselves are now becoming or are about to become, the secretaries

---

* Manchurian warlord army under Chang Tso-lin.

and clerks of the new Caesar. No one fears and no one respects the Kuomintang, which is now despised even by foes who used to blench and flee at the sound of its armies on the march.

What is the cause for this startling change in values and in men's opinions? The answer is to be found in the work of the reaction in Canton, in Nanking and Shanghai, in Changsha, and lastly in Wuhan. Peasants and their leaders, workers and their leaders, Communists and their leaders, who labored in order that the Kuomintang power might reach the Yangtze, have been ruthlessly and wantonly killed; and Soviet workers who gave of their best to the Kuomintang and whom men, in later and juster days, will adjudge to have deserved well of Nationalist China, have been forced to leave, because so-called "leaders" of the Kuomintang—petty politicians reverting to type—believe that they can violate Sun Yat-sen's Three Policies and rely on the new militarism to carry out the stupendous task of the revolution.

They will fail and go the way of those before them who have sought to rule in like fashion. But they must not be permitted to involve in their own ultimate ruin the heritage left to us by Sun. His true followers must seek to rescue the real Kuomintang from the degradation of becoming a mere secretariat of the new militarist clique emerging out of the intrigues and disloyalties now afoot.

My own course is clear. Accepting the thesis that the Three Policies are an essential part of the thought and technique of the revolution, I draw the conclusion that real Nationalist success in the struggle with Chinese militarism and foreign imperialism is possible only by a right correlation, under Kuomintang leadership, of the revolutionary forces issuing from the Three Policies. As the reaction led by pseudo-leaders of the Kuomintang endangers the Third Policy, it is necessary for the revolutionary wing of the Kuomintang—the group with which Sun would today be identified had he been alive—to leave no doubt in the Soviet mind that, though some have crossed over to reaction and counter-revolution, there are others who will continue true and steadfast to the Three Policies enunciated by him for the guidance and advancement of the work of the revolution.

I go, therefore, to Moscow to explain this in person.

GREETINGS ISSUED TO SOVIET WOMEN THROUGH "ROBOTNIZA", OFFICIAL ORGAN OF THE WOMEN'S SECTION OF THE COMINTERN

Moscow

September 3, 1927

Both as a Chinese woman and as a representative of the Left Kuomintang of China, I wish to extend greetings to the women workers of the Soviet Union. I, from the women of China, the most oppressed class in one of the most oppressed countries of the world, come to the women of the Soviet Union, who have seen the birth of a new social era in which it is possible to be free not only as a worker but also as a woman. To us, in China, the freedom of the women of the Soviet Union seems a wonderful thing. We are working to achieve a similar freedom for ourselves. In the struggle that is ahead we are counting on the sympathy and cooperation of the women of the Soviet Union who have known bondage and now know what it is to be free. I bring you the greetings of the revolutionary women of China.

FOR "SMENA", OFFICIAL ORGAN OF COMMUNIST YOUTH

Moscow

September 3, 1927

The young people of the Soviet Union who have met us at every station in the long journey from Vladivostok stand to me as the symbol of the assured victorious future of the U.S.S.R. It is the youth who protect the victories of revolution, who guard against slumps into reaction, who stand watch against counter-revolution. The spirit of the revolutionary youth of the Soviet Union is a force more powerful than armies or battleships. We, in China, need just such a youth as you, to act as our strong line of defence for the victories we have won and have still to win. In the name of the revolutionary Kuomintang, a party facing a critical struggle for freedom from oppression, I greet you, the youth of the Soviet Union who are your country's guarantee that she will remain forever free.

STATEMENT ISSUED IN MOSCOW

September 6, 1927

I have come to express appreciation for what the people of the Soviet Union have done for revolutionary China. During the recent crucial years of China's war against imperialist domination, it has been mainly to the people of the U.S.S.R. that we have been able to turn for sympathy, cooperation and counsel. Your people have stood side by side with us in our struggle to free China from oppression. In extending this cooperation, revolutionary Russia has fulfilled her mission as friend to the oppressed peoples of the world, and, in expressing appreciation, I am speaking in the name of one of the oppressed peoples.

A period of reaction has begun in China. The united front of the revolution is broken. There have been betrayals, desertions and a complete distortion of the nationalist movement. Millions of organized peasants, in accordance with Kuomintang teachings, joined the struggle for the realization of the slogan "Land to the Peasants". Without an agrarian revolution it is impossible to overthrow feudalism. All further progress in the revolution is impossible without the realization of the agrarian revolution. From this it follows that all who act against the agrarian revolution, i.e., against the economic emancipation of tens of millions of peasants, find themselves in the ranks of the counter-revolution.

Today the great central Yangtze Valley, which a few months ago was the focal point in the struggle for freedom from world imperialism, is in the grip of counter-revolution, and the greatest blot upon China is that this shameful counter-revolution is being led by men who have been intimately associated in the public mind with the nationalist movement.

As a result, there is confusion in the mind of the world, which looks to the leaders for an explanation of the nature and aims of a movement. Therefore, another important purpose of my present journey is to make clear to the world that the men on the Yangtze who are now representing themselves as the spokesmen of nationalist China do not voice the sentiment of the revolutionary Kuomintang and do not speak for China's revolutionary masses.

The revolutionary Kuomintang has violently opposed the present reaction. A new feudal-militarism has traitorously cropped up under the revolutionary banner and has stolen many of the material fruits of the victories won by the revolution. But the spirit of the revolution is still undaunted, and it is in the name of the revolutionary masses of China that I come to explain that the revolution, although for the moment despoiled of its territorial gains, is still strong, vital and confident. I speak for revolutionary China, which is distinct and apart from the present feudal officials and militarists on the Yangtze. These men, having alienated the people, are now trying again to drag China along the familiar road of petty feudalist wars for personal gain and power. The result is chaos, but it is a chaos that is only on the surface. Underneath there is the strongly entrenched and strongly organized revolution which cannot be crushed and whose voice will soon be heard around the world.

There is a third mission I would fulfill on my present journey. Death claimed Sun Yat-sen before he could carry out one of his most cherished desires, to come to Moscow, and here, in person, confer with the strong revolutionary friends of China. His death was hastened by the hardships of forty years of revolutionary struggle and by frequent breaches of revolutionary discipline on the part of the very men who are now again betraying him while pretending to speak in the name of his principles. Before he died, he asked me to visit Moscow for him. And so I come, in his name and in the name of the revolutionary masses of China, to assure the Soviet Union of our appreciation for the cooperation her people have given us in the past and to express our confidence that this cooperation will continue in the years of struggle that are ahead.

STATEMENT ISSUED THROUGH TASS

Moscow

September 6, 1927

To the workers of the Soviet Union, I bring the greetings of the Left Kuomintang of China, a revolutionary body pledged to the emancipation of the masses of China who are oppressed by foreign imperialism and the Chinese military and exploiting classes.

The Left Kuomintang speaks for the working classes of China, for the millions who live in conditions of oppression so that a feudal-military class may prosper and foreign imperialists grow powerful. These masses are the majority of the real revolutionaries of China's hope in her struggle for freedom from foreign exploitation and feudal oppression. In bringing the greetings of these revolutionary working masses of China to you, the revolutionary working masses of the Soviet Union, I declare that we Chinese revolutionaries recognize the close tie that binds us to our revolutionary brethren of the U.S.S.R. I wish to express our appreciation of the sympathy that has been given so freely by the working classes of the Soviet Union and to tell you how grateful I am for this opportunity of coming to your country to express in person the appreciation of the Chinese revolutionary masses. I greet you in the name of the revolutionary Kuomintang.

STATEMENT ISSUED THROUGH
LENINGRAD "PRAVDA"

September 6, 1927

To the Leningrad Workers:

In the name of the Left Kuomintang, I wish to greet the proletariat of Leningrad who were the first to light the torch of world revolution. During our revolutionary struggle in China, you workers of the Soviet Union have been our staunchest allies. We have appreciated your sympathy and your cooperation. In greeting you, I proclaim the conviction that we will continue our fight, shoulder to shoulder, against our common foes, world imperialism and the forces of reaction.

THE PRESENT SITUATION IN CHINA

Moscow

September 19, 1927

There is no slightest cause for discouragement about events in China. The defeat of the movement to secure by revolutionary methods the freedom of China from the exploitation of imperialism and militarism, and to free the masses from the intolerable burdens under which they are now laboring, is purely on the surface. Geographically it seems extensive, but geography can be deceiving.

The reaction sits in Wuhan, Nanking, Shanghai, and has seeming control of all the territory south of the Yangtze and considerable territory to the north, but although its authority is widespread it does not go deep. Six months ago the mandates of the revolutionary government of China at Wuhan were effective not only over a wide geographical area but also among all social classes. The word of the Kuomintang authorities was obeyed by workers, peasants, merchants, industrialists, and, reluctantly, by imperialists both in China and abroad. Today the word of the so-called "Nationalist Government" has no force either among the people of China or the nations of the world. This is a fundamental fact of the present situation. The reaction in China lacks power.

The other fundamental fact which bars discouragement is the reality of the strong organization of the people. The people of China, wherever the Nationalists have had control, are awakened. They know both the weakness of the reaction to win ultimate victory and their own power to rise above surface chaos and to conquer.

Today they are facing the future with straight shoulders and stout hearts. Women who during the past two years have marched down the streets of Canton, Changsha, Wuhan and scores of other cities, small and large, in south and central China are not the same women they were two years ago.

I have seen working women in China, hobbling along on their bound feet in workers' parades and Kuomintang celebration meetings. Many of them wore the union badges which are today the symbol in China of less bestial labor for a wage which can raise families out of squalid poverty. These bound-foot women, marching in victorious parade, have been to me one of the most convincing proofs of the fact that China has changed.

The great masses have changed everywhere. The women with their bound feet offer a striking example. But the transformation is no less startling among other classes. Workers are different today from what they were two years ago. They have learned organization and have had a glimpse of power. Peasants are different. They have learned that by their united efforts they can prevent the exploitation by landlords and militarists

which leaves them, the producers of food, without
sufficient rice to feed their families. They have discovered a new system of village organization, in which
they have a voice in the management of their own
affairs. The masses of China have learned that misery
is not inevitable, that there is another way of life, to
be won by revolution.

It is this knowledge that assures victory. With a
people aroused and confident, with the trained leaders
who have come through the drive of the past two years
and the oppressions of the past few months with unwavering confidence in ultimate victory and ever more
sure technique of leadership, China cannot fail.

The trained mass leaders are today in the ranks
of the Left Kuomintang, the only group in China which
is deserving of the name bequeathed the revolution by
Sun Yat-sen, as it is the only group that gives its
allegiance to his Principles and his Policies. The
masses have confidence in these leaders.

Already we are getting reports of outbreaks in the
territory under the nominal control of reaction. Today
these uprisings seem sporadic, one here, one there.
But the ferment which causes them is everywhere in
China. It will boil over from the far south of China
to the great wall and beyond. It expresses the concentrated determination of a people which will not be
vanquished, no matter how great the obstacles nor how
cruel the oppression. It is the guarantee that the
present period of surface chaos will pass and China
will be free.

WOMEN AND REVOLUTION

Moscow

September 25, 1927

One of the principal tasks of the Revolution in China is the emancipation of over two hundred million women from the bondage of semi-feudal and mediaeval social ideas and customs. As long as this great human mass—it is half the population of China—is not liberated, a real revolutionary change, not only in the institutions of the country, but in the general life and thought of the people, will not be effected.

A mere political revolution of the Anglo-Saxon type which took place in England in the XVII century, or in the American Colonies in the XVIII century, or a bourgeois revolution like the French Revolution, can be brought about without directly involving the woman-mass of the nation. Because the Bolshevist Revolution in this country is a fundamental social revolution and not merely a political or a bourgeois revolution, it is at once natural and logical that the women-masses of the U.S.S.R. should and must take part in the work of revolution, and thus assist and complement the creative labors of the men-masses and their leaders. In this way the profound changes in progress here and the new civilization under development promise to be enduring.

It is in this sense that I view the convocation of the First National Congress of All-Women Soviets in the U.S.S.R. In extending my greetings, I wish to ask their assistance in the cause of emancipating from mediaeval subjection the millions of Chinese women who, if the nation is not to perish, must raise fit workers and rulers for the China of tomorrow.

YOUTH AND REVOLUTION

Moscow

September 1927

By the youth of the Soviet Union, more than by anything else I have seen in the short time I have been here,
I have been thrilled and heartened. In their fervour,
their earnestness, their serious concern for the better-
ment of their nation and their intelligent understanding
of events and problems in their own and other lands,
I see the Soviet Union's greatest strength, the power that
will make her invincible. Youth is the bulwark of the
revolution. It forms the guard that stands sentinel
and protector over the gains of the revolution and the
force that hastens the course of history in its drive
toward a better world.

When I return to China, one of my first tasks will
be to start a movement similar to this great movement
I find in the Soviet Union. We in China have known the
value of youth, but we have not organized our young
people as you have. We, too, must now mobilize our
youth, for it is they who will make certain our victories
and carry on our unfinished work.

Sun Yat-sen always realized how indispensable to
the success of the revolution were the support and

enthusiasm of the young people of China. Even in his most hurried days, he never denied himself to the young boys and girls who came in great numbers to speak with him. He was often forced to ask men of affairs to wait a few hours or a few days—but never young students or young, eager, half-grown workers from the factories or the fields. To these, his door was always open. If anyone remonstrated that the young were young and had time to wait, he would answer that the principles of the Kuomintang could be carried out only by the youth of China, that older leaders die or become wavering with the passing of the years, that it is youth that is determined and will conquer.

His prophecy is fulfilled today. Tragically, during the past few months in China, the older leaders have deserted. Men who were associates of Sun fifteen years ago, are today in the ranks of reaction. That the revolutionary organization is still strong and vital is due to a younger generation of revolutionaries. It is for the most part younger leaders who have refused to compromise, who have opposed reaction and who will win victory despite the forces of counter-revolution.

But many of these younger leaders will also grow weary and old. They must hand the torch to men and women who are today boys and girls in schools and workshops. It is these we must organize.

It will be a great task and we are looking to the Communist Youth of the Soviet Union to help us. We need your cooperation. With it we can be strong. Working together, the Communist Youth of the Soviet Union and the revolutionary youth of China have it in their power to achieve the goal of freedom from oppression for all the oppressed people of the world. It is this cooperation for revolutionary ideals that is true humanity and true brotherhood and the essence of that internationalism which is the aim of revolution everywhere in the world. Together, the youth of China and the Soviet Union will constitute a great body, in number and spirit. Working side by side, they will have the force needed to create a new world.

THE KUOMINTANG IS NO LONGER A
POLITICAL POWER

Statement issued in Shanghai

December 19, 1931

It is no longer possible to hide the fact that the Kuomintang as a political power has ceased to exist. It has been liquidated, not by its opponents outside the Party, but by its own leaders within the Party. With the death of Sun Yat-sen in Peking in 1925, the national revolution suddenly lost its leadership and broke midway to its completion. The Party comrades in Canton at that time, however, adhered strictly to his doctrine by which the masses were made the foundation of the revolution, enabling the Northern Expedition to be successful in the Yangtze Valley within a short period of time. But soon after came the split between Nanking and Wuhan, caused by the personal dictatorship of Chiang Kai-shek and mutual conflicts among militarists and politicians, daily deepening the gulf between the Party and the people.

The revolution was driven underground by frightful slaughter and terrorism. Using anti-Communism as a screen for its treachery, the Kuomintang continued its reactionary activities. In the Central Government, Party members strove for the highest and most lucrative posts, forming personal cliques to fortify their positions, while in their local districts they likewise exploited the masses to satisfy their personal greed. By allying themselves with one militarist after another, they have been able to jump to high positions in the Party and Government. But faithful and true revolutionaries have been deliberately tortured to death in many cruel ways, the latest example being the murder of Teng Yen-ta.

Within the past five years civil wars and political intrigues followed in continuous succession, the result of the reversal of the revolutionary policy, each opposing clique capitulating to the imperialists, and not hesitating to use forces and tactics which are the most corrupting. All that the former militarists and politicians in the North dared not do, has been ruthlessly done under the cover of Party Rule. Is there any wonder that the Kuomintang is discredited beyond rescue, despised and hated by the entire nation today? Not for a single day has the Testament of Sun Yat-sen really been carried out.

Recently came the split between the Nanking and Canton factions, forming two conflicting forces. Each accused the other and boasted of its own virtues. Hypocritical catch-phrases, such as "open politics," "democratic rule", and "revolutionary diplomacy", have been used as weapons to deceive the Chinese masses. But in reality, both Canton and Nanking are dependent upon militarists, both are pleading for the favor of their imperialist masters, and both are betraying and slaughtering the Chinese masses.

Since Japan has openly invaded Manchuria, both the Canton and Nanking cliques, facing the national crisis and public criticism, have been forced temporarily to cease fighting openly, and have held a so-called "Peace and Unification Conference". Three months were spent in intrigues, the debates centering on the division of spoils in the Central Party Committee and the Government. Of the abject misery and desperate needs of peasants and workers, who form the over-whelming majority of the nation, not one word was uttered in this conference. Self-interest has completely blinded these rival cliques to the fact that personal dictatorship, demoralization of the Party, and partition of the country by foreign imperialists have all resulted from the gulf created by themselves between the Kuomintang and the masses.

Only a party that is built on the basis of a worker and peasant policy can establish a foundation for Socialism, break the power of militarism and throw off the yoke of foreign imperialism. If "peace" and "unification" go smoothly, enabling each clique to get all it wants, "peace" will mean nothing but a peaceful division of the spoils, and "unity" nothing but a united looting of the masses. It is utterly unthinkable that the masses of China should have any interest in such a "peace", or the nation should desire such a "unity".

We are now witnessing the first fruits of this unification in Nanking. Only three days ago, by the order of the imperialist ministers, the "United Government" tried to suppress the patriotic student movement. In less than 12 hours soldiers and gangsters surrounded the students, brutally beating and bayoneting them, and driving them out of the city like beasts. Many students were injured and killed; a great number are reported missing.

Such an atrocity has been staged at the very moment when a foreign imperialist army is advancing on Chinchow, and when all traitors and imperialists are honored, flattered and protected. This has been carried out following the arrival in Nanking of men who have been promising revolutionary diplomacy, national democracy, free speech, press and assembly. It is clear that the new unified government, composed as it is of Japanese, French, British and American agents serving masters whose interests conflict, will continue to take orders from imperialists to suppress any kind of mass movement aiming at the emancipation of the Chinese nation.

I, for one, cannot bear to witness the work of 40 years by Sun Yat-sen being destroyed by a handful of self-seeking and scheming Kuomintang militarists and politicians. Still more unbearable is it for me to see the subjection of a nation of 475,000,000 to imperialism, brought about by the Kuomintang's betrayal of its own doctrine.

I am therefore compelled to declare frankly, that since the Kuomintang was organized as a machine for the revolution, and since it has failed to carry out the tasks for which it was created, we need express no sorrow for its downfall. I firmly believe that only a revolution built on mass support and for the masses can break the power of militarists and politicians, throw off the yoke of foreign imperialism and truly realize Socialism. I am convinced that, despite the terroristic activities carried on by the reactionary forces in power today, millions of true revolutionaries in China will not shrink from their duty, but, urged by the critical situation facing the country, will intensify their work and march on triumphantly toward the goal set by the revolution.

activities carried on the revolutionary front ... in places
today, millions of these revolutionaries in China will
not shrink from their goals but, watched by the entire
situation facing the country, will unfailingly march ...
and march on triumphantly toward the goal set by the
revolution.

PART II

THE STRUGGLE
FOR CIVIL LIBERTIES

THE TASKS OF THE CHINA LEAGUE FOR CIVIL RIGHTS

Shanghai

December 1932

It is absolutely necessary to be clear on the character of the China League for Civil Rights. The League is not a political *party*. It does not aim to lead the political or economic struggle of the Chinese masses, and consequently does not aim at leadership of the struggle for the conquest of political power. While taking this view of our work, we must understand that the questions we have to deal with are nevertheless political in nature. Our tasks as outlined in our first manifesto are:

1. To fight for the liberation of political prisoners in China and to fight the system of imprisonment, torture and executions now prevailing. This League shall concern itself first of all and above all with the masses of unknown and nameless prisoners.

2. To give legal counsel and other assistance to political prisoners, to arouse public opinion by investigation of prison conditions and the publication of the facts in regard to the denial of civil rights in China.

3. To assist in the struggle for civil rights, i.e., rights of organization, free speech, press and assembly.

Because the League is not a political party, there is, therefore, room within its ranks for all those who really intend to assist in the fight for our demands. There can be no room in the League for people who assist the government in its suppression of the people or who defend or excuse this suppression. There is no room for those who only weakly "criticize" individual cases of arbitrary terrorism of the government while upholding the "legal" system of terror which forms the framework for the suppression of the people and the withholding of democratic rights by the Kuomintang— the political party of the landlords, capitalists, gentry and militarists.

If the League wants to fulfill its aims, it must resist any attempts from within or without its ranks to change its constitution, the character of its work, or to make it an appendix to the system of Kuomintang rule. Such a League would not be worthy of the support of those who honestly want to fight for our demands. On the contrary, such a reactionary League would have to be fought by us all. We have already had one such test case. The action of Hu Shih in starting a fight against the League, whilst a member of the League and whilst Chairman of our Peiping branch, was reactionary and dishonest. Hu joined the League by agreeing to its published fundamental principles. But as soon as the Kuomintang and Chang Hsueh-liang came out openly to oppose the League, he became nervous and started to find excuses and justifications for his own cowardice.

The League should congratulate itself for having got rid of such a "friend", and it must do everything to prevent such incidents and sabotage in the future. On such fundamental principles as this, there can be only absolute unity, and we must not permit wavering. People who do not agree with our principles should not join the League, but if they do, they must uphold and support it energetically.

Let us consider the question of democratic rights of the people. Enemies and critics of the League have raised a number of hypothetical objections to our activities and principles. Democratic rights cannot be separated from the struggles shaking the world as well as China, but are, on the contrary, bound up with and part and parcel of these struggles. There is also the revolutionary necessity for these democratic rights, and for the release of all political prisoners. By revolutionary necessity I mean the necessity for China to free itself politically and nationally. There is but one alternative to this, and that is subjection and dismemberment. There is no Chinese worth his salt and no friend of China who wishes to see the subjection and dismemberment of China, and I cannot conceive that any member of the League for Civil Rights wishes to see such a thing. So our work is part and parcel of the struggle to prevent this.

I wish to take up some of the most important tasks of the League:

Our enemies and critics have asked us a number of questions which they thought would embarrass or silence us, such as: "Are you going to demand the release of kidnappers?" Our answer is: Certainly not! Kidnappers

and criminal gangsters are part and parcel of the system
that controls China today—a system we must fight.
Such elements sit, not in the League, but in high official
and semi-official positions. They do not belong to the
Chinese masses, but very often are tools in the hands
of the authorities in suppressing the masses. Just as
the economic basis of gangsterism in the United States
is capitalism and the liquor traffic, so in China its
economic basis is the imperialist-feudal regime and
the opium traffic. But we are fighting the kidnapping
and arrest of anti-imperialist fighters going on all over
China, going on in the foreign settlements, carried out
by Chinese, and foreign imperialists, and very often
by their tools, the gangsters. We fight the cooperation
of the Kuomintang government with the imperialists
in suppressing the revolutionary movement in China.
This cooperation shows the corruption of the Kuomintang, shows how the interests of China are subordinated
to those of imperialism and shows the ideological and
political capitulation of the Kuomintang before imperialism. Those who are afraid to fight these evils had better
not join the League.

Still other enemies have tried to scare us by asking:
"Do you demand the release of political prisoners who
have committed acts of political violence?" To this
question our answer is equally clear: We do not believe
in individual terroristic acts. They can never supplant
the struggle of the masses, and more often they hamper
this struggle. But we know also that when all rights
of the people are suppressed, individual acts of terror
are more common than otherwise. Most often people
who commit terroristic acts have no connection what-

ever with the masses or their organizations. Yet even down to today, many civilized countries have given asylum to men who have committed acts of political terror against tyrants. The United States of America, as well as England and France, have received and given protection to many such men. Also, during the World War, Frederic Adler, now secretary of the Second International, was in prison for having shot the Austrian Minister of War. The masses rightly demanded his unconditional release from prison. The revolution in Austria in 1918 released him as well as tens of thousands of other political prisoners.

But we do not have to go to Europe to find such cases. China has had a number of well-known cases, including that of Wang Ching-wei, President of the Executive Yuan, who was a bomb-thrower in his revolutionary days. And did not the Chiang Kai-shek Government on March 11th release Cheng Chi-chen, the assassin of General Chang Tsung-chang? It did, and for once we did not oppose the government for this act. We demand that such acts of amnesty shall not be limited to cases in which even the Chiang Kai-shek Government has an interest. We demand the release of all political prisoners. They are not criminals, but pioneers in the struggle for human emancipation. Most of them are imprisoned because they have exercised, or attempted to exercise, their elementary rights of free speech, free press, assembly and organization. Our demand for their release is but a logical consequence of our demand for the realization of the civil rights of the people. It is an infamy without parallel that the flower of China's manhood are tortured with lingering death in prison, while gangsters, militarists, professional politicians, capitalists and feudal landlords sit in the seats of power and deliver our country to the imperialists. Our demand for the release of all political prisoners is a revolutionary necessity if China is not to become a subject nation.

Enemies of the League have called some of us Communists and have tried to argue that there are no democratic rights in the Soviet Union. True, there is a dictatorship of the proletariat, based on the alliance of the proletariat and the peasantry, in the Soviet Union. But this dictatorship is the rule of the overwhelming mass of the population. The institution of the Soviets combines both the legislative and executive power, and is the true democratic state organ of the dictatorship. The vast masses of workers and peasants have the right to elect and recall their representatives to the Soviets. Therefore the Soviets are the only true democratic state organs of the masses of workers and peasants The right of organization, assembly, press, speech, etc., has never in history been so developed as in the Soviet Union, and no other country has such powerful organizations of the masses. A political party with three million members brings the wide range of all political, economic and cultural questions before the masses, teaches and leads them, discusses all questions openly with them, bears the heaviest tasks and responsibilities, criticizes itself openly at every step and invites the criticism of the masses in order to avoid mistakes and in order to get the maximum of results in the interest of the masses. There is the League of the Youth of workers and peasants, with ten million members, the great educator and organizer of a new generation, freed from the individualistic outlook of capitalist society, growing consciously into the builders of a new Socialist society. The great children's organization, the Young Pioneers, carries on similar work. The Trade Unions, with their twenty million members, in unison with the workers' State, protect the interests of the workers, help to organize Socialist production and do great cultural work. The Cooperatives, with many million members, solve the tasks of distribution of the necessities of life for a great country. The numerous cultural, scientific and other organizations bring cultural development, science and art, to the masses. The enormous development of the press, literature, of the cinema and the theater—all this conclusively and irrefutably gives the lie to the statements of our enemies. Does anyone imagine that the great achievements of the Soviet Union—from destroying the landlords and capitalists, throwing out the imperialists, to the realization of the Five Year Plan—could be brought about without the conscious efforts of tens of millions of the masses, plus a leadership that represents the interests of the masses? Surely not. Equally sure is it that the conscious efforts of the masses could only be attained when they themselves are drawn into this whole work of administration, of Socialist economic construction and of cultural work. If reactionaries and philistines do not understand this, it is mainly due to the fact that they shudder at the thought that the old society based on exploitation is bound to pass into a new cycle of wars and revolution, the beginnings of which we can clearly see today.

There are other opponents of the League who ask: "Is not the democratic system of modern capitalist countries like England, the United States and France, superior to the Soviet system?" In my opinion, most decidedly not. Formal bourgeois democracy is never real in so far as the masses are concerned. It gives only a very small minority democratic rights. Even in the "freest" bourgeois democracy the rights of the masses are restricted. They may have a vote on such issues or in such elections and for such parties as the bourgeoisie permits to exist. However, the right to organize is more or less restricted, demonstrations must have permission or be smashed up. Besides, the workers and peasants are further handicapped; the great printing plants, the publishing houses, the educational institutions, the great halls for meetings are, with but very few exceptions, in the hands of the capitalists. Democracy is only formal and on paper in the wording of the constitution, and is permitted only so long as it does not interfere with the "right" of the capitalist exploiters to loot the people. In reality, such "democracies" are but a system of carefully guarded rights and powers of a small minority of the exploiters, and their "democratic rights" are but the screen for hiding the rule, the dictatorship, of this very small minority of exploiters over the broad masses of the people. But even this formal democracy is done away with when the interests of the bourgeoisie demand it. We have seen this in all capitalist countries during the last World War, and more recently we have seen the same development in other countries. After the War, the fascists established a dictatorship in Italy on the ruins of bourgeois "democratic" institutions. In Germany today there is taking place the liquidation of the last remnants of democratic rights which the German workers gained in the revolution of 1918. In every great strike in England, Belgium, France and the United States, we have witnessed a state of siege and terror against the workers, proclaimed to protect the interests of the capitalist minority against the majority of the population. The class struggle becomes ever more intensified and shatters the framework of formal bourgeois democracy. Where the European workers are not powerful enough, there fascism triumphs. In most cases, such triumph is due to the illusions about the possibilities of a peaceful development under bourgeois "democracy". Fascism is the child of bourgeois democracy, of capitalism.

While this state of affairs exists in Europe and America, what about conditions in China? The Kuomintang does even worse. Its laws alleged to benefit the "people" are openly and blatantly framed to serve the interests of but a very small minority of feudal landlords, capitalists and the imperialists. The paper laws about the "people" are for nothing but propaganda, and are entirely without substance. Daily instances of the most ruthless suppression of the workers, peasants and students, reveal the reality. Even during the Japanese invasion of Shanghai, the factory owners used the invasion as an excuse for lowering the wages and lengthening the hours of the workers, and the authorities used the occasion—just as they do down to the present—as a new opportunity to harness new reactionary restrictions on the people. The open presentation of Manchuria and Jehol to Japanese imperialism is used for renewed

oppression and suppression. In Hankow, the authorities
have recently used the Jehol invasion as an occasion
for issuing new decrees, one of which states that workers in foreign factories who attempt to negotiate directly
with the capitalists for the betterment of their condition,
thereby "creating a serious situation", shall be put
to death! The decree declares that anyone who attempts
to form a society or hold a meeting shall be immediately
arrested! The Kuomintang in Shanghai and elsewhere
has imposed a new censorship on all newspapers lest
the Chinese masses learn the exact situation, but the
Japanese and the other imperialists know accurately
every detail of the Chinese situation, every step taken
by Chinese officials and every move of Chinese armies.
It is the Chinese people alone who are kept in dark
ignorance that they may be more easily deceived and
exploited and that they may not arise to defend the
country against subjection.

The enemies and opponents of the China League
for Civil Rights are influenced in their mode of thinking
by bourgeois arguments and illusions about "democracy". They delight to charge that there is suppression in the Soviet Union. But let us take the Soviet
Union again as a point of comparison. There are, for
instance, armies and navies in the whole world—in
capitalist countries, in China, and in the Soviet Union.
But what a difference in their functions! The armed
forces in the Western capitalist countries serve aggressive purposes, serve to subject colonial peoples, to attack
weaker countries like China, to safeguard their established (established by force) "rights" of robbing the
masses of their own and colonial and semi-colonial

lands. In China the armed forces are used almost exclusively for the rival wars of the generals, and for the suppression of the workers and peasants struggling for their rights. In the Soviet Union, however, the armed forces serve to protect the people against a hostile capitalist world that is actively preparing a new war of intervention. An imperialist army can march unhindered over vast stretches of Chinese territory, but an imperialist soldier cannot stick his nose over the Soviet frontier without having it shot off. There is equally a difference between the use of force by an exploiting minority against the vast majority, and by the vast majority of the people against a small exploiting minority. In the first case, force is used for the purpose of upholding a system of brutal exploitation and slavery, for preventing the further advance of society to higher forms after capitalism has demonstrated its complete failure and has shown its inability to give the masses the necessities of life—food, clothing, shelter—in spite of increased productivity of human labor power. In the second case, force is used by the vast majority hitherto exploited, against a small minority, which is trying by all means to get back its lost power. Here force becomes a weapon employed in the interests of the great masses, a weapon for the advance of society to higher forms, a weapon to abolish exploitation of men by men, and not to enslave men.

Some people may ask: "Why are you fighting for democratic rights in China if you do not believe in bourgeois democracy?" The answer is very simple. First, there is a distinction between formal bourgeois democracy and the democratic rights of the masses. For the latter the workers and peasants will always fight because the right of free speech, press and assembly, and the right of organization, once attained, give a more favorable basis for the development of the struggle of the masses for their final liberation. In this struggle we must be with the masses of China, warning them not to put their faith in the paper promises of the Kuomintang, such as the newly-proposed "civil rights" of the new Constitution, but to rely solely on their own efforts and power.

Secondly, there is another important reason. China is threatened with partition and dismemberment by an imperialist world. This process of dismemberment, begun by the imperialists decades ago, is hastened by the war of imperialist Japan now in full swing. Does anyone imagine that imperialist Japan can be defeated without arousing the whole people of China for a national revolutionary war? Can anyone believe that the feudal Kuomintang militarists and generals can lead the people in this war? If he does, let him look at Manchuria and Jehol, and let him watch the further developments in the North where we see today a secret, underhanded intrigue going on for direct negotiations between the Chiang Kai-shek Government and the Japanese, via the route of the foreign imperialist ministers in Peiping. This secret selling out of China is the reason the Chinese press is being severely censored by the Kuomintang censors. They are preventing the Chinese people from knowing the truth. The Chinese people are the ones that must pay the price of this and other disasters. The ruin and dismemberment of China will

be the result if the masses do not stop it.   Surely everybody who has the interests of China and its masses
at heart must understand that democratic rights are
necessary to enable the people to organize on a broad
basis, to organize the resistance against imperialism,
to march shoulder to shoulder in unconquerable numbers, with a national revolutionary spirit against *all*
enemies of China.   These rights the masses will wrest
from the powers that be.   They will and they must do
it if they and China are to live.   That is the great aspect
of the struggle of which our League is only a small
part.   The more we have this in mind, the more will
we be able to fulfill our daily tasks, the more will we
command the confidence and trust of ever wider masses.

There is another frightful evil against which the
League for Civil Rights must wage an uncompromising
war.   That is the system of torture of political prisoners, a system unequalled in the world.   When an
anti-imperialist fighter and a member of the Communist
Party is arrested, he is nearly always beaten up or
otherwise tortured, sometimes even to death, in an
effort to make him confess what the police want to know,
and to compel him to betray his comrades and organization.   Combined with this torture goes the
regular system of exacting "confessions" from political
prisoners.   These "confessions" are generally public
statements in which the prisoners declare they have
repudiated their former convictions and now have
accepted the program of the Kuomintang.   All these
public statements, signed though they may be by names
of different men at different times, still all sound exactly alike, all use the same phrases, and all seem

to be written by the same person or persons, according to a set formula. These statements, exacted under torture, or falsely signed with the names of helpless prisoners, serve to discredit the present system of torture and corruption. They show the weakness of a system that uses such methods and that cannot maintain itself except by torturing and killing anti-imperialist fighters. They show that the Kuomintang itself can command no respect whatever among the masses of the people and must use the names of captive revolutionary fighters to gain a hearing. But such methods deceive nobody. We all know how they were extracted, and we know that had the prisoners believed in the Kuomintang, they would have joined its ranks while still in freedom. The fact is that only the torture rack and the shadow of death can force revolutionary prisoners to make statements in support of the Kuomintang.

There are many so-called "intellectuals" in China, of whom Hu Shih is typical, who do not believe that torture does exist in prisons unless it takes place right before their eyes. What prisoner would dare to speak openly in the presence of his jailers? What jailer would show a prison investigator a recently tortured prisoner, or permit an investigator to be present at torture? But even the mildest and most weak-kneed of persons admits that political prisoners in Chinese dungeons are chained like animals in their cells. They even take this for granted, and imperialists—who do exactly the same thing to prisoners and urge the Chinese authorities to continue it—use this as an argument why foreigners should not come under Chinese law. However, I am not interested in what foreign imperialists hypocritically say. I am interested in the youth of China with which the prisons are filled. Imagine men and women, often boys and girls, the flower of China, doomed for years to filthy jails, with rotten food, denied intercourse with the outside world, without books or papers, day after day, year after year, chained in heavy irons. Helpless against this torture, helpless against the barbarity of their jailers, they depend on us outside to release them from lingering death. To release these tens of thousands of prisoners from the dungeons of China is the great task of the League.

We must further try to organize legal protection for political prisoners, giving them legal assistance wherever possible to bring their cases into the open. We must demand the immediate repeal of all laws and regulations which impose restrictions in any way on the civil rights of the people, such as Special Emergency Laws. And we must fight against the hypocritical clauses in the newly proposed Constitution which speaks of civil rights in one breath, but withdraws them in the next by such phrases as "in accordance with the law". Such phrases mean in reality that civil rights are permitted to a very small minority of the population, the exploiters and their intellectual apologists, whereas the vast masses of workers and peasants to whom democratic rights are a vital necessity, are denied them.

Another of our tasks must be to destroy the secret tribunals before which political prisoners are brought, and where not only elementary justice, but the fundamental rights of man, are mocked and violated. In these tribunals prisoners are tortured, denied any right of self-defence, and sent secretly to a lingering death in prison, or to the execution grounds. We must further combat the secret torture and secret "railroading" methods of the foreign imperialists in the settlements who arrest men and women on the flimsiest pretexts and, on the manufactured evidence of their spies—who are generally gangsters—hand them over to the Chinese authorities to be further tortured, imprisoned, butchered. The hands of the foreign and Chinese torturers and butchers of the Chinese people must be stayed! While demanding the release of the tens of thousands of Chinese political prisoners, we must also demand the release of Paul and Gertrude Ruegg, and at once. They are friends of the Chinese people. But there are other people who should be jailed. For instance the British imperialist, Woodhead. What other country would allow such a reptile to run loose, to exhort Chinese generals daily to go over with their armies to the Japanese?

Those who think that they can prolong their rule of bloody suppression of the people indefinitely, are mistaken. The masses must struggle for their fundamental rights. This struggle will increase, will sweep China, will make it powerful and unite it. And this will answer the last question of our enemies: "Do you advocate revolution?" We are not a revolutionary party. Our task is more limited. But we live in a revolutionary epoch. One-sixth of the world has already accomplished the revolution, and the masses in the old capitalist countries are gathering for the great battles. The colonial peoples must mass their strength to break the chains of imperialist domination. China, seemingly helpless today, will free itself tomorrow. The imperialist war against China is a fact. But the revolutionary situation is also a fact. Either the revolution will triumph in China, or imperialism will conquer and dismember China. There is no alternative. Believing in the final victory of the masses in China, I am sure that the revolution will establish its own right, establish the unity, independence and integrity of China, and the right of the masses to govern themselves. And my conception of the China League for Civil Rights is that it is one of the instruments which will move us toward this goal.

ADDRESS TO THE PRESS AT A MEETING OF THE CHINA LEAGUE FOR CIVIL RIGHTS

Shanghai

December 1932

In the name of the China League for Civil Rights, I extend to you a sincere and hearty welcome. Members of the press and the Civil Rights League should stand shoulder-to-shoulder in their task of aiding in the advancement of human society. It is logical and proper that we should form a united front and cooperate loyally in our common task.

The purpose of our organization is to assist in the struggle for civil rights, i.e., the rights of free organization, free speech, free press and assembly. In other words, the Civil Rights League champions and defends the liberty of the press. It should, therefore, be to the interest of the press to earnestly support this organization.

One important fact I should like to lay stress upon. The chief concern of this League is to assist the masses of unknown and nameless political prisoners who are over-crowding our jails. As members of the press, you are cognizant of the countless numbers of illegal arrests and imprisonment of our fellow-citizens, the existence of secret military tribunals—relics of the mediaeval age. Are you going silently to witness these outrages without a protest, or will you whole-heartedly join in the efforts of the League to secure justice for the countless unfortunate ones who have no one to defend them? I feel a strong and courageous press could do a lot in establishing a current of public opinion in favour of liberty and justice.

TO THE CHINESE PEOPLE

A Call to Rally to the Protection of
Imprisoned Revolutionaries

Shanghai

April 1, 1933

The hearings in the Second District Court in
Shanghai on March 31, when five prisoners were
brought to "trial" and extradited to the Chinese
authorities by the Shanghai Municipal Police, were a
glaring example of how the Chinese authorities are
working hand in hand with the imperialists against the
anti-imperialist and anti-Japanese fighters of the
Chinese masses.

The cases of these prisoners constitute but another
example of a policy pursued by the Chiang Kai-shek
Government which has today brought China to the verge
of complete dismemberment and imperialist subjection.
This situation is so dangerous to China as a nation that
I feel it my duty to call once more upon the broad
masses of the Chinese people to struggle against it.

The cases in the Shanghai court yesterday involved
Lo Teng-hsien, Liao Cheng-chih, Chen Keng and
others. The procedure adopted in these cases was an
open, blatant violation even of the laws of the foreign
settlement. First of all, the prisoners were arrested on
nothing but the word of professional police informers.

No incriminating evidence could be produced against any of them. Throughout the hearing it was clearly demonstrated that there was no evidence upon which they could be charged, and that had the settlement authorities abided even by their own laws, they would have been forced to release them all immediately.

The settlement law requires that a "prima facie case" be made out against the accused before their extradition can be granted. This law, if adhered to, also requires that proof be given of a crime committed outside the settlement. In the case of murderers and kidnappers, opium traffickers and gangsters in general, the settlement has jealously guarded its jurisdiction. Yesterday, however, five revolutionaries were brought to trial and extradited merely on the unsubstantiated evidence of professional police informers who said: "I know these people and they are Communists." This was the sole "evidence" on which all five were handed over to certain torture and possible death. As in all these past six years during which reaction has raged in China, where evidence has failed the foreign and Chinese authorities always fall back upon the last weapon of tyrants and despots: torture and killing.

In this "trial" yesterday, it was nakedly clear that the Chinese and foreign authorities, by prearranged agreement, brought the prisoners to a hearing merely as a matter of form to deceive the public, and that the presentation of evidence or argument and the citation of law could in no way have altered the court's decision. It was only too evident that the decisions regarding them were made even before the farcical hearing was held. During the hearing, no attempt was made to establish a case against them. The municipal advocate sat silently in his place, while the judge merely tolerated the attempted defence of the lawyers. The accused completely refuted the charges of the police informers. The Kuomintang delegate in the courtroom, heavily armed, declared that he also represented the Bureau of Public Safety, and before the hearing opened he was heard to remark that "the whole matter has been arranged." When the miserable farce came to an end, the judge left the room for a few seconds, as a matter of form, then returned and read out the extradition order.

Despite the open farce, the prisoners conducted themselves in a manner and expressed ideas worthy of every anti-imperialist fighter in China. They all were types of which the Chinese people may be proud. Lo Teng-hsien was typical of them when, in his defence, he said:

"I am charged with being a 'reactionary'. I shall tell you my record. I helped organize and lead the Hongkong strike in 1925. I have just returned from the Northeast where I fought with the Volunteers. I have helped organize strikes in the Japanese cotton mills in Shanghai. That was all part of the struggle against imperialism. Is this what is meant when I am charged with engaging in 'counter-revolutionary' activities?"

Is it not infamous that anti-imperialist fighters like these are branded by the authorities as "reactionary", while treacherous men negotiating with the enemies of China call themselves the "saviours of China"?

The procedure adopted in these cases obviously exposes the fact that the Shanghai International Settlement, which the imperialists describe as an "island of security and justice", is also a paradise for imperialist enemies, traitors and betrayers of the Chinese people, opium traffickers and gangsters. Indeed, the foreign settlements are the headquarters for the auctioning off of China, and one of the chief bases of activities against the Chinese people and the existence of the Chinese nation. In this city now come and go, in absolute freedom and with official recognition and honor, representatives of Japanese imperialism that has invaded, conquered and annexed four of our provinces. Here representatives of the Chiang Kai-shek Government and of the invaders of our territory, make official and friendly calls to prepare for the secret treaty that will turn our territory and millions of our people over to a foreign imperialist conqueror. While this goes on, members and leaders of the Chinese revolutionary workers' and peasants' movement who are struggling against the dismemberment and subjection of China, suffer imprisonment, torture, death and a living death in mediaeval prisons.

These iniquitous conditions must be brought to an end by the united, determined struggle of the broad masses of the Chinese people. They can be terminated forever only when we take our fate in our own hands, free the country from imperialists and the Chinese henchmen of imperialists, and establish our own courts and other institutions of a free people. In order to free ourselves, we must recognize the necessity of this fundamental fact, and struggle with determination.

One of the first steps is to fight against the continued persecution of revolutionary fighters who are already leading this struggle. I regard the China League for Civil Rights as one of the means to obtain our end. And I declare that the five prisoners arrested and extradited to the Kuomintang yesterday, just like all their comrades who suffer a similar fate, are not criminals, but the highest type of representatives of the Chinese people. I, therefore, call upon the Chinese people to demand their release, to demand their protection from torture and death. By permitting their arrest, imprisonment and possible death, we are permitting the fearful reaction to strike at the roots of life of the Chinese nation. Their release, and the release of thousands like them, means the release of the unconquerable power of the national revolutionary spirit of China. Without this, China cannot live, cannot exist as a nation and as a people.

A DENUNCIATION OF THE PERSECUTION OF GERMAN PROGRESSIVES AND THE JEWISH PEOPLE

Shanghai

May 13, 1933

The China League for Civil Rights, which fights against the terror in China, for the civil and human rights of the Chinese people, and which allies itself with progressive forces throughout the world, feels compelled to enter an energetic protest against the brutal terror and reaction prevailing in Germany at the present time.

We learn from the most varied and reliable sources, representing all shades of political opinion, that since the fascist regime was established in Germany, 30,000 to 40,000 workers and thousands of working class leaders and intellectuals have been arrested. Prisoners are beaten up and tortured in jails, in the barracks of the Nazi storm troops and in the concentration camps. In the hospitals there are thousands of people with broken limbs, whose condition bears witness to the barbarism now prevailing in Germany. Hundreds have been killed and their corpses often thrown in rivers, lakes or forests. Others are shot and news is given out that they were shot while trying to escape, or that they committed suicide in their homes or in prison. Needless to say, all these cases are nothing but cold-blooded murder.

The organizations of the working class have been suppressed, their printing plants, property and funds confiscated or stolen by fascists. The rights of the working class in Germany, gained in decades of struggle, are torn to shreds. There is no freedom of the press, of speech, of assembly, no right of organization, no right to any activity of the masses to better their conditions.

All progressive intellectual and cultural life in Germany is blocked. The greatest scientists, like Dr. Albert Einstein, Magnus Hirschfeld and thousands of others, are persecuted and driven into exile. Lion Feuchtwanger and the Nobel Prize Winner, Thomas Mann, have been forced to leave the country and their positions in Germany taken by mediocrities. The fate of thousands of others, proletarian and progressive writers, is even worse.

Great artists like Max Liebermann and Kaethe Kollwitz, and great composers or directors like Bruno Walther, are deprived of any opportunity to work, are molested and their works smashed and burned. Libraries are denuded of rich collections of literature and thousands of books burned in the streets.

The press exists under the iron heel of the fascists, the entire working class press, and even such liberal intellectual organs as the Weltbuehne and others of an even milder nature, have been suppressed and their editors imprisoned. Foreign news despatches are rigidly censored before they are permitted to leave the country. Another sign of human and cultural retrogression to the Middle Ages and the darkest days of Czarist Russia, is the persecution of the Jews and the anti-Semitic pogroms, systematically organized and encouraged by the German Government and the Fascist Party.

The latest acts of vandalism in burning the books of progressive, proletarian and Jewish writers are acts such as have occurred only during the darkest days of ignorance and barbarism in human history. Such was the fate of great scientists and thinkers in the distant past when they paid for their advanced thinking by being burnt at the stake. These facts, with many others of a similar nature, have been reported in responsible papers in Europe and America. Even such conservative organs as the New York Times have published such reports daily. In its March 15th, 20th and 21st issues, the Times further reported the following facts:

"Reports of the torturing of Communists, Socialists, Radical and Jewish deputies, newspapermen, lawyers and writers are daily published in the newspapers of Vienna. Of common occurrence are such instances as that of Deputy Sollmann who was beaten unconscious, his ribs fractured, then he was repeatedly revived by burning the soles of his feet with a torch, only to lose consciousness again.

"Dr. Von Ossietsky, editor of the Weltbuehne, had his teeth knocked out by a revolver butt; the novelist Heins Pohl was made to eat his own manuscript. The eyes of other prisoners are gouged out, their hair torn out, hands burned, heads and bones broken. . . mutilated bodies are found in fields and forests . . . in the Nazi barracks men are confronted with levelled revolvers and compelled under threats of death to flog each other until they lose consciousness. Among the victims are fathers and sons . . . it is not unusual to find almost any morning in the woodlands surrounding Berlin the bodies of men killed by bullets or beatings; three such discoveries were made last week in a single morning. The police report them as 'unidentified suicides'! . . . Berlin proletarian homes have been raided and their occupants mistreated. . . ."

Lion Feuchtwanger, the great writer, writing in a special article in the New York Times on March 21, reports "despairing stories of women whose husbands and sons have been dragged from bed and inhumanly beaten, and about whom nothing more had been heard or seen . . . day after day bodies are discovered, mutilated beyond identification. . ."

The Volkscrecht of Switzerland reports among numberless other facts: "There are bourgeois newspapers in Germany which report that corpses of men with gouged out eyes and teeth knocked out, have been dragged from the Landwehr Canal in Berlin."

In the name of the human, social and cultural advancement of mankind, and in an effort to help preserve the social and cultural achievements of men and movements, the China League for Civil Rights protests in the most energetic manner against these facts, reports of which are duplicated in all the press of Europe and America. We protest against this fearful terror against the German working class and progressive thinkers, a terror which is crippling the social, intellectual and cultural life of Germany.

PART III

THE STRUGGLE FOR INTERNAL UNITY AND AGAINST IMPERIALIST WARS

WORKERS OF CHINA, UNITE!

Published in the "Nation" Magazine

New York

May 24, 1933

Before reviewing conditions in China, I should like to make a few remarks about the international situation today. The world crisis of capitalism becomes ever severer. Workers and peasants starve, the middle class is ruined, banks and business concerns crash, and even the United States of America has given up the gold standard. Only in the Soviet Union an entirely different development is taking place. Unemployment has been abolished, industry and agriculture are being organized on a socialist basis, exploitation has been done away with, the cultural and economic levels of the masses are being raised. The Five-Year Plan is a huge success. In fact, some capitalist countries are trying to adopt certain features of the Five-Year Plan. But they cannot succeed, because the laws of capitalist production and the rule of the bourgeoisie prevent it. Only the working class in alliance with the peasantry can build a socialist society.

The more precarious the existence of capitalism becomes, the more vicious becomes the ruling class against the workers and peasants. Fascism is spreading in Europe as the last desperate attempt of the bourgeoisie to maintain the existence of a bankrupt system of brutal terror. The greater the antagonism between the imperialist powers becomes, the greater becomes their enmity against the Soviet Union, the greater the preparation for new imperialist world wars, for a new war of intervention against the Soviet Union.

With this international background in view, what are the conditions in China? Economically, the workers are unemployed, or starving with miserable wages. They work long hours and have no protection. Peasants suffer, starve, and are robbed by high rents, usurious interest rates, and taxes. They have not sufficient land and they groan under feudal exploitation by the landlords and gentry. They suffer by the wars of the generals and the marauding armies of the warlords. Politically, there is no right of free speech and free press, no right of assembly and organization. Radicals and revolutionaries are imprisoned, tortured and killed. Culturally, there is no money for the education of the people, because 90 per cent of the revenue is squandered by the various local and provincial governments for the maintenance of their armies.

All of these conditions are aggravated by the war of Japanese imperialism against China. How is it possible that Japan can wage a war against China? There are two reasons: first, Japanese imperialism is assisted by imperialist England and France, which also aim at further dismemberment of China. The League of Nations has given Japan a free hand, making only such reservations as aim to guard the imperialist-robber interests of the other powers and to deceive their own and the Chinese people. The second reason lies in China itself. The Chinese people want resistance against Japanese and every other imperialism. The Chiang Kai-shek Government stifles this resistance by suppression of the boycott, sabotage of the Volunteers and abolition of the democratic rights of the people. The main forces of the country are employed to fight not the Japanese but the Chinese people, the workers and peasants of China. The leadership of the armies of China is in the hands of reactionary, treacherous generals.

Who "defended" Jehol? The opium general, Tang Yu-lin, chairman of Jehol Province. He opened the gates of China to the Japanese invaders. He left the Volunteers in the ditch without arms and supplies; he stabbed his own soldiers in the back. Who is responsible for this treason? The Chiang Kai-shek Government. Why? This government employs its main forces against the Chinese people; it puts treacherous generals in command and prevents their removal; it prevents the arming of the people and the organization of volunteer military detachments for the waging of a national revolutionary war against Japanese imperialism.

Today even members of the Chiang Kai-shek Government raise the cry: "Death to Tang Yu-lin!" We agree, but we doubt that Nanking will shoot him. He should have been shot long ago. But did not T. V. Soong, Minister of Finance, declare a few weeks ago that the suggestion that Tang Yu-lin is on the Japanese side of the fence is an insult to the nation? So, only when the Chinese people overcome the treason of their leaders will China live.

And now for the Chiang Kai-shek Government—the so-called "central authority". The time has come when its phrases about "prolonged resistance" can no longer hide the facts of betrayal, cowardice and non-resistance. No preparations for real resistance were made by General Chiang Kai-shek and the Kuomintang leaders of Nanking. Only the utterly foolish hope was expressed that Japan might stop at the Great Wall, and that Japan's war of aggression would break down of itself owing to internal revolution and financial bankruptcy. But Japan will not stop. Jehol is the key for the invasion of Mongolia as well as of the north of China. Japan will not only take the territory north of the Yellow River, but will repeat its bombardment of Shanghai as well as other Yangtze ports, in order to win greater power in the Yangtze Valley and dictate terms to the Chinese people. In its future war against the Soviet Union, Japan will even attempt to use the Chinese masses as cannon-fodder, as it is already to-day using the Chinese soldiers of Manchuria against their brothers and sisters in Jehol and Hopei. When a nation can be driven to fight the robber wars of another imperialist power, it has reached the lowest depths of its humiliation.

What is our task, the task of the Chinese people? It is clear. We must take the road of national and social liberation. The Chiang Kai-shek Government cannot unite China, cannot lead the national revolutionary war of the armed people against imperialism, cannot give land to the peasants. Why not? Because it is seeking always to compromise with imperialism. Because it fears the armed people more than the imperialist invaders, because it is the representative of the landlord-bourgeois bloc which exploits and suppresses the masses and ruins the country.

I call upon all men and women, the youth of China, and especially the workers, peasants, students and Volunteers, to unite and organize this struggle for the liberation, unity and integrity of China, a struggle inseparably bound up with the efforts for the emancipation of the toiling masses from exploitation, with the fight for the rights of free speech, free press, assembly and organization, and for the liberation of political prisoners. Only through such effort will be developed the unconquerable national and social forces which will break the power of imperialism and its treacherous allies. Let us remember that the Soviet Revolution demonstrated the superiority of a revolutionary people and its revolutionary armies over the forces of the whole capitalist world. The Chinese people with its already great revolutionary tradition will conquer in the same way. Not imperialist domination and the dismemberment of China, but a free, united, revolutionary China of the workers and peasants!

We must fight in every city and village for these demands:

(1) That at least 80 per cent of the armed forces of the country, with adequate equipment and all airplanes, be sent against Japanese imperialism to regain Manchuria and Jehol and to defend China;

(2) That the people be armed and that voluntary military detachments be formed;

(3) That democratic rights — free speech, free press, right of assembly and organization — be granted at once, and that the imprisonment, torture and killing of revolutionaries cease immediately;

(4) That the advance against the Soviet territories in China be stopped. Let it be emphasized that not only has the Soviet Government of China declared war on Japanese imperialism, but in January of this year it offered its co-operation with any army or military detachment in the fight against Japanese imperialism, upon the condition that the advance against Soviet territory cease, that democratic rights be given to the people, and that the people be armed.

If we want to carry through these demands we must prepare to fight. We must organize in every factory, every school and university, every city and village. Our demands must be discussed in every house, shop, and factory. Our demands must flood the streets. Only by arousing the masses to the seriousness of the situation and to the task of the future, will we bring action. This action will be the broad and anti-imperialist struggle culminating in the national revolutionary war of the armed people against Japanese and other imperialism. It is the duty of all national revolutionary elements to prepare for this struggle.

STATEMENT ISSUED AS CHINA REPRESENTA-TIVE OF THE WORLD COMMITTEE AGAINST IMPERIALIST WAR

Appeared in the magazine "China Forum"

August 6, 1933

In the West, successive conferences and endless negotiations among the capitalist powers seeking a way out of the world crisis have only served to deepen it and to bring out into bolder relief than ever the conflicts and antagonisms which are rapidly leading the world toward a new conflagration. The hopeless failure of the World Economic Conference showed how clearly these conflicts are daily being accentuated, rather than attenuated, by the march of events. Today the entire capitalist world is in a state of intense economic warfare. It will scarcely be long before the war of currencies and tariffs is transformed into a war of poison gas, air bombs and artillery.

In the Far East, imperialist war, with its attendant devastation of cities and wide areas, its terrific toll in human lives, in suffering and privation, has already been a fact for nearly two years. Japanese imperialism has carved out huge areas of China and is racing ahead, trying to outdistance the other imperialist powers in the partitioning and dismemberment of China and the enslavement of its people.

Fully aware of the value of these international conferences* and fully aware that the crisis and its conflicts are inevitable forerunners of imperialist war, the powers have been and are building their war machines to a level and capacity for destruction of human lives unknown before in the history of the world. The coming of fascism in Germany, the signature of the Four-Power Pact directed against the Soviet Union, the outspoken "reversion" to nationalist policies, and the launching of a monster naval building program by the United States, the feverish scrambling for alliances —the headlong march toward war and death and destruction—are the outstanding features of the present period.

The United States is seeking a temporary palliative for her own crisis in inflation and concurrently is driving forward with a program which will make her the greatest sea power on the face of the earth. Great Britain, crushed between the pressure of American and Japanese competition on all the markets previously her uncontested domain, and the threatened collapse of the Empire on the basis of economic conflicts, is leading the movement to secure a military-naval bloc of powers which will attack the Soviet Union before the inter-imperialist antagonisms themselves thunder through

---

* Referring to the founding Congress of the World Committee Against Imperialist War. This statement was issued in the capacity of Chairman of the Shanghai Preparatory Committee for the Far East Conference which would relate the struggle against imperialism in this sector to the international fight for liberation and peace. The conference was banned and had to be held in secret and the foreign delegates were not allowed to leave their ship. I defied the prohibition and went aboard to personally greet them.

the surface of diplomatic niceties in a catastrophic explosion.

France is carefully threading her way through conflicts that demand the maintenance of the Versailles system, the Little Entente and her alliances with Poland, and the nurturing of the anti-Soviet bloc (Four Power Pact) which signalizes the active entry of fascist Germany into the imperialist arena, an entry which France watches with mistrust and suspicion. Fascism in Germany knows it cannot bring bread but bullets to the workers, and is now striving to hurl them to death on battlefields which must inevitably one day become the graveyards of the whole capitalist system.

Japan in the Far East is steadily and consistently building up her war machine in the territories she wrenched from China and is preparing with a series of studied provocations for the ultimate and inevitable attack on the Soviet Union. In this task she is clearly being aided by international imperialism, despite the inner conflicts that make both England and the United States regard her progress with misgivings.

Thus, through a maze of inner conflicts and contradictions, while millions starve and warehouses burst with grain and foodstuffs, while millions go cold and unclothed, while factories remain idle, capitalism is bringing the world ever closer to a new bloodbath more ghastly than any conflict that has ever in history left its fields strewn with dead. This steady progress toward murder and destruction is being accompanied by a wave of war propaganda in every capitalist country on the face of the earth,

Every means in the possession of the ruling classes, the enormous facilities of the press, the radio, the cinema, the schools, are being bent to the task of hoodwinking and deceiving the people, driving them to fight against their fellow-workers and fellow-sufferers in other lands.

This wave must be met and fought. Against it must be marshalled the fighting forces of the world working class and all toiling masses who are alone capable of nullifying the war plans of the imperialist powers. Only the united action of the masses of the world can prevent and forestall the forthcoming slaughter. Throughout the world today a campaign is proceeding to awaken the masses to a realization of their impending fate, to instill in the hearts and minds of exploited men the knowledge of their own ability, by united action, to determine their own destiny and the fate of the millions who will follow them.

One aspect of this anti-war movement is the World Committee Against Imperialist War, established on an international scale at the Anti-War Congress held at Amsterdam in August 1932, where more than 2,000 delegates, representing 30,000,000 workers in 30 lands, gathered to organize the struggle against the impending imperialist war. This committee has now sent a delegation to the Far East to unify the campaign against war here, where Japanese imperialism has already reached out its dripping talons over the body politic of China, and where the base betrayal of the Chinese ruling classes and the Kuomintang has consistently sabotaged the efforts of the Chinese masses to resist and repel the invader.

Under the international auspices of this committee, an Anti-War Congress will be held in Shanghai during the month of September, uniting all elements actively prepared to enter the struggle against war. The Shanghai Anti-War Congress is not organized along political party lines. It will welcome to its sessions all who are prepared to help prevent the advent of a new world slaughter, a new imperialist war.

We appeal to all who are willing to join in this movement to send delegates to this Congress. Especially do we invite delegates from factories and unemployed workers, from trade unions and workers' clubs, from peasant organizations and members of local Kuomintang branches, from universities, schools, and student-youth organizations, from among intellectuals, writers, artists and cultural organizations, from anti-imperialist, anti-Japanese organizations, boycott groups and Chinese Volunteers, from handicraft guilds and from all organizations desirous of participating in the struggle.

CHINA'S FREEDOM AND THE FIGHT
AGAINST WAR

Translation of the main address delivered before
the Shanghai Anti-War Congress
September 30, 1933

Comrades and Friends:

If we were able to hold an open conference, free
from the terror and interference of the imperialist and
Kuomintang authorities, there would be thousands of
delegates, raising their voices on behalf of China's exploited millions. Although the number of delegates to
this conference had to be limited for obvious reasons,
this smaller gathering represents in no smaller degree
the interests of the toiling masses and their protest
against the carnage of war, carried out by the Japanese
and other imperialists against the Chinese people.

I do not want to deal with the ever-increasing war
danger in its totality. Suffice it to say that we in
China are at war already and that it is only a question
of a very limited period before the war waged against
China will develop into a world conflagration.

The present epoch is that of a dying system. Capitalism is desperately seeking a way out of its contradictions. The only way open to the capitalists is to
intensify the exploitation and oppression of the people
and to prepare and carry out new wars for a redivision

of world markets. The capitalist system falls into ever deeper chaos. The collapse of its economic system, the sharpening of imperialist antagonisms, the rise of fascism and intensification of the most barbarous expressions of national chauvinism, the use of the most brutal forms of oppression, torture, and murder against the toiling masses and their leaders, the retardation of cultural and productive progress, are all features of decaying capitalism.

But the capitalist system has brought forward the class destined to smash it—the proletariat. With its dominant role in production, its separate and distinct class interests, the proletariat developed its own ideology and has assumed today the leadership of the struggle of all exploited and oppressed peoples throughout the world, workers and peasants in all capitalist, colonial and semi-colonial countries.

Therefore, the present epoch also marks the birth of a new system of society—Socialism. Because the class interests and class forces of the bourgeoisie and landlords stand in the way of the peaceful development of society to a higher form, because the masses cannot live if the means of production and distribution remain longer in the hands of the few exploiters, proletarian revolution becomes the most urgent social necessity of our day.

While the capitalists seek their salvation in war, the toiling masses seek and must seek theirs in revolution.

History shows us clearly that wars become ever more destructive, more catastrophic, and occur at ever shorter intervals. But at the same time, war does not solve but heightens the contradictions of the capitalist system. With each successive war, the forces of revolution gather strength, assert themselves, and draw nearer to their ultimate triumph.

The Franco-Prussian war of 1870-71 produced the Paris Commune; the Russo-Japanese war of 1904-05 accelerated the development of the bourgeois-democratic revolution in Russia. The world war of 1914-18 gave enormous impetus to the revolutionary movement throughout the world and led to the triumph of the revolution of the workers and peasants in Russia, laying the foundations for the construction of Socialism on a gigantic scale.

It is clear that the drive for the dismemberment of China, led by Japanese imperialism, will hasten the development of the revolutionary forces throughout Asia, China, and the whole capitalist world.

I should like to make clear my position towards the different forms of war. War is always an instrument of politics, an instrument designed and used to enforce a specific policy. Most wars are waged for conquest of territory and peoples, for domination of new markets, and for the acquisition of new sources of raw materials. All these wars are directed against the broad masses. They lead to untold miseries and increased sufferings for all who toil and die. Unless they lead to revolution, they result in further enslavement of the workers and peasants. These wars and their "peace treaties" increase the danger of new wars on a still larger scale. It becomes the task of the masses, therefore, to oppose such imperialist wars with all their power and to try to "transform them into civil war for the overthrow of the bourgeoisie", for shattering the regime of the ruling class.

At present, great attempts are being made by the imperialists to overcome the sharpening antagonisms which rend them asunder by temporary agreements for a new division of China and a war of intervention against the U.S.S.R. Japan's robber war on China is by no means the beginning. Long before Japan seized Korea and Taiwan (Formosa), the other imperialist powers had acquired control of all the strategic centres of China; had forced opium on its population; dominated the financial and economic policies of the country; retarded its economic development; and had begun to use the Chinese militarists and others as cat's paws for their different imperialist aims.

The attempts of Sun Yat-sen to secure China's independence were nullified by the Kuomintang, representing landlord and capitalist interests, which betrayed the mass movement of 1925-27 and has been pursuing ever since a policy of terror against the workers and peasants, hostility towards the U.S.S.R. and of cowardly opportunism towards imperialism. It is this policy of the Kuomintang which enabled Japanese imperialism to embark successfully on its war against China, tearing Manchuria from China, penetrating and dominating the North, and now looking ambitiously southward towards the rest of the country.

It is this same policy which encourages and aids British imperialism to extend its influence on our western frontier. It is this policy which is helping France in its imperialist designs on Yunnan. And it is this policy which is helping the U.S.A. establish its financial and political hegemony over China, and the League of Nations (Britain and France) to further its nefarious schemes for joint imperialist control of China. The end is not yet in sight. We are only at the beginning of the most gigantic imperialist robbery in China's history, aided and abetted by the successive Kuomintang betrayals. If the imperialist powers and their Kuomintang puppets are not stopped by the masses, the end will be the complete partitioning and dismemberment of China and the deeper enslavement of its people.

Moreover the imperialist powers will fight out their battles at the expense of the Chinese people. A whole series of wars will develop in which the human and material resources of China will be used by the different imperialist powers for their own ends. Just as the Chinese population of Manchuria today is already being used by Japanese imperialism, so will the people of the whole of China be used as cannon-fodder by the different imperialists, aided, as now, by the Chinese militarists, landlords and capitalists.

Japanese imperialism is building up Manchuria as a base for the future war against the U.S.S.R. It is trying to broaden its base by first dominating and ultimately occupying the territory north of the Yellow River, by invading Inner Mongolia and the Mongolian People's Republic and by completely subjugating all of China. British imperialism, with its bitter antagonism toward the U.S.A., its growing struggle with Japanese imperialism in Asia, its fear of revolution in India, its hatred of the U.S.S.R., is trying desperately to form a bloc of the European imperialist powers against the U.S.S.R. and thereby postpone the inevitable war among the imperialist robbers.

This is the true state of affairs at present and it is criminal treason to look for help from any of the imperialist powers or from the League of Nations. It is folly to hope for salvation from the policy of the Kuomintang, which today is planning more consciously and deliberately than ever before the complete and unconditional surrender to the Japanese and other imperialists. The leaders of the Kuomintang have only one demand and hope, that they be allowed by the imperialists to remain in power with the privilege of continuing to extract their share of the tribute from the misery and exploitation of the Chinese people.

Help and salvation can come only from the masses themselves. China's millions, the great masses of the peasantry led by the working class, are irresistible if they unite in the struggle for rice and land against imperialism and the Kuomintang.

Already millions of workers and peasants have taken up this struggle and the fact that for a number of years big Soviet territories have existed in China is the hope, the promise, the guarantee, that the broad masses of China will travel along the same path.

Out of these struggles alone will develop the power and strength capable of freeing and uniting China; rejecting the imperialists; liberating Manchuria and the other stolen territories; giving land, bread, and freedom to the Chinese people, including the freedom of the different races to develop their own national existences.

These struggles alone can save China from the untold miseries of successive wars and the brutalization of prolonged capitalist exploitation. Only the realization of the proletarian, the agrarian, and the anti-imperialist revolution can form the basis for the future development of China toward Socialism.

Supporters of imperialism ask us, "You oppose imperialist war and white terror. Why don't you oppose the use of force in revolution?"

To this question we can answer plainly, "The use of force by a revolutionary class against oppression is fully justified. The use of force by a suppressed people fighting for its national liberation is fully justified. In both cases armed struggle is necessary because the forces of reaction never relinquish their power voluntarily."

Imperialist wars, militarist wars, wars of intervention against the Soviets in China or against the U.S.S.R., oppression and terror against the masses, all serve reactionary ends. *Reactionary force can be met only by revolutionary force.* Only by taking this stand do we come to a clear understanding of our tasks in the present national revolutionary crisis of China. We are not against every war. If so, we would be playing directly into the hands of the imperialists and help to disarm the Chinese people in its present and future struggles. *We are for the national revolutionary war of the armed people of China against imperialism.*

China will become free only when its people will rise in their tens and scores of millions. The example of the struggle of the French people during their Great Revolution against superior foreign invaders, the struggle of the workers and peasants of the Soviet Union who repelled the combined forces of all imperialist powers, point the way out for the Chinese people.

It is now fashionable to ask: "How can our suppressed people in China wage such a successful struggle against such powerful enemies?" But has not the history of our own country already given us our answer? The Northern Expedition taught us that a revolutionary force is far superior to reactionary forces and can win victories against overwhelming odds.   The Workers' and Peasants' Red Armies in China have fought many times against armies tenfold their strength—and they have won! Armies are not the only decisive factor, ideas also have their role to play.

Certainly the combination of a ruling revolutionary ideology with good arms is the best guarantee of success and victory over the imperialists and the reactionaries. It is obvious that the struggle of the heroic Volunteers in Manchuria who resisted Japanese imperialism for so long a time (and are still doing so) would have reached far higher levels if the Volunteers had not been so criminally sabotaged.

In addition to sabotage on the part of the Chiang Kai-shek Government, there was another factor which retarded the movement. The anti-Japanese Volunteer leaders were afraid of the masses and disarmed them, giving arms only to those whom they considered "safe" from the class viewpoint of the landlords, gentry and capitalists. The workers and peasants of Manchuria had to take up arms in opposition to these leaders of the Volunteers, Generals Ma Chan-San and Li Tu, as well as the Japanese. Under such conditions, success was no immediate possibility.

Before we can successfully struggle against the great military machine of Japanese and other imperialisms, the Chinese people must free themselves from the shackles which the militarists, landlords and capitalists in China have fastened upon them.

The Kuomintang is cropping the powers of resistance inherent in our great toiling masses. It suppresses any mobilization of the masses for any form of fight against Japanese imperialism. It suppresses in the most brutal way the workers, peasants, students, and Volunteers in the territory under its rule. It mobilizes all available forces for great campaigns against the Soviet districts. It negotiates with Japanese imperialism about the conditions under which Manchuria and the North shall become Japanese and the rest of China an imperialist colony. It begs for help, money, arms, munitions to fight the Chinese people, and becomes more completely dependent upon the imperialists. This is not the road to salvation; it is the road to the death of the Chinese nation.

Hand in hand with the struggle for the national revolutionary war against Japanese and other imperialisms, must go the struggle for the establishment of a real people's government in China. Such a government can only be formed by the workers and peasants themselves. The Provisional Central Government of the Soviet Republic of China is pointing the way to all the toilers of China. And the proposals of the Soviet Government and the Workers' and Peasants' Red Armies to conclude military agreements with any army in the struggle against Japanese imperialism (with the attached condition that the people be armed and democratic rights be given them), shows the seriousness of the Soviet Government's readiness to fight imperialism. So far these appeals, although they have won the sympathy of the masses and soldiers, have not met with any successful response. This shows that the commands of the different military units are either pro-imperialist, Kuomintang tools, or else are afraid to take up a real struggle.

To sum up, we are against imperialist wars but we are for the national revolutionary war of the armed people which can alone free China from the imperialist combination. A successful national revolutionary war can only be carried through when the people free themselves from the rule of the Kuomintang and establish their own government of workers and peasants, as has already been done in several different parts of China.

We are strongly opposed to militarist wars in China. Different groups of militarists are constantly fighting for the exclusive right to exploit certain provinces or territories. Different factions of the Kuomintang are constantly fighting among themselves for power and pelf at the expense of the people. Different groups of the imperialists use the militarists to further their own ends and to weaken China. These wars cause untold suffering for the masses of the population and the soldiers. It is clear that China's militarists, hitched to the wagon of the Kuomintang and the imperialists, must be smashed and exterminated.

There remains our one appeal to the whole Chinese people, to the toiling masses, an appeal for unity now in the struggle against the Japanese and other imperialists, the struggle for the unity, independence and integrity of our country. Let us unite in the struggle against all those who betray our country and sell it, province by province, to the imperialists! Let us join and defend to the best of our ability the workers and peasants in China who have already freed themselves from the yoke of imperialist domination and feudal exploitation, and who are today threatened by the fifth and largest offensive of the Kuomintang forces. This offensive is directly aided by sixteen of the fifty American millions loaned to the Chiang Kai-shek Government, by American planes, bombs and flying instructors, by Japanese, British, American and French warships which rush to the aid of the Kuomintang where they can (as recently in Fukien), and by every other possible form of material and moral imperial support.

Let us rally to the defence of the U.S.S.R. against the threatening war of intervention! Let us develop a powerful movement against imperialist war throughout the Far East and above all in China.

STATEMENT UPON THE ASSASSINATION OF YANG CHUAN

Shanghai

1934

Last Friday, Yang Chuan came to see me and show-ed me many of the threatening letters he had received in recent weeks and told me of verbal warnings he had been given concerning plots against his life. He told me that on several occasions friends had come to him directly from Nanking to warn him that certain people were planning to kill him.

On Friday, his particular mission was to warn me that several of the letters he had received included my name among those who would soon feel the blows of the terror. I told him I had likewise received many such threats—often in the vilest possible language—and urged him in turn to be careful. That was the last time I saw Mr. Yang.

These people and their hired murderers think they can crush the slightest movement of struggle toward freedom by sheer force of violence, kidnapping, torture, murder. These are the weapons of their rule. They signalize and characterize the entire regime. The China League for Civil Rights represents one such movement for freedom, and it was because of his activities in this organization that Yang was murdered in cold blood.

But far from crushing us, the penalty he paid for his sympathy for liberty must mean renewed struggle and renewed efforts to carry on until events develop to their logical conclusion. Let the murderers of Yang Chuan realize that political crimes inevitably carry with them their own penalties.

STATEMENT ISSUED UPON THE ARREST OF THE "SEVEN GENTLEMEN"

Shanghai

November 26, 1936

As one of the members of the Executive Committee of the All-China Federation of National Salvation Associations, and in view of the arrest of seven of the leaders of this organization, I wish to enter my protest against these unwarranted arrests and the groundless charges made against them.

It is obvious to any thinking person that these arrests and these charges are the result of Japanese influence. That the hand of the Japanese can be seen in these arrests is evidenced by the report of the Shanghai Mainichi,* issued on November 25th (yesterday) in which it is stated that I was arrested early this morning by the French authorities, charged with Communist activities, in connection with the Third International. Perhaps the "Mainichi" and the "Nippo"*, which published similar rumors, have advance information!

The well-known object of the National Salvation Association is to bring the Government and the people

---

* Both Japanese Government-supported newspapers.

together into one united front of resistance to Japanese aggression. Contrary to the provocative assertions of the Japanese, the National Salvation Association is neither pro-Communist nor anti-Government. These charges are deliberately fabricated by the Japanese as a means of inciting the Chinese Government against the National Salvation Association, thus driving a wedge between the Chinese Government and the people for their own advantage.

Despite these arrests and malicious charges, the National Salvation Association reaffirms its position: It is not anti-Government; it is not pro-Communist; it is for a united front of all people, regardless of their political beliefs or party affiliations, and for a national war of liberation.

May I point out the fact that such tactics on the part of the Japanese, contrary to their intention, will only serve instead to further arouse the wrath and patriotic indignation of the people against them.

As to the personal charges made against me, they are so ridiculous that it should be unnecessary to refute the slanders of the Japanese press, which is notorious for its libelous and dirty disseminations.

Seven leaders of the National Salvation Association have been arrested, but there are still 475 million Chinese people, whose patriotic wrath and righteous indignation cannot be suppressed. Let the Japanese militarists beware! They may cause the arrest of seven leaders, but they must still reckon with the Chinese people!

FOLLOW THE WILL OF SUN YAT-SEN

A speech delivered to the Third Plenary
Session of the Kuomintang

February 18, 1937

The eyes of all the Chinese people are anxiously turned toward the Third Plenary Session of the Kuomintang Party that is being held in Nanking at this critical period of our history. China has been driven to its last extremity by Japanese aggression. The final sacrifice is inevitable. Japanese provocations have raised the anti-Japanese movement to a high point, and it is gaining great momentum. All Japanese efforts to take over North China have signally failed. Japanese bandits have met with defeat in their efforts to attack Suiyuan, while their efforts to force demands upon the Chinese Government resulted in failure. The determination and resolution of the Chinese people to make no more concessions to Japanese imperialism but to prepare to recover our lost territories is of greatest political significance in the life of our nation.

Humiliating negotiations with Japan must cease!

It is most unfortunate that there are still politicians who do not understand the real situation, and who are victims of the "fear of Japan" sickness. They overesti-mate the strength of Japanese imperialism and underestimate the power of the Chinese people. Such erroneous ideas are without foundation.

Japan cannot defeat China because, first, she is economically and financially too weak to withstand a long war; second, because the Japanese people themselves are opposed to war. The upheaval in their political life indicates their worry and dissatisfaction with the militarist-adventurist policy which has brought heavy burdens and impoverishment to the Japanese toiling masses; third, because the military strength of Japan is numerically inferior; lastly, and this is the determinant factor, because the Chinese people themselves have resolved to fight to the end.

It would be ridiculous to think that Japan can send from 15 to 20 divisions to fight in China when the general situation in the Far East is so unfavorable to them. This number would be too insignificant a force for them ever to hope to accomplish their purpose, and the fact remains that neither their industry nor their reserves will permit the sending of greater numbers. This small force, scattered over our immense territories would be shattered by our numerically superior Chinese soldiers, fighting for their lives and country. They have saved Suiyuan from the aggressors, and they will save the nation.

There can be no doubt to whom the victory would go! If only the Government would execute the last will of our late party leader, Sun Yat-sen, who on his deathbed declared that the salvation of China lies in the faithful execution of his Three Policies!

Improvement of the peoples' livelihood is essential for every Chinese government. Although in the last few years there has been some small progress in the field of railway construction and road building, still the living conditions of the people remain unchanged.

Poverty, misery and distress are evident in all rural districts. Our farmers are suffering from exorbitant levies, taxes and extortions from still unabolished feudal remnants in the villages. And we must not forget that the peasantry is the backbone of the Chinese economy. Unemployment in the cities is affecting the toiling masses. Not only are the workers in a miserable state, but the young intelligentsia is without work. Educated in schools and universities, our Chinese youth must idle in the streets without hope of applying their knowledge.

The only solution to this problem is to promote rural construction and industrialization of our country. To carry this out it is necessary to act in accordance with the teachings of our late party leader. The government must free the mass movement, sponsor mass initiative and enthusiasm for reconstructive purposes. Only then can the principle of livelihood be fulfilled. We must never forget that the late party leader always taught that the promotion of the mass movement in every field of activity is the basic condition of success. Reconstruction and rural improvement will go speedily forward only when we follow Sun Yat-sen's will and teaching.

Practically, to bring the masses into action the Government must bring to an end the period of tutelage, convoke the National Congress as speedily as possible and attract people of talent, notwithstanding their party affiliations, to the Government. The National Congress will fulfil its task only when the electoral system is so arranged that the masses can really participate.

To facilitate the election, the Government must immediately abolish censorship, grant freedom of assembly, organization and speech, release all political prisoners and give living reality to the late party leader's will for a democratic government.

It is very regrettable that even now we have in the government certain individuals who have not yet understood that for the salvation of the country, we must liquidate every civil war. How ridiculous it is to hear today the antiquated theory that first we must suppress the Communists and then resist Japanese aggression! Shall we go to war with one arm broken? We have had ten years of experience in civil wars, when the country's energies have been wasted on internal strife and the country devastated while Japanese militarists were slicing off one piece after another of our territory.

Every Chinese patriot now rejoices that after these painful experiences, the Government is beginning to understand that internal strife must cease for the sake of national salvation and that all forces, including the Communists, must be utilized to preserve Chinese national integrity. It is self-evident that Chinese must not fight against Chinese. The Chinese people do not want to fight against their own brothers. They know it is against the interest of the nation. Every internal conflict can and must be solved peacefully and amicably. There must be no more civil wars. There must be peace and unity. We must speedily build up Chinese national defence against foreign aggression.

Although the salvation of China depends on the Chinese people themselves, yet the late party leader has advised us not to isolate ourselves from the outer world, but to cooperate with those nations who treat us on the basis of equality. World-wide sympathy is with China in her struggle to meet Japanese aggression. The task of the government is to utilize such sympathy in the most effective way.

I have said nothing new in this article, only what our dead party leader has instructed us. I firmly believe that if the Government will faithfully follow the will of Sun Yat-sen and take effective steps to execute his three fundamental Policies, then China will quickly recover from her internal turmoil and distress, and externally will be greatly respected by the world.

CONFUCIANISM AND MODERN CHINA

Published in "Asia" Magazine

New York

April 1937

Many discussions are now going on in China regarding the practicability of applying Confucian teachings to modern life. In the past twenty years, many scholars, politicians and statesmen have been trying to revive Confucian teachings in the belief that in these years of disorders, calamities and foreign invasions, Confucianism would be able to consolidate, strengthen and unify the Chinese nation, as it had done many times in early Chinese history. But there are other scholars and educationalists who are equally convinced that Confucianism must be banished from every schoolbook if modern China is to survive.

There began three years ago a movement entitled "The New Life", which is flavored with Confucianism. This makes it of great practical importance to find the right approach to Confucianism. Therefore, let us look back into the age when Confucius was alive, into the era of the old Chinese sages. It was in the 5th and 7th centuries B. C. that the two most popular Chinese sages, Laotse and Confucius, were living and teaching. Both gathered around them many followers and disciples. First we must answer the question whether there was need for their teachings or not.

In the epoch when these sages were living, there were great disorders everywhere in ancient China. Feudal states were jealous and constantly engaged in contending with one another. The various feudal states were fighting for supremacy and there was uncertainty in all vital human relationships. Many feudal groups succumbed in war. The fate of other feudal states continuously hung in the balance. One day the feudal lords were powerful, the next they were banished or put to death. And the great masses of the people were increasingly oppressed and exploited. Not only was compulsory labor imposed upon them, but added to their other calamities was the burden of military service. The most important obligation of the government then was to maintain irrigation systems, to dig canals, to prevent floods and to erect dams. But these most vital functions of state were neglected owing to wars, corrupt officials and disorders which impoverished the people. The people were unhappy. Tears and sorrow were evident everywhere. It was a period of bloodshed, flood, plague and famine and not only was there warfare between the feudal lords, but there were also uprisings of the peasantry, together with the suppressions of these uprisings by the lords. Thus, we see that in this era, 500-700 B. C., the class struggle existed. At that time came two Chinese philosophers, Laotse and Confucius, whose influence upon Chinese life and thought are felt even today.

Laotse was inspired with hatred against the state and the feudal landlords. His teachings possessed many points in common with the anarchists of later periods. He expressed the protest of the peasantry against oppression. In his teachings we find great hatred towards the ruling class, the heads of states with their wars and armies trampling upon the growing grain, destroying dykes, robbing farmers of their crops and animals, forcing sons and husbands away from their families, turning them into soldiers to fight for the interests of landlords. Laotse taught that weapons, even when they are victorious, are not blessed among the tools. Today we Chinese should say instead, "Blessed are the weapons which help to defend our national independence." The masses hated the state, government and kings, and Laotse expressed their hatred. The people would have been contented had there been no government at all. This idea of indifference to the state is expressed clearly in our ancient poetry and folklore. For example, I cite here the following verse which is perhaps more than 3,000 years old:

> "We rise at dawn,
> And rest at sunset,
> We dig wells and drink,
> We till our fields and eat,
> What is the royal power to us?"

But Laotse was not revolutionary. He did not call upon the people to fight the existing evils and master them. Passive resistance, indifference and quietism were the ideals of Taoism which sprang from the teachings of Laotse and became the religion of the oppressed Chinese masses.

The original teachings of Laotse were not for the ruling class, the landlords or the literati who were receiving their bounties from rich patrons. They needed another philosophy to express their ideas of statehood. And although there was great need to bring order out of chaos, Confucius came along with his teachings and obscured this need.

As a reformer, Confucius played a great historical role. He created moral codes for feudal society. In attempting to strengthen this feudal order, he based his teachings on historical traditions. The stories about the semi-mythical model kings, Yao and Shun, were perhaps manufactured by Confucius himself, or his disciples. No one can prove whether Yao and Shun really lived. But based on the myths about them, Confucius and his disciples evolved conceptions of the feudal order. People cannot govern themselves, they declared. People must be governed by wise and judicious officials. They taught that obedience is the general principle of every human society. Wives must submit to husbands, children to parents, and every man to his ruler and king. To make people submissive, Confucius created a whole structure of ceremonies to consolidate the position of feudal order. He set forth vindications for patriarchal authority. Sovereignty in the Confucian state is built upon the authority of the father in the home; the patriarchal family is the cell, the sub-structure of feudalism.

Out of the five relationships in Confucian teachings, four are concerned with the family: relationship between father and son, between husband and wife, between brothers and between family friends. I think such great emphasis on family relationships in Confucian teachings was in harmony with the economic conditions of ancient China. The large families of feudal China were the foundation for the economic structure of the country. All products which the family required were produced in the family, and every member of the family was obliged to work and maintain the family. The family was an economic unit. And although this family system existed thousands of years ago, its strong influence extends even to our modern times. Confucian teachings contributed largely to make the Chinese family-minded instead of national-minded. Confucius put emphasis upon obligations toward family and he said very little about obligations toward the state, the nation as a whole.

Confucian teachings are feudalistic and autocratic from beginning to end. Society was divided into two classes: the ruling class—the landlords, and the subjugated class—the peasantry, and between these were the literati. In the Book of Rites, we find such a characteristic saying: "Courtesy is not extended to commoners, and punishment is not applied to lords."

There were many speculations around Confucianism during more than two milleniums, as well as different interpretations of his teachings. There were periods in Chinese history when Confucianism was banned and his books burnt. But notwithstanding, Confucianism survived and dominated Chinese thought. And there is little wonder, Confucianism is the philosophy of feudalism, and so long as the feudal system existed, there was need of Confucian teachings. But Confucius' ethical system degenerated into mere rituals and ceremonials, while his precepts enslaved the intellects of the scholars, limited the scope of learning and kept the masses of the people in ignorance.

Confucius was conservative. He based his teachings, as we have seen, solely on tradition. It is natural that Confucian conservatism has hindered the development of science and social order in China. Confucius taught the old truth. Never had he anything to do with revolution. His teachings are hostile to every change of social order. It is strange indeed that in our modern times there are still Chinese intellectuals zealously advocating the revival of Confucianism. Efforts to turn back the clock of history are not only fruitless and futile, but they obstruct human progress and advancement. Instead of reviving anachronistic Confucianism, it is of utmost importance for us to eradicate all remnants of feudalism in rural economy as well as in urban life. We must cleanse the Chinese mentality and free it from the cobwebs of Confucian ideology which block our cultural development. Revival of Confucianism is pure reaction disguised as concern for social order.

History tells us that the old sage was very rational-minded, and despised superstitions. In his teachings there was no mention of god. But now in this enlightened day, we see people who would make of him a god. Indeed the old sage would turn with horror in his grave could he but know that posterity would make a god out of him.

The structure of our present society is radically changing, transforming and remodelling. Naturally the new social order demands new ideology, new moral codes and new relationships. There is confusion in many minds and it is difficult to solve the problems that arise from the great changes that are taking place in

China. Confucianism cannot help to solve them; it has lost every practical value. Only the reactionary-minded seek its restoration. Only in our history books will Confucius live and occupy many important chapters because of his definite role in Chinese civilization.

But Confucian ideology has permeated the brain of Chinese intellectuals during a longer period than any other philosophical system. We must realize how deeply Confucian influences have been imbedded in our art, literature, social sciences and morals. We must exert great efforts to uproot Confucian ideas out of every nook and corner of our life and thoughts.

China today needs another ideology. New economic and technical developments of people's life and new conditions demand new ideology. What China needs, the late party leader, Sun Yat-sen, has pointed out. Although he did not develop his teachings in detail, he has given general lines and principles. To enforce Sun's teachings is of paramount importance today. If they had been put into practice everywhere, many difficulties and problems that have faced us during the past ten years would have been overcome. Our party leader has summarized his teachings in his Three Principles: Nationalism, Democracy and People's Livelihood. These Principles are applicable to the present situation of China. Just as Confucianism represents autocracy, oppression and misery of the people, Sunyatsenism means democracy and the well-being of the people.

Happily, in the past year, we have observed a phenomenal growth of the Chinese national spirit. Chinese nationalism is growing in the form of the anti-

Japanese movement. However, it would be wrong to think that Chinese nationalism is directed against the Japanese people or any other foreign nationals. In all our past history, the Chinese people have been peace-loving. Now more than ever, they have no thought or desire to conquer another nation. The idea of Chinese nationalism is to resist the Japanese warlords who are invading our country. And there is no doubt but that China will not only be able to preserve her present territory, but will surely recover all her lost territory.

The most significant proof of the development of Chinese nationalism is the successful defence of Sui-yuan. In order to keep alive and increase the patriotic flame, the example of Suiyuan must be publicized and made known to every Chinese worker and peasant. Our poets, novelists, writers, painters and actors must popularize the heroic Chinese struggle for national liberation and glorify the national heroes who defended our country from foreign invaders. Society and government must care for our wounded soldiers and the families of the martyrs. When a man has spent his life in the service of his country and returns crippled, it is the obligation of the state to care for him.

We must become military-minded and make every effort to change the mental attitude of our people towards the soldiers who are fighting for the salvation of China. Naturally, our attitude towards soldiers could not be positive when China was suffering so much from her own armies during periods of disorders, especially in the last ten years, when her armies were employed in civil wars against her own people. The people hated these armies for ravaging, massacring workers and peasants and destroying their homes, leaving in their wake misery and devastation. But when civil warfare has ceased and armies are properly used to defend the country's independence, then the people's attitude towards soldiery will naturally change.

"Good iron is not used for nails, nor good men for soldiers". On such pernicious slogans were we educated. Now we must smash this slogan. When the Japanese warlords are menacing the independence of our country, military education must be enforced among the masses. Only in the rising of the masses to defend national independence lies the salvation of China. To defend our country is the most important art which we must learn today. Let us learn to operate machine guns, organize air defence and other military arts. Military virtue, as self-sacrifice, should be glorified and patriotism exalted.

It would be foolish to think that the country can be saved from Japanese encroachments without enlisting support from a mass movement. Sun Yat-sen said that the success of the revolution depends upon the participation of peasants and workers in governing the country. The Kuomintang must help to promote the labor and peasant movement, invite workers and farmers to join the Party so as to secure a real united front against Japanese imperialists. The last plenary session of the Kuomintang decided to convoke the National Congress in November of this year. But what about the electoral system? Nothing has been done to help the people participate in this congress. Evidently the congress will consist only of Kuomintang officials and bureaucrats. This is contrary to Sun's principle of democracy. It is of vital necessity to change the electoral system immediately and introduce universal suffrage, thus enabling the masses to take part.

Although civil warfare has ceased, nothing officially has been heard of the reconciliation with the Communist Party. It is useful to remember what Sun Yat-sen said about the Communist Party: "Not only should we refrain from declaring that Communism conflicts with the People's Livelihood Principle, but we should regard Communism as a good friend. The supporters of the People's Livelihood Principle should study Communism thoughtfully. If Communism is a good ally of the People's Livelihood Principle, why then do members of the Kuomintang oppose the Communist Party?" In 1924 when there was discussion going on as to cooperation with the Communist Party, I asked Sun Yat-sen why it was necessary for the Communists to enter the Kuomintang. He replied: "The Kuomintang is dying from degeneration and therefore fresh blood is required to revitalize it". What did he mean by "degeneration"? He meant that members of the Kuomintang were lacking in revolutionary spirit, morale and courage, forgetting that the Kuomintang was founded for revolutionary purposes—with the disastrous consequence that personal interests began to dominate the actions of its members. More than once, disgusted and disappointed by what he saw around him, Sun remarked to me: "The Kuomintang is composed of the best and worst people in China. The best are attracted to it by its ideals and objectives, while the worst join us because they think it is the stepping-stone towards becoming officials. If we cannot get rid of these parasites, of what good is the Kuomintang?" Even today how true are Sun Yat-sen's words!

As a result of the ten years' fight with the Communists, we have wasted immense numbers of lives, great quantities of materials, energy and money, and have forgotten to defend China against Japanese encroachments. Now although late, it is better late than never to correct this great mistake. China has suffered too long from autocracy during her 5,000 years existence. Let us at last become democratic and create a government of the people, by the people and for the people. From this viewpoint, we must, therefore, cleanse our brains, our schoolbooks and our hearts from the pernicious remnants of Confucian ideology.

But to raise the national spirit and really enforce a democratic government, it is necessary to make great strides to enforce people's livelihood. "Livelihood" said Sun Yat-sen, "is the driving power in all social movements, and if livelihood does not go right, social culture cannot advance, economic organizations cannot improve, morals will decline and many injustices, such as class war, cruelty to workers and other forms of oppression, will spring up—all because of failure to remedy the unfortunate conditions of livelihood. All social changes are effects; the search for livelihood is the cause."

During all these years of Kuomintang rule, we have done nothing to improve the life of the masses. The peasantry is impoverished; many provinces have suffered heavily from civil wars. We must bear in mind that

agriculture is the chief industry of China and that about
90 per cent of the total value of Chinese exports belongs
to agriculture, yet our farming remains in the same
backward condition as in the time of Confucius. As a
result, we have lost valuable markets for our tea, silk and
cotton industries. To improve the livelihood of the peasantry, we must organize nationwide campaigns to improve and promote modern methods of agricultural production.

But in the "New Life Movement", there is nothing
new to be found; it gives nothing to the people. Therefore, I propose to replace this pedantic movement by
another, that is, a great campaign to improve people's
livelihood through the improvement of methods of production.) This would be a revolutionary outlook on life
rather than Confucianism, since the aim of revolution
is the uplifting of the material welfare of human beings,
of the masses. If that is not reached, then there has
been no revolution.

The point is that China has all of the necessary
factors to achieve the well-being of our people. We
possess the earliest history in the world. It had already
reached a high cultural stage when Europe was still
barbarian. Our frugal and industrious people were
harassed by many foreign invasions during our long
history, but we have survived. The great vitality of the
Chinese race conquered even the worst circumstances
and conditions. Hard-working and enduring, our
people labored in many different climes, from the polar
region to the tropics. We not only managed to survive,
but we prospered and multiplied. There is not the
slightest doubt but that we shall overcome the present

crisis and successfully repel every foreign invasion and push forward the revolution as Sun Yat-sen has enjoined us in his last will. In order to achieve this result, we do not need Confucianism. We need unity. We need to cease every internal struggle and prepare to recover our lost territories. We need to learn from the industrial and agricultural achievements of Europe, America and especially the U.S.S.R. Then we will march forward confidently to a glorious future.

CHINA UNCONQUERABLE

Published in "The Forum and Century"

New York

August 1937

I

Hundreds of books and thousands of articles have been written on the subject of the Sino-Japanese conflict. It seems to me that most of the authors overestimate the Japanese strength and underestimate the Chinese power of resistance. But if one examines the policy of the Chinese Government during the past ten years, that impression will be strengthened. Concession after concession has been made to the Japanese. It was only necessary for Japan to make some new bluff, and her aim was achieved. Japan had only to threaten the Chinese by landing some troops and a handful of airplanes, and immediately the Chinese Government made new concessions.

The unfortunate policy of the Chiang Kai-shek Government, which followed the course of internal pacification before resistance of external aggression, has even more played into the hands of the Japanese militarists. But during the past year the situation has changed. The anti-Japanese movement of the people reached a high level, and it became no longer possible for the Japanese to obtain their aims by threats and bluffs. The Chinese people have realized that it is possible for them to resist. They are no longer afraid of their "friendly neighbor".

Mass opinion has made itself felt in China. In the growing demand of the people for resistance to the Japanese, all political differences have become of secondary importance. Military satrapy has given way to the rise of an intense patriotism, which gives hope for a genuine unification of the country.

From my viewpoint, the most important task before China is the realization of Sun Yat-sen's principle of democracy. To guide us in the Chinese revolution, Sun Yat-sen gave us Three Principles—democracy, nationalism and the people's livelihood—and Three Policies, which are the instruments by which these principles can be achieved. The democratic nations have witnessed how neglect of the first principle during the past ten years has brought great calamity to China. There has been endless civil war; the country has been devastated; millions of our people have perished and millions more have been rendered destitute and desperate. The best minds of China have always demanded the cessation of civil warfare and conciliation between the Kuomintang and the Communist Party. Long ago, public opinion condemned the insidious belief that before resisting Japan we must first crush the Communists. Naturally, this policy was provoked by Japan.

As a result of ten years of internal warfare, many parts of the country have been ravaged. And, far from being defeated, the Communists have become the advance guard of the anti-Japanese resistance. From the articles of Edgar Snow, correspondent of the *London*

Daily Herald, who recently visited the Red regions, we know the actual conditions there and realize what a lot of nonsense and false propaganda was written by persons who had never ventured within speaking distance of the "outlaw". In fact, it is quite probable that most of this propaganda originated in Japan.

It is a matter for congratulation that General Chiang Kai-shek has stopped further civil warfare and that the Kuomintang at last, in a recent plenary session, discussed the question of reconciliation with the Communist Party. But it is very regrettable that, in the manifesto of this plenary session, conditions for conciliation with the Communist Party have been laid down which will make a ready compromise difficult of achievement. There are such unreasonable demands as that the Communists cease propagandizing and abandon their political program of class struggle. How can the Communist Party renounce propaganda and the class struggle when those are the basic reasons for its existence? In France and elsewhere, the Communists have not renounced propaganda and the class struggle, and bourgeois parties are successfully cooperating with them. Chinese Communists have repeatedly declared that they would not attack the government if the latter would really resist Japan. To work hand in hand to save the country is their only condition.

Therefore, for reconciliation with the Communist Party, it is necessary only to put into action Sun Yat-sen's principle of democracy, convoke the National Congress, change the electoral system so that the people could really participate and have a voice in the government, release the political prisoners, grant freedom of press, organization and assembly, mobilize the masses for reconstruction of the country and resistance to Japanese militarists.

The sincerity of the Communists in wishing to co-operate with the government was proved clearly through the Sian coup. They exerted every effort to maintain peace between the central government and the north-eastern army. It was the Communists who sponsored the release of General Chiang Kai-shek and the peaceful settlement of the Sian affair. They have done their utmost to preserve unity in China. Therefore, if the Kuomintang desires to follow Sun's policy of alliance with workers and peasants, it must not reject the assistance of the Communists in saving the country. Co-operation between the Kuomintang and the Communist Party is absolutely essential. All forces must be united.

II

Regarding China, there are many untrue opinions in circulation to the effect that China is so weak that she cannot stand against Japan. It is my confident belief that China not only can resist every and any Japanese aggression, but that she can and must prepare to recover her lost territories. China's greatest strength lies in the awakening of her masses. If, some time ago, the Japanese imperialists had hopes of making the Chiang Kai-shek Government their tool to subjugate China, this fond hope must now disappear. Every new act of Japanese aggression strengthens Chinese resistance more and more. The Japanese policy of dismembering China is a failure. On the contrary, there can no longer be a government in China which would dare make new territorial concessions to Japan. Popular indignation rose very high when leaders of the National Salvation Association were arrested last year by the Chiang Kai-shek Government, as well as when there appeared signs that the government was considering making new concessions to Japan. The growth of the anti-Japanese movement has made possible financial reforms, caused the peaceful settlements of the threatening Fukien and Sian affairs and the cessation of civil warfare. All these are indisputable evidences of the new strength of China.

China must now prepare to recover her lost territories. There must be preparation of the masses politically and militarily. Freedom of speech, press and assembly will arouse the masses. Military training of the able-bodied population must become compulsory. China's defence cannot be built up to resist the aggressor on the basis only of the standing army, which is deficient in technical equipment. But behind this army stand the masses of the people, prepared to give the last drop of blood for their homes and their country. Fighting in guerrilla warfare, they would be an invincible force before which Japanese militarists must tremble.

To give living reality to Sun Yat-sen's economic policy, the mass movement of the people must be given free expression. This is also a prerequisite for the reconstruction of the country, the firm establishment of our industries and communications, and the improvement of our rural economy. This basic upbuilding of our country can come only when genuine democracy is achieved.

Sun Yat-sen advised China, in her conduct of foreign policy, that she should ally herself with those countries who treat her on a basis of equality. There is no doubt that Japanese aggression has aroused world-wide sympathy for China and serious dissatisfaction in other nations with Japan's imperialistic policy. Japan is in an isolated position. Her attempts to fight a way out through the German-Japanese agreement have also ended in complete failure. In Japan itself there is growing dissatisfaction with this move. The Chinese people have never entertained aggressive designs, but the Chinese people will no longer remain homeless slaves, driven from their native abodes, or endure the taunt that China is the sick man of Asia.

III

To appreciate the strength of any country, we cannot do better than to analyze her economic possibilities and the strength of her social structure. Economically, Japan is a weak country. Her chief weakness lies in the poverty of raw materials, such as iron ores, cotton, oil, nonferrous metals, gold and platinum, all of which Japan is forced to import in great quantities every year. This poverty in raw materials is a most dangerous weakness for Japan in case of war, because she will then be dependent on other countries, who at any moment might cut off her supply.

There is no possibility of Japan's establishing great reserves of these raw materials in a period of peace, because of her lack of capital. She cannot invest huge sums for that purpose. To cite a few statistics: Japan now expends from 200,000,000 to 250,000,000 yen yearly to import raw materials for her metallurgical works. Let us imagine how much she must expend in wartime when the requirements will be increased many times. And all the gold reserves of Japan amount to only 600,000,000 yen. Of the total volume of Japanese imports in 1934, raw materials comprised 70 per cent; in 1935 they were 80 per cent; while in 1936, 82 per cent of her total imports consisted of raw materials. If we consider the steel industry alone, which is the basic factor in war industries, we see that in 1936, 40 per cent of the raw materials (iron and scrap iron) had to be imported. The weakness of Japan becomes even more evident when it is noted that in 1936, 87 per cent of all iron ores used were imported. And most of these imports were secured from China. If we take another important raw material—oil, we discover that Japan produces only 8 per cent of her requirements and must import the other 92 per cent. Of other raw materials such as tin, cotton, wool, quicksilver and antimony, Japan must import 90 per cent of her requirements.

For all these immense imports, Japan must pay with her exports. It is most difficult for her to do this even in peacetime. Her difficulties increase every year, and last year her adverse trade balance was approximately 130,000,000 yen. Thus, it is quite evident that Japan's industrial basis is not sound, especially for waging war.

If we turn our attention to Japanese agriculture, we see, according to the latest statistics, that the volume of production is decreasing year by year. In 1929 it was 45,000,000,000 yen; at the end of 1935 it was 32,000,000,-000 yen. A growing discrepancy between market prices of agricultural and industrial products becomes ever sharper, rendering conditions more and more unfavorable for agriculture. In 1936, the impoverished farmers accumulated debts amounting to 5,000,000,000 yen, while Japan had to import one fifth of the foodstuffs necessary to maintain her already low standard of living. The Japanese peasantry is suffering from three different kinds of exploitation. Landlords take from 50 to 60 per cent of the crops in rent, while the state has increased taxes every year in order to pay for military expenses, and, lastly, industrial capital is impoverishing the peasantry by sponsoring high prices for industrial products.

The Japanese newspapers are discussing this problem of an impoverished peasantry, and the Japanese themselves are pessimistic over their rural districts. Since 70 per cent of the soldiers come from those districts, the Japanese militarists themselves are conscious of the danger and are worried. Social unrest in the villages is evident, and herein lies one of the weakest points of Japanese imperialism. In the last Diet, there was proposed a new six-year rearmament program, to cost 3,000,000,000 yen. And this year, in 1937, the Japanese military budget was increased more than 300,000,000 yen over that of 1936.

Most of this money will again come from the villages. This means added financial burdens on the already impoverished peasantry. It will impose new difficulties and new strains on an already weakened structure.

Japanese economic and social conditions are not robust enough for a long war. And certainly, the Japanese militarists cannot hope to conquer China in a war of short duration. If peacetime Japanese economy is strained to the utmost and her social structure is threatened by unrest, how could these weakened structures withstand a great war on the Asiatic continent?

It is no longer even an open question whether China can be defeated by imperialistic Japan. Japanese efforts to expand their control in North China have failed. In Suiyuan, Chinese troops have successfully repulsed Japanese bandit encroachments. Japanese demands to our government have been rejected. Japan is losing face in China. New bluffs of Japanese militarists, threatening the Chinese with military invasions, can have only one result: to promote China's unification and strengthen the determination of the country to struggle for her independence.

With the spontaneous desire of the Chinese people to mobilize themselves, with China's immensely vast territory, rich in natural resources, with a population of 475,000,000 people, the might of Japan becomes a mere paper tiger. Japanese economic and social structures cannot hold out in a long war with the Chinese people.

No! China could not be defeated even if she had to fight Japan single-handed. But China will not be alone. For China has the sympathy of the world.

PART IV

**THE STRUGGLE TO PRESERVE
UNITY AND TO DEFEAT FASCISM**

LETTER TO THE BRITISH LABOR PARTY DELEGATES CONDUCTING A SURVEY OF JAPANESE AGGRESSION IN CHINA

Shanghai

October 3, 1937

Friends:

I am most grateful that your delegates have given me an opportunity to write to you and at the same time appeal to you for your understanding and active support in our war of resistance, the aim of which is to strive for the national liberation and freedom of our invaded land. China, at present, is engaged in an historic struggle of world importance. China is fighting for the preservation of her nationhood and for the survival of her people.

For the past thirty years, the Japanese imperialists and militarists have been carving up the Chinese soil bit by bit. I am sure that you still remember how the four northeastern provinces were snatched away from China in the years of 1931 and 1932. In so doing, Japan crushed the Nine-Power Treaty and Kellogg Pact. The British government, as you recall, though herself one of the signatory nations of these treaties, made no protest to halt the Japanese from disintegrating China. From 1933 to 1935, when the Japanese imperialists began to extend the influence of their rule to North Chahar and Hopei, the League of Nations and the treaty signatories still made no response to this atrocity. Naturally, such an attitude greatly encouraged and objectively aided the Japanese bandits in invading China.

The intensification of the Japanese aggression has provoked the rise and the strengthening of the anti-Japanese movement in China. Salvation associations have been organized by the masses of workers, peasants and intellectuals, with the purpose of preparing themselves for the nation's war of resistance. The atrocities of the Japanese militarists rather than intimidating, on the contrary, have greatly aroused the anti-Japanese feelings of the Chinese people. The vicious cruelties and oppression in Manchuria and Jehol have highly stimulated local guerrilla anti-aggression activities.

But the Japanese imperialists were not content with the subjugation and economic exploitation of the Chinese people in Manchuria and North China. They have deliberately set about destroying Chinese culture and reducing the people to the status of ignorant and uncultured slaves. Everywhere we witness the ruthless destruction of Chinese universities, schools and libraries. All schoolbooks have been revised, curricula altered to provide the barest minimum of cultural education and a maximum of training in so-called "labor education", which in essence consists in doing the menial work for the Japanese. Meanwhile the teachings of Sun Yat-sen, leader of the Chinese Revolution, are listed among the strictly prohibited. Practically all writings on the Chinese nation are forbidden. The Chinese history textbooks have all been rewritten and undergone falsification. Subjects in social science listed in the curricula have been eliminated. Moreover, a limit has been enforced on the number of Chinese attending schools in Manchuria. As a consequence, the number of students has been decreasing year after year. Thus, is it not obvious that the Japanese militarists are deliberately destroying Chinese culture which has a history of four thousand years?

It is but natural that such a policy of the Japanese imperialists can only arouse our hatred and determination to resist. Seeing this, the Japanese Government has again demanded that the Chinese Government suppress the spread of anti-Japanese sentiments. What a foolish demand! For who on earth can suppress the hatred of a people towards its oppressor? On the other hand, the people of China have no bad feelings towards the Japanese workers, peasants and intellectuals, who are only deceived by the Japanese militarists and fascists.

During the past two months, you have observed the trespassing and massacre conducted by the Japanese aggressors in China. With the bombing of the Nankai University of Tientsin as a prelude, they occupied all the cultural organizations in North China by force, and set fire to those that were of no use to them. They bombarded and bombed the colleges and schools of Shanghai and Nanking; they raided the American missionary hospitals, sending the nurses, doctors and wounded soldiers to their deaths. In order to threaten our people, in order to make us bend our knees, they ruthlessly dropped bombs on those women and children escaping from the war districts in search of refuge. Their airplanes, in a similar way, strafed the innocent

dwellers of the peaceful cities and villages. Trains and
ships on which refugees evacuate, railway and other
stations where the poorest people are concentrated, have
all become the targets for the outlet of their malice.
They have stamped international law and morals
under their feet, by exhibiting themselves as the devils
of the human race. These are all clear facts, not propaganda. After breaking into the various provinces of
North China, the Japanese "Imperial" Army again with
its deadly cannons, tanks, machine-guns, poison gas and
bombers, landed at Shanghai. They have only one
aim. That is to butcher the Chinese soldiers, workers
and peasants, so that the Japanese military rule may
be extended over the whole of China. In the eyes of
the Japanese imperialists, treaties or agreements have
never existed.

The Chinese nation has now stood up like a giant
to resist the Japanese aggression. Such solidarity of
spirit, action and will is unprecedented in our history.
The 475 million Chinese people will never be driven to
extinction. No force in the world can annihilate them.
All the parties and factions, by putting aside their past
discord, have rallied together around one common purpose of resisting and defeating the Japanese aggressors.
The Chinese Red Army, headed by General Chu Teh,
is now fighting shoulder to shoulder with all the other
troops of China under the leadership of General Chiang
Kai-shek. All internal conflicts have ceased voluntarily.
All dissension has also disappeared before the threat
of foreign aggression. In this unity of all forces lies
our insurmountable strength.

China is resisting with her heart and soul. You have no doubt observed how our armies, consisting of workers, peasants and intellectuals, have made the landing of Japanese invading troops difficult, although we have pitted against us overwhelmingly great odds. Notwithstanding the fact that the technique and equipment of the Japanese land, sea and air units far surpass those of the Chinese army, we know that this war cannot be won with mere military techniques. The present war of resistance has verified that China is in a much more commanding situation from the aspect of the morality and morale of our soldiers and people. Japanese militarism can never enslave such a great nation as China fighting for her national existence. There is no doubt that the final victory will belong to us. Although we must go through many years of suffering and sacrifice, yet we are all set to face them.

Friends: I entreat you not to keep aloof from the heroic war of resistance waged by the Chinese people. Only through careful scrutiny can you realize that China is not only fighting for herself, but also for the whole human race. The Japanese fascists and militarists, together with their bloody and inhuman acts of destruction, are not only threatening China's independence, but are also a menace to all the democratic countries, and to the peace and freedom of the human race. Friends: Behold and you will see that only within the short lapse of two months, the Japanese imperialists have already greatly impaired and damaged the British interests in China. The British ambassador was chased by a Japanese bomber, and nearly lost his life; British merchant ships were intercepted by Japanese warships, which insisted upon the right of going on board to inspect the passengers and documents; they deliberately detained and crippled the custom's patrol-ship, sailing within the territorial waters of Hongkong. In Shanghai alone, millions of pounds of British properties have been damaged by the Japanese warships and bombers. Although war has not yet been formally declared, yet Japan has already impeded British trade in China, rendering a tremendous loss to the British industrial and commercial circles. These are only a few instances of injury inflicted upon the British interests by the Japanese, during the short period of two months. If the war continues, the loss will consequently become bigger.

Therefore, not only from the point of view of righteousness and justice, but for their own essential interest, the British people should do everything in their power to put a stop to Japanese aggression in China. It must be clearly understood that if China should fail in her resistance, then there will be an end to British economic interest in China.

The war of aggression has been going on in China for almost two months, yet it is regrettable that we still have not seen any definite response from you in giving us your active support to halt the fascist invaders. The British sailors on board the S.S. Severnleigh once went on strike in protest against the transportation of cargoes to Japan which would enhance her strength of aggression. We can never express how grateful and happy we were when we heard such news of cooperation from the British sailors. While this action has been greeted as an obvious expression of alliance to our war of resistance, we sincerely hope that your party will also show your sympathy with concrete action.

The struggle of the Chinese nation is indeed of international significance. While China has the moral support and sympathy of other nations, this in itself is not sufficient to prevent Japanese militarists from their mad venture of subjugating all China. It is to the interest of foreign nations, and especially of England, to check Japanese aggression by strengthening the Chinese power of resistance. Your party, being the pursuer of freedom and democracy, is striving for the welfare of the masses of your people. The purpose of our war is to resist the oppressor, fascism and militarism, which are also your foes. It is upon this common basis that we are here taking the privilege to appeal to you for your support and assistance.

Hence, with strong confidence and hope, I wish that the British Labor Party will muster her every effort and take every possible step to support our heroic war of resistance in fighting against brutal and culture-destroying barbarism.

TWO "OCTOBERS"

From the Magazine "Resistance"

November 6, 1937

On October 10th, we celebrated the twenty-sixth anniversary of the founding of the Republic of China. That day marks the overthrow of the decayed Manchu Dynasty and the birth of a new democratic regime. These were epoch-making events in the history of China. It was the day when 475 million people, having thrown off their shackles and chains and emerged from the darkness of feudalism, advanced along the path of having a government of the people, by the people and for the people. That was our hope and conviction and the goal for which we had been struggling.

As early as 1905, when the Russian people were still living in a world of depression, when their revolutionary upsurge was ruthlessly suppressed by the terror of the Czarist regime and Socialism remained but a dream in the minds of millions, Sun Yat-sen was envisaging and planning for the freedom of China. He mapped out a number of programs, all aimed at the raising of the people's livelihood and the industrialization of the country. He advocated a thorough reform of China's society. From the very beginning, Sun believed that only through a radical change of her economic system could China achieve her emancipation. Then came the year 1911, when the Manchu Dynasty was overthrown. In an article published that same year in the Geneva magazine, "The Socialist", Sun Yat-sen pointed out that all social and economic reforms in China must be based on land reform. Everything he planned was meant for the improvement of the livelihood of the masses. In his opinion, peasants and workers constituted the most reliable force in the building of a new and free China. He believed that in the great struggle for the overthrow of imperialist rule and the unification of the country, these two laboring classes would be the foundation of our strength.

In order to enable the participation of the broad masses of people in the work of government, Sun Yat-sen introduced freedom of speech, press and organization. Surprising progress was made thereafter. Students, peasants and workers zealously joined in various social and political activities of the time. The country was travelling along the road of freedom and democracy.

But immediately after his death, tragic changes took place. These helped bring about the present national crisis and the suffering of the people. Warlordism became rampant in every province. Corruption and conspiracy were prevalent and besmirched the existence of our nation. Thousands of Sun Yat-sen's loyal followers who were struggling for the complete realization of his principles and policies, were killed, and those advocates of more democracy also met with disaster. Ten years of ruthless civil war corroded the country and undermined the strength and vitality of our people. This was the situation in the past. However, now the long night of disappointment is being replaced by a day of hope. The Double Tenth of this year means something new to us. We are holding high again the ideals of Sun Yat-sen. Our hearts are beating with the hope of freedom. Today, in every corner of our country, we can hear the cannons roar, saluting our national unity, a stirring reply to the probings of the Japanese fascists now threatening the existence of our nation. Civil war has stopped. The painful memory of the past internal strife is now buried in the new dawn of the country. We are now a united people, standing firmly behind our government. We believe our government will faithfully and courageously deliver the country from its dangers. Our solidarity will solve all problems and remove all obstacles. After such a baptism, we are certain to win.

The October sky was darkened with war clouds. Yet, at the bottom of our hearts we glowed with hope. Had we not as our great neighbor the Soviet Union, also born of an October, when the situation was much more threatening? Now our neighbor has passed her most trying moment, and is there one Chinese person who does not show his deepest sympathy and admiration for the Soviet Union's struggle for freedom?

The Soviet Union was once a battleground for all imperialists as they sought an outlet for their fury. The interventionist armies were threatening Soviet cities. The Russian traitors and the "White Guards" were conspiring with the imperialists for a sell-out of their country. At one time these armed forces reached the outskirts of

Leningrad. All the reactionary forces of the world came out to smother this newborn child of freedom. They surrounded the Soviet Union with a "Cordon Sanitaire" and blockaded all her seaports. The Japanese occupied Vladivostok, the Entente troops entered the region of Arkhangelsk, the Germans took the Ukraine, the Czechs held the Volga basin and the "White Russians" occupied the Don-Kossack region. The situation was indeed desperate. Despite this, the Soviet people looked ahead to their future of freedom and hope.

It was under this banner of freedom and hope that they resolutely marched forward and attained their eventual victory. Their country was disrupted by the corrupt, feudalist rulers. The people had sustained sufferings in the First World War and withstood another three years of civil war, inspired and financed by the imperialists. Counter-revolutionaries were loose in every corner of the country. Famine, calamities and poverty swept over the land. But they were not a people to be subjugated, nor would they seek compromise with their enemy. They fought on with any available weapons, however poor they were, and by every available means. They distributed leaflets among the German soldiers, calling upon them to overthrow the Kaiser. They turned their war with Poland into a war of emancipation for the Polish people and swung from the defensive to the offensive. They appealed to workers all over the world to come to the defence of the first state of workers and peasants.

The Soviet people were triumphant. This year the Soviet Union celebrated her twentieth anniversary. Her record of progress and prosperity is now establish-

ed in the history of mankind. She is no longer a backward and exploited country, but has become one of the
great powers of the earth. She has made her contribution to the world in all fields of human endeavor. We
witness for the first time in history a country which is
steadily progressing toward set goals according to a
plan. The Soviet people, plain peasants and modest
workers, are now masters of their own destiny. The
Soviet Union, which used to be a straw floating in the
turbulent sea of the imperialist world, has now become
a ship sailing in all safety and toward a definite destina-
tion. She is holding high the torch of hope for millions
of people all over the world and for the disillusioned
and despairing people everywhere.

Peace is the cornerstone of this great and powerful
country's foreign policy. She has extended her hand
of friendship to people of all lands and has negotiated
treaties of friendship, neutrality and non-aggression
with many countries. When China signed her non-
aggression pact with the Soviet Union, we not only joined hands with one of the mightiest forces of peace in
the world, but also with a country likewise threatened
by the same enemy. The fascist invaders of Japan once
recklessly broke past the border of this land of peace,
but were halted midway and made to know that the
Soviet people are well prepared for the defence of their
country and every venture of an invader is dearly paid
for. Japan now has resorted to sending her spies into
Soviet territory and has brought over some Russian
traitors to prepare an attack from within. But all of
these manoeuvres, the demonstrations of strength and
the espionage activities on the part of the Japanese have

proven powerless before the Soviet Union. (Neither will they be of much avail in our country!) They have met with strong resistance.

After long years of darkness, the Soviet Union has at last found her way, the way to peace and progress and the way of freedom. The October Revolution succeeded in welding a broken country into one whole and made it strong and powerful. The Soviet people have been steadily building up their country. A new world has taken shape, where there is no more human suffering nor natural calamities, where men have learned to constrain their individual desires for the common good of society, where nature has been made to serve the purposes of man.

Returning to the situation in China, the aggression of the Japanese fascists, their savagery and brutality, have brought chaos and terror to our land. But we are certain to defeat these butchers of our culture and progress. Their modernized weapons of destruction will be battered by our unabated courage. We will be holding high the beacon of our rebirth in our fight against the corrupted "bushidoist" war. We will not be enslaved by feudalism at home or the fascist aggressors from without. The shackles of slavery will never again fall upon us. Our country, having long been a filthy and despicable stable, is now cleansing herself of all the deep-rooted evils detrimental to her existence. Let us follow the example of our great neighbor, the Soviet Union! Let us sweep away all traitors, the selfish and corrupted people! Let them perish by the fire of our fury! We will not only win our war of liberation on the battleground, but in the process will build up our new democratic state. Then, the principles of Sun Yat-sen will be completely realized.

We have displayed courage in the war of resistance. But politically, is our courage as indomitable as that of the soldiers at the front? Have we conveyed our faith to our fellow-countrymen and told them that in our present arduous fight against the frenzied fascists dwells the hope of having a better life? If we lack such confidence in this result, we shall not be able to lead the people and we will not be in a position to criticize the people when they are reluctant to follow us. Therefore, this hope of a bright future must be cherished by people all over the country, the future of emancipation from feudalism and improved living based on freedom, democracy and peace!

What the Soviet Union has achieved in the lapse of a mere twenty years can also be achieved by us, if we have the confidence and determination!

ON THE RECONCILIATION

Statement issued in Shanghai

November 1937

Following the Japanese attack at Lukouchiao (Marco Polo Bridge) July 7, 1937, in the interests of anti-Japanese unity, the Kuomintang and Communists laid the groundwork of a formal alliance to replace the truce that had obtained since Sian.

Throughout his life Sun Yat-sen advocated the principle of joint struggle for the existence of China. That is why he held that the Kuomintang and Communists should work together. The Communist Party is a party which stands for the interests of the working classes, both industrial and agricultural. Sun realized that without the keen support and cooperation of these classes, the mission of completing the national revolution could not easily be carried out. If the cooperation with the Chinese Communist Party, which he advocated, had continued uninterruptedly until the present time, China would by now have been a free and independent power. Past events are a good lesson. During the present crisis, all former differences should be forgotten. The whole nation must join together in opposing Japanese aggression and fighting for the final victory.

AN APPEAL FOR AID TO PARTISAN FIGHTERS

The text of an address delivered before a gathering of
women in Hongkong on International Women's Day
March 8, 1939*

I bring you greetings from the heroic Chinese
defenders of justice and democracy, the men and women
at the front who by their indomitable courage and spirit
of selflessness have won the admiration and the right
to the support of all right-thinking people. They rejoice
with me that on this great day, commemorating the
international women's movement against force and
oppression, women of different races in Hongkong have
gathered for the first time to express their solidarity with
us and to identify themselves with a cause which is
indisputably the cause of every democratic citizen, of
whatever nationality.

We are living in a most critical epoch in the history
of mankind. Our present day world is witnessing the
life and death struggle of two irreconcilable forces, of
the forces of peace and democracy against the forces of
war and fascism. In China, as in Spain, this struggle
has already assumed the form of open war. The Japan-

---

* Some 300 foreign women attended the meeting. The Hongkong press did not publish a word of the speech.

ese fascists have launched a savage attack to destroy our national independence, and with it the whole structure of our material and cultural life, the heritage of thousands of years of the labor of our people. Our cities, towns and villages have been devastated. The bodies of our best sons and daughters have been broken on the wheel of war. Our women have been violated, our children maimed and invalided for life. Tens of thousands of our people have been driven mad by the bombings and other atrocities of these fascist beasts. Tens of millions have been rendered homeless, destitute and starving.

For over a year and a half now, our Chinese people have fought this horror of fascist aggression. And it is no figure of speech to say that during this time they have also fought the menace of war that hangs over the whole world, that they have also fought for your peace. We have all seen how the arrogance of the fascist powers of Europe has grown since they have been allowed to triumph in Czechoslovakia and encouraged to proceed undisturbed with the murder of the heroic people of Spain. Nearer to us here, we have seen the increased attacks on the British and American positions in the Pacific that have followed every success of Japanese arms in China. If China had capitulated, if she had lent herself without a struggle to be a material base and reservoir of manpower for the military machine of Japanese fascism, do you think we would be able now to sit quietly here in Hongkong?

China, the most peace-loving, non-military nation on earth, when faced with the choice between slavery and struggle, chose struggle. Because this struggle most truly represents the interests of all groups of our population, our Chinese people have not allowed themselves to be conquered in a single town or village occupied by the Japanese. Millions have preferred to leave their homes, facing privation and sacrifice rather than remain under the Japanese yoke. Greater millions have stayed and are carrying on the fight. At this moment, the largest part of the Japanese forces in China is not engaging our national army at the front, but is fighting unsuccessfully to suppress the people's army of hundreds of thousands of partisans which has grown up in the so-called occupied territories.

The unity in the aims of all classes of our people is expressed in our national anti-Japanese united front, the consolidation of our 475,000,000 people into one united power which is the surest guarantee of our final victory in the protracted war of resistance against Japanese imperialism. This unity is the chief obstacle that our enemy has to face, and the Tokyo militarists know it. Time and again, they and their agents have tried to weaken our resistance, not only by naked and ruthless terror against defenceless civilians, but also by cunning offers of "compromise", the real aim of which is the subjugation of our beloved country. They have tried to split us by creating new dissensions among us and by trying to revive those which existed in the past by provoking differences between the Kuomintang and Communist parties. But they have succeeded only in buying over a few historically known double-dealers and defeatists, and these traitors had only to show their hand to be categorically expelled from the ranks of our party and government. Instead of splitting us, as they hoped, their self-exposure has had the result of strengthening our ranks and clearing the muddy atmosphere, which for a time confused our friends and well-wishers and undermined their confidence in the resolute determination of our government to fight on until the final victory is won.

I assure you most solemnly, that we will continue to fight until we have achieved the liberation of our soil and people and have driven the fascist invader off the continent. We will hold our section of the front of struggle for peace and democracy throughout the world.

What is our place in this struggle, yours and mine, as women of all countries? The fight against war and fascism and the fight for the rights of women are one and inseparable. Throughout the ages, war has brought women endless suffering and pain. Fascism, the bully's doctrine of the war of the strong against the weak, has made all womankind one of its "inferior races". In Spain and China, invaded by fascist aggressors, women are bombed, tortured and violated. In every country where domestic fascism rules, women are being pushed back into medieval slavery, while their husbands and sons are trained for the slaughter of the husbands and sons of their sisters in other countries. In Germany and Italy, women are systematically excluded from the universities and professions and from the opportunity of achieving economic independence. Daily, they are insulted by the official insistence that they are fit for nothing better than to be breeding machines for cannon-fodder—"the mothers of the warriors of the race". In Japan, laboring under vicious feudal-fascist domination, the body of woman is a commodity to be sold in job lots for sexual or industrial exploitation; the wife is the slave of her husband, and every woman is taught from girlhood that her highest destiny is to be an endlessly tractable servant to man. In the fascist countries, the rights of women as citizens, won through decades of struggles, have been utterly destroyed. When they have continued to fight for their democratic rights as human beings, they have been subjected to the same brutal terror as their male comrades-in-arms. In Germany, the heads of young women have fallen under the axe.

The place of all women, of every race and every class, is in the front ranks of the struggle against this infamy. Shall we permit these fascist brutes to control the fate of the world, to abolish our rights and to take our husbands and sons for their raiding expeditions? Do not think that this danger exists only in certain areas. Abyssinia and Austria have disappeared. What is left of the independence of Czechoslovakia exists only in name. The legally-elected government of Spain is fighting for its life against overwhelming odds. The Chinese people are opposing a wall of flesh and blood to the military machine of Japan. This is the record of little more than two years. Can you say for certain that you yourselves will not be involved tomorrow?

Our Chinese women are taking a full part in our country's fight for survival. On every front there are thousands of girls in uniform. Some have engaged in actual fighting. Others perform auxiliary duties in the line of fire. In the rear, our women have shouldered the tremendous task of providing care for our wounded, winter clothing for our armies, shelter and education for our war orphans, and cultural activities to teach our people the meaning of their struggle. There are many women in the People's Political Council, our first approach to a democratic parliament. Women of all classes are among the notable names of the leaders of the nation's fight. Ting Ling, a writer and intellectual, leads hundreds of girl students and former industrial workers in cultural work on the northern front. There are many other names, not yet known to our foreign friends but famous throughout China, and behind their names the work of millions of women, millions to whom the struggle has not only brought new burdens to shoulder, but also growth and development and a new sense of worth and of confidence in the future.

This is what our people and our women are doing in the war of resistance against Japanese aggression, which is at the same time a war to check international violence throughout the world, a war against the dark reaction of fascism, a war for the preservation of democracy and for the rights of women everywhere. In China and Spain today, whether you admit or repudiate this fact, two heroic peoples are fighting for all peoples. By helping China and Spain now, you will do no more than help yourselves.

In the name of the Chinese people and of the women of China, I feel that I have a right not only to appeal, but to demand your aid. You have all given thought to the misery and distress of our 60,000,000 refugees and orphans. Now I want you to think of our heroic partisan fighters, who not only face similar conditions, but continue in spite of them to deliver blow after blow at the well-equipped invader. Not only do these heroes battle with obsolete rifles, scant ammunition, homemade grenades, scythes, swords, clubs and bare hands against an enemy equipped with all the technical devices of modern warfare; not only do they lack even the most elementary medical supplies, but having abandoned farm and workshop rather than submit to slavery, they are in desperate need of clothing and food. Our government is doing all it can to help. But every day new battalions of our people rise to fight for the recovery of their homes and their freedom, and all the help that can be given is yet not sufficient. As the popular basis of China's struggle is broadened, and as greater and greater numbers of our people voluntarily throw themselves into the struggle, so our own responsibility increases to extend the amount and scope of outside help to these obscure heroes, fighting not only for the liberation of China, but for freedom and democracy throughout the world.

WHEN CHINA WINS

Appeared in "New Masses"

New York

July 11, 1939

Writing on the second anniversary of our war of resistance, it is no longer necessary for me to tell readers of New Masses and all our friends in the United States that we will fight on, that our struggle shall not cease until the final victory is won. Everyone now understands this. Everyone knows that the invader has failed to destroy our fighting forces and spirit, that he has proved unable to inflict either the smashing military blow with which he planned to wipe out our army, or the political stab in the back which he hoped would break up our anti-Japanese united front. Our armies are seizing the initiative on the battlefronts. Our people and government, the Kuomintang, the Communist Party, and even the provincial militarists whom the enemy has so often tried to seduce from their allegiance, have stood together against Wang Ching-wei and his band of traitors, unanimously approving their expulsion from all state posts and the orders issued for their arrest.

Our will to resist and our ultimate victory are no longer in doubt. But serious misconceptions still surround many aspects of our struggle. These misconceptions cluster most thickly around the question: "After the war, what?" How is China changing during her fight? Will she return, after the great effort, to the paths of development she was following before Marco Polo Bridge? Or will she, as our enemies constantly assert and so many of their dupes believe, "go Red" in some sudden, violent and mysterious fashion?

Neither supposition, of course, is true. As revealed in the statements of our national leaders, the unity of the Chinese nation in the present struggle will continue after our victory in a united effort for national reconstruction and the realization of the San Min Chu I, the Three People's Principles of Sun Yat-sen, which the Kuomintang and the Communists recognize as a common national program. Only the Three People's Principles offer a solid base for the continued collaboration of all anti-Japanese political groups now and in the future. To defeat the enemy and to build a San Min Chu I republic is the aim and goal of such collaboration today.

What kind of republic will this be?

In accordance with the teachings of Sun Yat-sen, the Chinese republic must be based on direct rule by the people through their elected representatives. The hsien or district must be the basic unit of self-government, as well as the constituency for electing deputies to the National Assembly. This system can grow only on the foundation of the fullest and most widespread extension of democratic rights.

The National Assembly shall be the supreme authority from which the central government will receive its mandate, and to which it will be responsible. The relationship between central and local governments will change. There will have to be a thorough reform of the present system of provinces, completely eliminating the traditional autonomy of the local armies. Sun Yat-sen advocated the creation in China of provinces of a new type, provinces which will be no more than convenient administrative divisions of a united nation, like the French departments, instead of, as too often hitherto, separate political and military domains.

The organization of the army will also be altered. Its numbers will be restricted to conform with the requirements of national security and defence and the carrying out of China's international obligations in connection with the maintenance of collective security. Superfluous military formations will be disbanded and their members transferred, in a planned way, to national reconstruction projects, industrial and agricultural. In the China of the future, mercenary armies will have no place. The principle of general conscription will be carried into full effect.

The united front of national resistance, the cooperation between the Kuomintang and Communist parties, the unification of all the armies under the generalissimo and his simultaneous leadership of the government: all these represent an important step forward in the process of centralization which, with the accompanying growth of democracy, is the prime essential of our national revolution. It would be wrong to view these things simply as "wartime measures". The tendency they represent has been accelerated by the war but is, in itself, a part of a necessary historical process which will continue

after the victory. The fact that the most vigorous
growth is witnessed precisely at the present moment
proves that the progress of our national revolution is
impossible without the united front of the entire Chinese
people, the collaboration of our two chief parties, the
combination of our armed forces with the people's anti-
Japanese movement, and determined resistance to
Japanese aggression. These conditions, created by the
anti-Japanese struggle, have assured our independence
thus far. Further progress in national unification and
democratic reforms will strengthen the foundations
already laid down for the people's China of the future.

Sun's first two principles dealt with the achievement
of national independence and the introduction of
democracy. The third, the principle of livelihood, was
concerned with the improvement of the living conditions
of the Chinese people. In our agrarian country, the
land problem is of paramount importance. Sun Yat-sen
formulated the slogan "land to those who till it". For
the period of industrial growth which would follow
political unification, he laid down the policy of state
control of natural resources, railways, and public
utilities, and the regulation of private enterprise, which
was not to be repressed but, on the contrary, encouraged
to develop in directions serving the needs of national
economic construction. Although progress in this direction is still inadequate, we see today, in the course of
our struggle, the beginning of the realization of Sun's
economic ideals. Rents and taxes have in many places
been reduced. Wasteland has been put to tillage Our
wartime reconstruction is taking place under state
auspices and, through organizations like the Chinese

Industrial Cooperatives, on democratic lines. After the war, we look forward to a type of economic development in which all groups of China's population will share.

It should be clearly understood by those who, through malice or ignorance, paint the national united front of the Chinese people a deep red, that it is just because this front represents a real effort of all classes toward the common aim of national emancipation, that the Three People's Principles, which were first propounded as a program for such united action, form an actual basis of its policy. The Three People's Principles represent a program for the anti-imperialist democratic revolution. Within this program, the institution of private property cannot and will not be attacked or abolished, and the only feasible interference with it is the confiscation of the possessions of enemies and traitors and general legislation to distribute more equably the burden of the common struggle against the invaders.

As with domestic so with foreign capital, China welcomes foreign trade with and investments by all countries wishing to assist her reconstruction. Sun Yatsen consistently declared, throughout the years of his leadership of the Kuomintang and the entire national revolutionary movement, that we would strive in every way to promote economic relations with foreign nations willing to deal with us on a basis of equality, non-aggression, and sympathy for our desire to bring China to her proper place as a member of the family of nations.

Today China fights not only for democracy and for the peoples of the world, but also for the national and economic interests of all countries threatened by the encroachments of Japanese imperialism.

To give a clear picture of the aims of our struggle, to expose and refute the lies by which the enemies of our people seek to split the forces which together would be able to swing America to a stand consonant with her interests, sympathies and great democratic tradition —these are the duties of every American friend of China, of every American who abhors fascist militarism and national oppression, who feels that the stand his country takes in these matters is a question vital to his own future as well as to his self-respect as a citizen of the United States.

CHINA NEEDS MORE DEMOCRACY

Written in Hongkong

Prepared for the magazine "Asia"

New York

October 1941

The international situation has turned in China's favor. The vicious German attack on the Soviet Union has put all the nations friendly to China—England, America and the U.S.S.R.—on one side in the World War. And now, by using every ounce of our energy and every particle of aid we can get from friendly nations, we can bring victory nearer, both to ourselves and to all democratic forces.

But the international situation, though favorable to us today, can change. If friendly foreign governments suspect that compromisers and appeasers have free play among us, that we are tired and ready to lay down our arms, they are likely then to make their own arrangements with Japan, in fear that if they do not, some traitor in our camp will beat them to it. The quickest way for us to lose our present international advantage is to forget that the advantage would not exist at all, unless we had shown our own ability to resist.

China's war is the key to the situation in the Far East, and not only in the Far East. Our continued resistance safeguards the future of that quarter of the human race which inhabits the Pacific's western shores. Its international importance can be gauged from the fact that it has thus far kept Japan both from wresting an empire in the south from Britain and America, and from attacking the Soviet Union in the north.

The key to China's war is our internal unity. Every one knows that in recent months, our national unity—that great cornerstone of the world struggle for decency and progress—has been in serious danger. Early this year it looked as if incendiaries of civil war might again rend our country and open wide the gates to the enemy. I need not apologize, therefore, for devoting this article to our National Anti-Japanese United Front, its nature and prospects, the dangers that it faces, and the question whether it still exists and can continue to exist.

In the four years since its formation, our united front has been subject to many misinterpretations, some malicious and some due to ignorance of the truth. Writers too superior to inform themselves on its simple essentials have paraded their confusion by putting the words in quotation marks, or talking of the "so-called united front". Some took the view that there never was such a thing, others that it existed until a certain event put an end to it, still others that it is on the point of final break-up today. Since all these views have gained wide currency, we will begin with a definition.

The name, "National Anti-Japanese United Front", is no accidental phrasing. It is a precise, scientific and historic term.

The word "National" means that it is open to every class, every political party and every individual in the nation, and that its aim is the preserving of our common national independence against an imperialist aggressor.

The word "anti-Japanese" reflects the fact that Japan is today the chief threat to China's national existence, and that our national united front cannot include any group that does not struggle against the Japanese invaders.

The words "united front" mean that all cooperating groups must keep a common face to the enemy and support one another against the enemy.

The National Anti-Japanese United Front does not mean that the groups belonging to it cannot have different philosophies and aims. It does not mean the dictatorship of any one party or group. The presence of friction, even of armed clashes, between groups does not mean that the united front has ceased to exist, although such clashes are without doubt bad for the war, and the reactionary elements who provoke them are aiding the enemy.

Finally, the National Anti-Japanese United Front can change its composition. The desertion of the traitor Wang Ching-wei and of similar turncoats to the Japanese was such a change. As our difficulties increase, many profiteers, political adventurers, cowards and weaklings may go over to the enemy, or work for him by undermining internal unity and crying for an early peace.

But to the vast majority of the Chinese people, from whatever walk of life they come, the prospect of being enslaved, as their relatives in the Japanese-occupied territories are enslaved, is absolutely intolerable. They will fight to the death to avoid it, and will support any internal or external measure needed to carry on the war. So long as there is a Japanese soldier in China, the National Anti-Japanese United Front will certainly exist. And it will exist afterwards, because the tasks of reconstruction, no less than those of resistance, call for prolonged unity. Democratic China, based on the Three People's Principles, which we hope to build after the war, will have place and opportunities for worker, peasant, manufacturer, merchant, scholar and professional man alike.

I have purposely avoided thus far speaking of the united front in terms of relations between the Kuomintang and the Chinese Communist Party because the survival of the National Anti-Japanese United Front, on which the future of our struggle depends, is a question not of parties, but of the alternative between war and capitulation, between fighting for national aims and the collapse of that fight through treason. The principles of our united front are based on the actual needs of our country; they are not fixed by any party. The test of any party or group in China is the extent to which it recognizes and works for those needs in practice. In today's concrete situation, however, the relations between the Kuomintang and the Communists are of first importance. Their cooperation is the foundation of unity; any conflict between them is a danger to national unity. In considering this problem, we are first of all struck by the fact that, with two great parties and several smaller ones, there is not sufficient machinery of democratic representation to allow each party to play its proper part, commensurate with membership and influence, in the administration of the war.

Lack of democracy in war-time Free China is the chief cause of the military clashes that occur between Chinese units, to the benefit of the enemy. Lack of democracy is perhaps the greatest single threat to the common anti-Japanese front, and offers the greatest opportunities to those who wish to break it. Since the Kuomintang is the ruling party and holds the monopoly of political power in Chungking, the extension of democratic government has been its responsibility. The Kuomintang rank and file has undoubtedly been in favor of reforms in the direction of increasing democracy. Opposition has come mainly from a reactionary minority within the leadership which has forgotten the teachings of Sun Yat-sen. Significantly, we find in this same group China's chief proponents of a Rome-Berlin Axis orientation and of a speedy compromise with Japan.

China's lack of democracy is valuable only to fifth columnists and potential compromisers and appeasers. By no stretch of the imagination could the granting of democratic rights impede China's prosecution of the war. On the contrary, our people overwhelmingly support the struggle against Japan, and hence the suppression of their initiative is definitely harmful. For the sake of the war, for the sake of the united front that makes our resistance possible, our countrymen and our friends abroad should support the demand for increased democracy in our country.

The fight against appeasers of fascism and misusers of the banner of democracy is the same all over the world. Only in the bright light of political democracy can we detect capitulators and traitors, move forward to the solution of our problems and strengthen our war for independence and the unity without which our resistance to the invader would not have begun, without which it cannot lead to victory. Lack of democracy makes it possible for compromisers and appeasers, many of whom are linked not only with our enemy but with the entire Rome-Berlin-Tokyo conspiracy against mankind's progress, to work in the dark and prepare a capitulation.

Thinking patriots of China know well that we can expect no aid from friends abroad if we give them reason to believe that appeasers may gain control of our political life. I want to tell our foreign friends that we know this and that we fight against any such possibility, for them as well as for ourselves.

On the other hand, we expect something from every foreign sympathizer of China. Changes in the international scene have revived the hopes and machinations of groups in Great Britain and America which seek to "wean Japan from the Axis", to "stabilize the situation in the Pacific", to compound a Munich in the Far East.

These are the same groups who, while the sympathy of the American and British peoples was entirely with China, made deals with the aggressor and sold him oil to fuel his air fleet and steel to make his bombs. Having helped the Japanese to strengthen their military machine, they may now seek to help them achieve their political aim—a peace of capitulation in China.

The Chinese people will continue to fight the invader and to defend the united front on which our resistance is based. I hope that our friends in America and Great Britain will help both us and themselves by supporting the demand for democracy in China, and by insisting that their governments give all possible aid to China and abandon all support, material or political, of Japanese aggression.

THE CHINESE WOMEN'S FIGHT FOR FREEDOM

Appeared in the Magazine "Asia"

Written in Chungking

July 1942

China's women, no less than her men, are fighting the battles of their country. In the present struggle, in which its entire future is at stake, they have shown themselves worthy daughters of the heroines of our past.

From ancient times, individual women have participated actively in the defence of the nation and the moulding of its destiny. Hua Mu-lan, a Chinese Joan of Arc, is reputed to have led the armies against foreign invasion from the north. Her exploits are remembered to this day in the songs and the theater of the people. Liang Hung-yu, the wife of a famous Sung general, also fought against the invaders. In the field of our culture, Pan Chao helped to compile and edit the Han Chronicles; Tsai Wen-chi was one of the most famous of the ancient composers; Li Ching-chao, Chu Shu-cheng and Yu Wan-chih wrote poems that are still read. Despite the fact that in the old Chinese society their position was unvaryingly that of obedient servants of the men of the family, the education, breadth of vision, adminis-

trative capacity and even military prowess of exceptional women left their mark on the history of the land.

Contact with the West, and the rise of the national
revolutionary movement, opened new and greater vistas
for Chinese women. Many entered the factories and
became independent wage earners. Though it was
still a long way from potentiality to fact, the basis had
been laid for the participation of women in national
life not merely as the wives and mistresses of the great,
but in their own right as citizens.

The process began with the upper and middle classes. Women began to appear as doctors, public health
workers and teachers. On the political scene, many of
them were self-sacrificing members of the revolutionary parties.

An outstanding part was played by the latter in
the struggles for the overthrow of the Manchu Dynasty.
Chiu Ching, one of the noblest martyrs of the revolution, was second in command of an underground republican organization with its own armed forces in Che-
kiang. She lost her life when she failed in an attempt
to assassinate En Ming, the Manchu Governor. Ho
Hsiang-ning (Mme. Liao Chung-kai) who at sixty-four
is still among our foremost progressives, was an original member of Sun Yat-sen's first united revolutionary party, the Tung Meng Hui. Many women of this
period helped both in the direction of the movement and
in the execution of its most difficult and dangerous
enterprises.

The proclamation of the Republic was not the end
but only the beginning of the fight for a new China.
The form of government had changed, but the power

was still substantially in the same hands and life remained what it had been. This was apparent in the field of woman's rights as everywhere else. When two woman leaders of the Kuomintang, Tang Chun-ying and Chang Chao-han, presented a bill for legal equality of the sexes to the first republican parliament, the reactionary majority easily voted it down.

During the first World War our own industrialists were able to build many new factories. A natural accompaniment of this was the rise of a labor movement. The conscious political fight for democracy in China widened to include not only the middle class but also the working people and the peasants. China began to witness not only the outstanding deeds of individual women, but also examples of heroic activity by women in the mass striving to create a better Republic.

Tens of thousands of worker, peasant and student women participated in the great military campaign for the eradication of the northern warlords in 1925-1927. They performed auxiliary services, spread the slogans of the national movement far and wide and on many occasions fought shoulder to shoulder with the troops. In the course of the struggle, large numbers of girls from field and factory grew from the status of semi-slaves and the stupor of endless toil to full human stature and leadership. It was not for nothing that the feudal leaders of reaction paid the homage of bitter hatred to the "bobbed-haired girls" of the time and made the gutters of our cities run red with their blood.

Women were represented also in the directing body of the great campaign. The Central Committee of the Kuomintang elected at the First National Congress in

Canton in 1924, included, among others, Ho Hsiang-ning, Teng Ying-chao (Mrs. Chou En-lai) and Tsai Chang, who were two leading workers in the Communist Party which contributed so much to the progress of the movement. Ho Hsiang-ning organized the Kuomintang Woman's Department.

From its inception, our national revolutionary movement has made the liberation of women one of its basic demands. The advance of our women to equality in legal status, educational opportunities and social position has been and is an essential part of China's march toward full independence and democracy. No nation can claim to be free when half its citizens are dominated by the other half. From the very start, our women fought not under the banner of a barren feminism but as part and parcel of the democratic movement as a whole.

When the forces of domestic and foreign reaction proved too strong for the first heroic assault of the people and China's initial effort to achieve democratic unity broke on the rocks of renewed civil war, it was natural that the trend towards women's emancipation should also suffer a check. Careers in medical, educational and welfare work remained open, but politics and administration were again barred, as if one out of every two human beings in China had no conceivable right to participate in the ordering of the society in which all lived.

The Kuomintang, captured and held securely in the grip of its right wing, abolished the woman's department that had done so much to bring it victory. The woman members who continued nominally to belong to its Central Committee remained there not in recognition of their own work but on the strength of the previous leadership of their dead husbands. They did not acquiesce in the new trend and, from exile, declared their opposition to the flight back to the past. But unfortunately there were other women who made their peace with things as they were, and counseled their less privileged sisters to abandon their seeking for a wider life. This was the dark period during which civil war raged for ten years and a policy of external appeasement allowed the Japanese to get a grip on large parts of our territory and much of our political life.

The new democratic movement that broke this discouraging pattern arose, some two years before the war, in circumstances of great danger to the country from Japanese encroachment. Ever since the seizure of Manchuria in 1931, the students in our universities had been active in pressing the government to fight Japan. Thousands of young people marched in protest demonstrations, moved on foot to the capital itself, starved in hunger strikes, braved the beatings of the police, imprisonment and execution to make their voices heard. At the end of 1935, the students of Peiping came out into the streets, ready to stop with their bodies the attempt of the Japanese to establish a puppet government in the capital of China's culture. The time was ripe, and their action not only accomplished its purpose but launched the new, organized wave of popular sentiment that we know as the National Salvation Movement. As many girls as boys took part in this heroic initiative, and the casualties among them were as great. Chinese women will always remember that it was a girl

marcher who, when the gates of the city were locked
against the procession, squeezed her slim body through
the space under them and, ignoring the swinging broad-
swords of the guards, explained the purpose of the demonstration and appealed to them to let the students
through.

Within a few weeks, hundreds of National Salvation Associations had been organized in all parts of the
country and among all groups of the population. Not
the least of these was the Women's National Salvation
Association established in Shanghai on December 22,
1935, only two weeks after the Peiping demonstration.
On the day of its founding, a thousand members paraded through the city with slogans identical with those of
the general democratic upsurge:

"Stop civil war!"

"Chinese must not fight Chinese!"

"Form a united front against Japan to save the
nation!"

"Women can emancipate themselves only through
participation in resistance!"

The new body soon organized many separate occupational sections—for professional women, teachers,
students, workers, housewives. It established close relations with others working in the field, such as the
Y.W.C.A. Woman writers formed discussion groups
and planned the production of literature. Three
woman's magazines, "Woman's Life", a monthly,
"Woman's Masses", published every ten days, and
"Little Sisters", a fortnightly, began to appear.

After the student marches, the next great action
of the people against Japan was carried out by the tex-

tile workers of Shanghai and Tsingtao, who walked out in tens of thousands from enemy-owned cotton mills. Among them there were far more women than men. Their courage was even greater than that of the students, because they faced not violence alone but immediate starvation. These miserably underpaid factory girls, with patched clothing and wisps of cotton in their hair, working sixteen to eighteen hours a day from early childhood, many of them already coughing from the tubercular-seeds of death in their chests, will always remain heroic figures in the annals of our awakening.

When the strike broke out, the various National Salvation Associations in Shanghai formed a committee of leading intellectuals to support the workers. Under Japanese pressure, seven members of this committee were arrested by the government, charged with "endangering the safety of the Republic", for which the maximum penalty was death. Among these seven, who submitted voluntarily to trial, was Miss Shih Liang,* one of our few woman lawyers. They remained in jail until after the outbreak of war.

The countrywide movement against the imprisonment of the patriots served further to strengthen the anti-Japanese mobilization of the people. In the Sian Incident, the next great landmark on the way to unity and active struggle against the invaders, the release of the seven was one of the important demands made on the Generalissimo. These events, and ever-increasing Japanese pressure, led rapidly toward the achievement of the immediate goals for which every progressive,

---

* Now Minister of Justice.

patriotic, anti-fascist Chinese had been working—the cessation of civil war, and armed resistance to external aggression.

For the patriotic women of China, as for every other group of the population, the war was the great test. They rose to meet that test well. In the very first days after the clash on the Marco Polo Bridge, they organized nursing, bandage-making and political propaganda units to work in conjunction with the local garrison— the 29th Army. But within three weeks the bulk of this courageous but ill-led and ill-equipped force had been smashed, and the whole region fell into the hands of the enemy. Peiping and Tientsin witnessed consider-able fighting, but they did not suffer as other cities did later from the occupation. There was nothing except their patriotism to stop the more active young women who lived there from going back to their very comfort-able homes for the most part, and reconciling them-selves to fate. But this is precisely what they did not do. Thousands left the two cities for points behind the Chinese lines. Many went by boat to Tsingtao and overland to Nanking. Some slipped through the Japan-ese cordon, joining the regular Chinese forces along the Peiping-Hankow Railway and the Grand Canal. Still others entered the guerrilla detachments that were springing up in the hills around Peiping or struck west to meet the advancing Eighth Route Army, in whose schools they received training. They traveled in groups, and everywhere, in boats, on trains, in way-side villages, they spoke to the people of resistance.

Those who remained behind did not stay idle. They published underground papers, assisted in organizing secret contacts between the occupied cities and the ever-growing strength of the guerrillas, carried on propaganda among the Japanese troops, garnered intelligence and in general constituted a fighting column operating in the rear of the enemy.

While these developments were taking shape in the North, the tremendous battle for Shanghai broke out and raged fiercely for a full three months. Volunteers helped to bring the wounded back from the front, rolled bandages and sewed hospital clothes for their needs, nursed them, wrote letters, organized entertainment. Hastily set up classes trained two thousand emergency nurses in two months. Many women worked right in the zone of fire, mill girls, society matrons, students and girl scouts side-by-side. Thousands gave money, strength or both.

The barbarous sack of Nanking proved conclusively to every Chinese that life under the invaders would be impossible. In particular, the Japanese army showed there that it was warring not only against men, but against women also, taking special and brutal advantage of the defencelessness of the sex. Chinese women replied with the formation of the Kwangsi Woman's Battalion and training in armed self-defence in many places. But the deeper and more important reply was their greater activity everywhere in the task of helping the war.

The first nine months of 1938, during which the government had its headquarters at Hankow, marked the high tide of democratic unity for national resistance in China. It marked the high tide also of the woman's movement. All woman's organizations—the National

Salvation societies, old neutral bodies like the Y.W.C.A., new wartime products like the National Woman's Relief Association with over one hundred branches throughout the country, the National Association for the Care of War Orphans and others—were united at the Kuling Conference of July 1938 into an all-embracing woman's organization. This was the Woman's Advisory Committee, and its plan of work embraced not only aid to the orphans and the wounded, but also club activities for the troops at the front, education of village women, publication of magazines, encouragement of local production through the revival and improvement of handicraft methods and the training of skilled leaders and organizers along all these lines.

The Committee grew rapidly because it began as a truly united front organ. Kuomintang, Communist and nonparty women participated equally in its deliberations. Delegates to the Kuling Conference included many extremely able women whom the civil war had driven underground with a price on their heads, such as Teng Ying-chao, whom I have already mentioned as an active leader in the 1925-1927 period. Moreover, it could lean on organizations that had been created by the needs of the war and acquired much experience applicable on a broader scale. These organizations were widely different one from another, but all had something to contribute. The Hunan War Service Corps, for instance, accompanied one military detachment through a battle-studded march from Shanghai to Hankow. The Yunnan Woman's Battlefield Service Unit, starting from that remote southwestern province, proceeded by foot almost two thousand miles to the Central China front. The aforementioned Kwangsi Woman's Battalion covered fifteen hundred miles from Kweilin to the Fifth War Zone north of the Yangtze and worked among the soldiers there. Ting Ling's Northwest Woman's Battlefield Service Group, the most versatile of all, carried on every conceivable type of educational and agitational work. It drew posters, composed and acted its own plays, initiated production and recruiting campaigns, organized the people for specific tasks and was in almost every way an example of what such a unit should be.

The women's work in the Northwest and in the new guerrilla bases behind the Japanese lines needs stressing because, although the Advisory Committee rendered extremely important auxiliary service, it was only in the Shensi-Ningsia-Kansu, Shansi-Hopeh-Chahar and other border areas that a true woman's movement was created, carrying on the great tradition of 1925-1927. Here the women organized into associations numbered not thousands but hundreds of thousands, and their functions did not deal only with relief but involved full participation in the war and in political and economic self-rule. The organizers of the Eighth Route Army came to some of the most backward regions of China, devitalized by long misrule and shaken further by periods of Japanese occupation. In large sections of Shansi and Shensi provinces, women still had their feet bound. Illiteracy was ninety-five per cent or higher. Oppressed and embittered husbands made up for the hopelessness of existence by exercising boundless tyranny over their wives. Girl babies were sold or killed almost as a matter of course.

The very sight of the uniformed organizers, these strange and terrible free-striding "girl soldiers", frightened the local women indoors. They had to be approached carefully, first only with offers to help with their washing and their baby-minding, and with suggestions for better methods of doing these things. They had to be encouraged to talk about their lives, to be told of their rights in relation to their men, to be given a sense of their worth and their own importance, then to be helped into fighting with their families for the few hours needed to attend meetings and receive education, then to be entrusted with responsibilities. And the results of this patient and painstaking labor? Today, women in the border areas have become real people and real fighters, not only matching but often outdistancing the men. The system of democratic self-rule has placed women in administrative positions put there by the votes of their fellow-villagers of both sexes, and it is not uncommon to find women district magistrates, mayors of townships and heads of villages. In North Shensi alone, women hold two thousand elective positions in local administration. Woman's organizations are responsible for livestock raising, for the weaving of uniforms, for the care of wounded and children, aid to soldiers' families, control of travelers and, when the men are away fighting, the farm work of their villages as well. In many cases they have brought traitors to book, done intelligence work among the enemy, guarded wells and crossroads and performed other functions of military value.

No one who comes back from these areas fails to tell of the part played by women in every phase of life, of how, in the midst of the war, they have moved from the darkness of the feudal past to a position which, for their sisters in the rest of China, lies only in the future.

On a more limited scale, the Chinese Industrial Cooperatives have also made a great difference to the position of women wherever they have been established. One such body began with the opening of two textile cooperatives for some factory girls evacuated from Hankow. Today, after three years, it has organized some twenty-five thousand soldiers' wives, refugee and peasant women for home spinning of wool, runs schools for over seven hundred children and adults, and sponsors a production program for crippled veterans and Japanese war prisoners. Its efforts have been responsible for giving the country twelve hundred and forty tons of wool for army blankets and have saved great numbers of women from beggary. Literacy groups, clubs in which the women learn collective self-management, training classes to give them the skills that lead to independence, clinics for them and their children have been built up from the profits of the common productive effort In C.I.C. centers throughout the country, many women hold positions as district organizers, and they head some of the best and most efficient units, famous far and wide throughout the movement. In the recent enforced evacuation of cooperatives from the Shansi bank of the Yellow River, where a large-scale Japanese offensive achieved success, the workers put themselves voluntarily under semi-military discipline. "Desertion in the face of the enemy" became one of the statutory justifications for the displacement of officers and expulsion of members. Not one woman was so disgraced. On the other hand, it was the woman chairman of a textile unit who ordered her colleagues to go ahead and stayed behind herself to bury immovable machinery and carry away some lighter equipment on her own person when the Japanese had surrounded the cooperative on three sides at a distance of less than a mile. In the ranks of the cooperatives there are also women who a short time ago were mill-slaves under the galling conditions to which Chinese labor is subject. They were unskilled peasants, uprooted from their land and seemingly condemned to slow starvation as refugees, or local girls and housewives whose existence had been dislocated by the war. Now they have become people worthy in themselves and valuable to the country's present and future, no longer "just women", but full and respected citizens.

In 1938 a very real effort was made to unify all women's activities under the Advisory Committee, to which Teng Ying-chao reported in detail on the work in the guerrilla areas which was then in its exciting early experimental stages. Under the Committee, the groundwork was laid for the friendly cooperation of Chinese women of all classes and parties.

During the past two years, however, and especially in recent months, conditions on our united front have deteriorated greatly. Defeatists and fifth columnists have had altogether too much success in straining relations between the two major parties, between the guerrilla areas and the rear. Reactionaries who have lain low since the beginning of the war have been enabled to raise their heads and set to work busily to annul the democratic gains won by the people in four

years of war. Once again, this process has shown how
intimately the position of women is connected with the
relative ascendency of the forces of progress or backwardness. In the summer of 1940, women who, in
Chungking and elsewhere, had worked faithfully in government departments since the outbreak of the war,
carrying on through repeated evacuations, bombings
and war-time economic earthquakes, began to feel once
more the weight of the old prewar type of discrimination. The post office, for instance, suddenly declared
that it would no longer employ married women. Education projects of the Y.W.C.A. in the countryside were
closed. A meeting of all woman's organizations in the
capital, held under the auspices of the Advisory Committee, was called to devise measures of self-protection,
and the Committee itself immediately attracted the attention of the secret police and pressure-group political
manipulators. When reaction reached its zenith in the
attack on the New Fourth Army, the wave of arrests
throughout the country took in many workers in
woman's organizations, including one member of the
highest coordinating body. Under these circumstances,
some of the most active organizers were compelled to
leave the country.

Finally, the official convening message of a conference of woman's work leaders called by the Central
Organization Department of the Kuomintang in the
spring of 1941 showed that, despite all the gains that
had been registered, and despite such outward signs
as the presence of a number of woman members in the
appointed People's Political Council, the reaction had
by no means been defeated. The message advised

women to strengthen their organizations, to increase
their individual skills, to join the party and to have
more children. On the participation of women in politics it had this to say: "It is harmful for every woman
to strive to take part in politics. . . Work in the woman's
movement should be concerned with general education,
vocational training, woman's service, and welfare and
family problems. The woman's movement will have
succeeded when women reach the level of men in
character, knowledge, physical condition and technical
abilities." In other words, women are urged to equality
of attainment but denied equality of rights. It is hardly
necessary to say that such a conception is opposed both
to the ideas of Sun Yat-sen, who held strongly that it
is the duty of every one to take an active part in the
workings of government and its improvement, and to
the whole trend of painfully won progress in China.

Nevertheless, forward-looking Chinese women are
far from discouraged. They know that so long as the
war against aggression continues, the objective pre-
conditions for the growth of democracy, and the demand
of life itself for such growth, will increase and not
diminish, whatever the resistance of those who can only
look back. Also, they know that the awakening of
our womanhood is only beginning. Every traveller in
China can tell how much the vast majority of women,
even in their still backward state and whom the wave
of emancipation has not touched, are doing for the
common effort. The Burma Road and the great Northwest Highway to the Soviet Union, those two heroic
break-throughs of fighting China to the outside world
after the Japanese had blockaded her by sea, were

largely built by the labor of women. The Kwangtung trade route which, dodging the blockade for more than a year secretly moved far more goods each week than the Burma Road could manage in a month, was composed of endless lines of sturdy Hakka woman-porters, carrying hundred-pound loads in thirty-mile stages.

Women have not only worked but fought. I know personally of an instance in which the female population of a village in Hainan Island fought off a small Japanese landing made when their menfolk were away. They had only farm implements to fight with, and many were killed, but the enemy force was compelled to re-embark. Similar happenings must have occurred in a great many places throughout the country, unheralded and unknown. As for individual cases, there is a story in almost every district of some girl who, emulating Mu Lan of old, changed into men's clothing and fought in the army.

The fighting record of our women does not permit us to believe that they will ever again allow themselves to be enslaved either by a national enemy or by social reaction at home. Only an extension of democracy, including the rights of women, can bring real victory in this war. Such a victory, won by the united efforts of the people, will leave no room for any scheme of things other than democracy.

When the victory over aggression is achieved, Chinese women will stand with the women of all countries, as those who have suffered so much more than even the men in the mad revel of fascism and war that has spread throughout the world, ready and willing to see that in the future all movement shall be forward,

that the earth's present frightful testing-time shall be
the last of its kind.

OPEN LETTER TO FRIENDS OF CHINA ABROAD

Chungking

September 18, 1943

Dear Friends:

This is the third time that I am addressing you, at the head of a general report of the China Defence League, to thank you for the aid you have already given and to appeal for your continued support of the Chinese people's struggle.

The first time was five years ago. How much has happened since. I asked you to help China then because she was "one of the battlefields on which the great struggle of the peoples of the world against fascist aggression and darkness has already taken the shape of open war". I said that it was "because the Chinese people, like those of Spain, refuse to be conquered, that even the capitulation of Munich has not enabled the fascist wave to engulf the world".

Neither you nor I could have known at that time that the people of Spain would go down fighting gloriously in the face of the incredible blindness of the other lands whose forward ramparts they held. We could not foresee that the nightmare of a fascist victory would all but materialize, that because the world could not unite to prevent this war, it would be forced to fight it on the enemy's terms, that terribly late—but not too late—the anti-Axis powers would come together and, at the cost of millions of lives, finally achieve the turning of the tide.

Today, in sight of the military defeat of the fascist powers, it is not less but more necessary that we should keep and strengthen the unity won at such cost, that we should keep and extend democracy, that all peoples should work together untiringly for the things that are to the common interest of the common man everywhere.

The armies of China on the anti-Japanese fronts, the people's forces that by struggle and the practice of democracy have welded isolated guerrilla centers into strong anti-Japanese bases in the rear of the enemy, still stand as the vanguard of the war against fascism in the Far East. Now they no longer stand alone. They are fighting side by side with millions of other soldiers, of all nations, who are gradually tightening the noose around the enemy of the peoples. That is good. That is what they always expected and believed would come.

The best of our fighters do not expect to rest on the efforts of the past. Now that others are in the battle, all they ask is that on the whole global front, the battle be fought with maximum effect. For themselves, they want no exemption, just because they have fought longer, from any of the responsibilities of the Allies. They take the sharpest issue with those of our countrymen who think now others can be left to win our war. They realize that our responsibility to our partners is also our responsibility to ourselves, that we are entitled to claim aid only if we use it and all our own strength to fight harder than before. Only in this way can China's soil be freed. Only by our own efforts can we build China as part of the new world.

Most of this report is taken up with telling you what has been done in the guerrilla areas* to save our wounded and put them back into the ranks, to fight disease and hunger, to prevent these allies of the enemy from undermining the struggle. Why this preoccupation with the Border Regions? Are we advancing their claims beyond those of other parts of China and other Chinese armies? The answer is no, we are not. We lay stress on the guerrilla areas because although they engage and have engaged almost half of the Japanese forces in China, it is three years since they have received any aid, in ammunition, money, or particularly in our own field, medical supplies. When Spain alone stood in arms against fascism in Europe, the ill-starred policy of "non-intervention" denied her arms. The forces that have bit the deepest into the lines of Japanese fascism in China are subjected to a "non-intervention" policy even more drastic and more cruel. An internal political blockade denies them doctors, surgical instruments and drugs, even those that are sent by friends abroad. We do not ask for these forces to receive preferential treatment. We ask for equality of treatment, for a stop to the practice, and to the acquiescence of others in the practice, that has drawn an imaginary line through China on one side of which a soldier wounded in the

---

* Meaning the border areas held by the famous 8th Route Army under the leadership of the Chinese Communist Party.

fight against Japan is assumed to be entitled to have his wounds healed, and on the other, not.

The China Defence League is concerned entirely with relief, but with relief for a purpose. In its own field, and in its own field only, it wants to help win the war against fascism. When the great issue was not yet joined throughout the world, it fought against the conception of "neutral" relief and maintained that aid should go first to the fighters against aggression, who by their struggles were barring the way of those whose victory would cause such a tidal wave of suffering that not all the relief efforts in the world could cope with it. Today, it stands for relief that will help the great final efforts for victory and ensure that the unity of anti-fascist forces is maintained, that no new split be allowed to arise to jeopardise what has been won and expose the world to new and devastating wars, both civil and international. The China Defence League does not, and has never stood for "non-intervention". It stands for the right and obligation of all peoples to help the popular struggle for freedom, to cry a halt both to aggression and regression and to those who wittingly or unwittingly open the gates to aggression and regression. It stands for the spirit that brought Dr. Norman Bethune to China, to fight and die in defence of people everywhere on the Chinese battlefront against Japanese imperialism.

Our first slogan was, "Help the Chinese people to help themselves". Today it is still the same. Help the Chinese people to help themselves—and you. Without unity in China, and in the whole anti-fascist camp, there can be no victory. Without democracy there can be no unity. Without the people's initiative, based on understanding of the problems we all face, there can be no democracy. In the field of Chinese relief, as positive, democratic action, this means the principle of equal and proportionate aid to all those who fight the Japanese invaders. Every dollar given, every voice raised towards this aim, is a blow not only at suffering, but at the things that have caused it, and that, if we do not destroy them, will inevitably bring new seas of blood and tears in their train. There is no truer humanitarianism than this.

So we say today what we said five years ago. Relief —but relief against fascism. Relief—but relief for democracy. Only in this way can you help the people of China—and yourselves.

A MESSAGE TO AMERICAN WORKERS

Issued through "Allied Labor News"

February 8, 1944

Every American worker and every thinking worker throughout the world, now understands his stake in strengthening democracy and in the war against the Axis. Labor is fighting in this war, and producing for it, because its hope for a better life is bound up with the beating down of blackest reaction, represented by fascism—fascism that begins by reducing its own workers to helots and then goes on to reduce the peoples of other countries to slavery. Labor works and fights for the extension of democracy everywhere because only under democracy can workers organize and move forward toward the fuller enjoyment of the fruits of their own efforts. The nightmare of fascism in Axis strongholds and the slave farms of their "New Order" have shown the workers of the United Nations the value of democracy at home.

China has one-fifth of the world's people. For years she has stood as the great barrier to Japanese fascist domination over all Asia which holds half the people of the earth. Today United Nations forces, as well as her own, are striking at Japan from her soil. The more effectively she fights, the shorter the war against Japan will be, and the less the cost in American lives. That is why American workers have an interest in China's resistance. Chinese resistance has been greatest and most effective at times when and in places where democracy has been strongest, where the people's initiative has been encouraged, and where the people's war—the only weapon with which an economically backward and relatively unarmed country can beat back a better equipped invader—has been given the freest rein. China's resistance has faltered and failed at times when reactionary forces have committed open treason by going over to the enemy or made the enemy's task easier by suppressing the people and their initiative, and by fearing and sabotaging the democratic effort of all. That is why American labor has a stake in China's democracy.

The Chinese people are strong in defence of their own soil, as proved by their resistance through seven years. But reaction and fascism in China are strong also. This is proved by the betrayal of Wang Ching-wei and of many army generals, by the increased ease with which the Japanese can operate in different parts of our country, by the diversion of part of our national army to the task of blockading and "guarding" the guerrilla areas, by the fact that some still hold private profit above the national interest, by the oppression of the peasantry, and by the absence of a true labor movement in most of our territory.

American labor can best express its interest in China's resistance by insisting that the products of its efforts and the gifts it makes be equally distributed to every force in China, wherever situated, that is actively

engaged in operations against Japan—and to no force
that is otherwise engaged. It can express this interest
in China's democracy by going on record against the
threat of civil war which some Chinese reactionaries are
preparing in order to destroy a democratic sector of our
struggle. That sector is the guerrilla bases in North
Shensi and behind the enemy lines where the labor
movement is fostered and encouraged and where many
detachments of armed miners and railway workers cooperate with the guerrilla fighters to pry Japan loose
from her main continental base in North and Central
China.

Our government has promised—not for the first
time—that we shall have constitutional government, and
that one year after the war all parties will be equal and
compete politically through the ballot. We need democracy during the war because we must have equal
treatment for all anti-Japanese forces. Let the first
step be the lifting of the inhuman blockade which prevents wounded fighters of the guerrilla armies, that have
inflicted such a large part of all Japanese casualties,
from receiving vital medical supplies. Talk of democracy cannot be worth much at a time when even this
first step towards simple humanity has not been taken.

American labor needs no praise from me for what
it is doing for fighters against fascism everywhere.
American workers know, as we all know with warmth,
fellow-feeling and gratitude, that ships built by their
hands are carrying the weapons they have forged to
many fronts of our common struggle. I ask American
labor to make known its desire that the men who fight

fascism behind Japanese lines get a share of its efforts commensurate with the task they are doing.

SUN YAT-SEN AND THE DEMOCRACY OF CHINA

A broadcast from Chungking on the occasion of the celebration of Sun Yat-sen Day in America on March 12, 1944

Nineteen years ago Sun Yat-sen wrote in his will, which ever since has been one of the basic political documents of Chinese progress: "For forty years I have devoted myself to the cause of the people's revolution with but one aim in view—the elevation of China to a position of freedom and equality among the nations. My experiences during these forty years have firmly convinced me that to attain this goal we must bring about a thorough awakening of our own people and ally ourselves in the common struggle with those peoples of the world who treat us on the basis of equality. The work of the revolution is not yet done. . . . . . Above all, our recent declarations in favor of the convocation of a national convention and the abolition of unequal treaties should be carried into effect with the least possible delay."

What do the principles of this document mean to-day? We must seek their meaning, first of all, in the linking of the words "freedom" and "equality" as between nations or states, and the linking of "thorough awakening of our own people" with the common struggle in which we ally ourselves with those peoples of the world who treat us on a basis of equality. The linking of the abolition of the unequal treaties, achieved as a result of our anti-Japanese struggle, with the convocation of a democratic convention at home, not yet called, shows the same dominant thought—stable peace can only come to the world when international democracy is attained. Today we all recognize this in words, though not all do in deeds. International democracy means both equality among the nations and a government in each country based on the interest and freely signified will of its people. When Sun Yat-sen was called upon to crystallize in a few words the results of a long lifetime of thought and experience for the greatest need of the people of China, he put these two things first of all.

Every one knows that the aim of the Chinese people in this war is the aim of Sun Yat-sen's lifetime—full national equality. For almost three hundred years China was ruled by the Manchus. In the past century she became a semi-colony of other powers and narrowly missed becoming a second Korea. Today our occupied areas are colonial in every sense while other sections of the country are at different points of transition from a semi-colonial status to full national freedom. Nationally we must and will shake off every form of subservience and imposed dependence. But this does not mean that the Chinese people are or will be anti-foreign or that they will ever forget the precept of Sun Yat-sen regarding collaboration with friends of common purpose—true friends, whether they be states, popular movements or individuals—because this precept represents the Chinese people's true needs. All national revolutions have drawn on progressive thought and action everywhere. The American Revolution had its friends among the English people and in its turn influenced the French. Our movement to overthrow the Manchus drew deeply on the American revolutionary tradition. And the movement against the warlords, for people's rule and for full national equality, was inspired and sustained by the revolution in Russia. In his fight against the Manchus and imperialist encroachment, it would never have occurred to Sun Yat-sen to regard as interference detrimental to our sovereignty the support given to our people's movement by foreign friends, and it would not occur to our people today. We claim the right to criticize such things as American isolationism and the holding down of India, and we admit the right of others to examine and criticize the situation in our own country.

Speaking of criticism of foreign tendencies, I want to say that while every Chinese patriot believes that our forces fighting against Japan are entitled to all possible help, only those Chinese who have been spectators and not full participants in our national struggle have so little faith in our people that they can weep and wail and declare that if help does not come tomorrow we will collapse on the day after. The men who fight for our land and our future ask for help, but they make no conditions involving the end for which they have already sacrificed so much.

STATEMENT URGING COALITION GOVERNMENT AND AN APPEAL TO THE AMERICAN PEOPLE TO STOP THEIR GOVERNMENT FROM MILITARILY AIDING THE KUOMINTANG

Shanghai

July 23, 1946

In recent years I have devoted myself entirely to war relief, to add strength to China's resistance. I avoided political controversy lest it injure this work. I kept silent because all attention had to be centered in winning the war.

Today no foreign enemy threatens our land. We are threatened only from within. We are threatened by civil war, into which reactionaries hope to draw America, thus involving the whole world. Such civil war, though undeclared, has already begun.

This calamity must be stopped at its beginning. Every person with human feelings must speak out. Though I still wish to give my energies to relief, and in no way do I wish to jeopardize my work, I feel it necessary to speak at this time.

The present crisis is not a question of who wins— Kuomintang or Communist. It is a question of the Chinese people, their unity, liberty and livelihood. It cannot be settled by balancing armed forces, or bargaining for this city and that territory. Not party rights but human rights hang in the balance.

People keep anxiously hoping for something to come from the ever-continuing negotiations. But after every patched-up truce, the conflict flares anew. Negotiations between the Kuomintang and the Communists cannot give the final answer. The final answer must be given by the Chinese people.

The solution is clear, even if difficult. It lies in the correct understanding of People's Nationalism, People's Democracy and People's Livelihood, the Three Principles of Sun Yat-sen, and their correct application today.

People's Nationalism today means that China is one nation, one people. Within this nation are many political ideas. We must have a government to which all people may contribute their ideas.

People's Democracy today means that the time of Kuomintang tutelage is over. The time for constitutional government must begin. Our people have won this by eating much bitterness. They have shown themselves worthy of self-rule.

The coalition government must be set up immediately. It must not be brought into being solely by delegates appointed by the Kuomintang. Every party and political group must elect its own representatives. The Kuomintang delegates must also be elected by the membership and not appointed by a ruling group. There are many able, progressive members in the Kuomintang who have had no chance to speak. Now is the time to build democracy by practising it.

Once these delegates have been democratically chosen, let them prepare a constitution that the Chinese people will recognize and ratify. Let these delegates write into this constitution that the Chinese people will have their inalienable freedoms, nut in any way contingent upon the whims of a few who seek to control, but exclusively in the people's own hands.

People's Livelihood today means that the people must no longer starve while corrupt officials pile up their fortunes and honest officials despair. It means that the agrarian question must be justly settled. This is not Communist or foreign agitation. It is logic derived from our own history. A century ago the peasants' unrest caused the Taiping rebellion. The people's right to rise against starvation, feudalism and colonialism could no longer be denied. The people can no longer be denied now.

"Land to those who till" was Sun Yat-sen's program. It was also adopted at the Kuomintang First Congress. It is the cure for China's starvation. Has not CNRRA's director recently stated that in the Communist areas there is no famine? Why? Because they have followed Sun Yat-sen's program and give land to the tillers. This same consideration for People's Livelihood must be given all over the country.

The Kuomintang must perform its historic mission in leading the Chinese people to full liberation through a coalition government, the people's democracy and agrarian reform. If this is done, there is no doubt that the Kuomintang will be the leading party in any coalition. It will be supported by Chinese of many parties, including those who have no army and therefore no voice with which to negotiate. Free criticism must replace corruption, terrorism and political assassination.

Unless the Kuomintang fulfils these tasks at once, it must bear the responsibility for provoking civil war.

Civil war cannot bring unity, liberation or livelihood. Civil war brings chaos, hunger and destruction to the Chinese people. We will see the cities cut off from the countryside. The peasants will support the Communists, who give them land and lower taxes. Where then will the Kuomintang cities obtain raw materials, exportable products or even food? Bayonets cannot gather harvests. Inflation that already devours the cities will increase a thousandfold. The Kuomintang cannot win in such a war.

All this is known. Why then do the reactionaries inflame a war which they cannot win? Because they hope that civil conflict in China will incite war between America and the U.S.S.R., and thus at last crush the Chinese Communists.

The American people, who are allies and long friends of the Chinese people, must be clearly told of this road to disaster. They must be told that the American reactionaries are teaming up with Chinese reactionaries, each encouraging the other. They must be told that the presence of US armed forces on Chinese soil is not strengthening peace and order among the Chinese people. They must be warned that loans should be given only to a recognized and truly representative Chinese government. They must be told that if America makes it plain that she will not supply munitions or military assistance, there will be no spreading of the Chinese civil war.

The first flame of world conflagration is burning today in our land. It must be quenched lest the fire destroy the world. I appeal to the Chinese leaders of the two major parties and other parties and groups to form a coalition government at once.

I appeal to our American friends to foster such a move by stopping all military supplies and providing assistance only to a government which will belong to the Chinese people.

MESSAGE TO THE WORLD FEDERATION
OF DEMOCRATIC YOUTH

January 1948

Allow me to indicate my wish that your Festival has every success. The importance of youth meeting at this particular time to determine a program that will foster international friendship and world reconstruction cannot be underestimated. I hope that out of your Festival comes a concrete plan to promote these vital ingredients for global peace.

The youth of the world faces grave problems and grim conditions. However, this is no signal, neither is there time, to despair. The youth of today is also faced with a world in which the common man all over is alert. The atmosphere in which we live is charged with an energy that is filtering into the minds and bodies of ordinary people in all countries, an energy that will eventually smash all obstacles that selfish individuals and groups plant in the path of the people. The common men and women of the world are going to work out their own destinies; they will achieve their political freedom and economic liberation in the face of any and all opposition.

In this momentous emancipation, youth is not without its responsibilities. Its first responsibility is to recognize its roots. These must be buried deep in the heart of the people. Secondly, youth must know its roots intimately. You must go to the people to learn. Thirdly, there are no short cuts. You move with the people. It is hard work, but if you go too fast, they will correct your pace. If you go against them, they will destroy you. They are the prime movers. You must calculate their speed. You must integrate yourself so well that every step you take can be counted off by the millions taking that same step.

What must world democratic youth guard against? There are leaders in the world who in their youth once professed the same ideals as you do at the Festival. Yet these same people, compromised by opportunism, mellowed by expediency and divorced from their roots, are leading reactionary governments and forces against the general welfare.

The countries they rule are haunted by the moans of starving millions, the screams of police victims, the mouthings of democratic phrases echoing against the empty walls. This you must guard against, deviation. It leads to corruption of self and principle.

Therefore, world youth, if it is to continue to include the word "democracy" in its title, has its obligation. It is obliged to act. It must act against those who would divide the world into two sides, against those who would repudiate the sacrifices of the past war by withholding the very freedoms for which it was fought; against those who in the name of stopping aggression, bolster reactionary forces against the will of the people;

against those who would resist the trend and strain for the retention of power, even to provoking a third world war.

These are the forces the people will fight against. You must join the people in their struggle for victory.

PART V

THE LIBERATION AND PEOPLE'S GOVERNMENT

A MONUMENTAL PERIOD

Issued in Shanghai in celebration of the 28th anniversary of the Chinese Communist Party

July 1, 1949

This is a monumental period in the lives of the Chinese people. Their complete victory is at hand. A salute to their victory!

This is the impetus for the reconstruction and advancement of our land. Production and more production is our standard. A salute to the people's might!

This is the new light in our land. Freedom is dawning. It is spreading its warmth into every reactionary-darkened corner. A salute to the people's freedom!

This is a high tide of victory, rippling to every shore. People's movements in all lands take heart, add our strength to theirs and reinforce the good fight. A salute to our world-wide comrades in democratic strife!

This is to give strength to those who fought through to this victory. Their valor, a match for any. Their heart, one with the people's. A salute to the Chinese People's Liberation Army!

This is an extended hand to the leadership born in Shanghai, bred in the hills of Kiangsi, tempered into steel over 8,000 torturous miles and matured in the dust of our countryside.   A salute to the Chinese Communist Party!

Yes, this is a monumental period—a milestone in the Chinese people's revolutionary struggle. We divest ourselves of our burden of imperialism and colonialism. We uproot feudalism. The people move to new and more glorious heights. A salute to and long live the victory of the Chinese People's Revolutionary Struggle!

SPEECH AT THE PEOPLE'S POLITICAL CONSULTATIVE CONFERENCE

Peking

September 1949

There is a momentum in this land today. The Chinese people are moving and they have the impact of revolution. There is a pulsation, a building, a new China!

We have arrived at this historic position because of the leadership provided by the Chinese Communist Party. It is the only party which has the strength of the masses infused into its ranks. As a result, it is the surest guarantee that Sun Yat-sen's Three Principles —People's Nationalism, People's Democracy and People's Livelihood—will be successfully carried out.

This has been proven in the countryside, where the Communist Party has given land to the tiller. That we are here attests to the correctness of such a policy. Now the Communist Party is in the process of proving its right of leadership in our cities. It was on the backs of our peasants that the burdens of the first phase of our revolution were carried. The Communist daily, has shifted the emphasis of revolutionary vanguard from the peasants to the workers. Production has been made the keynote. And it is about to put solid flesh on the

skeleton plans which Sun Yat-sen drew up for the industrialization of China.

But there are doubters among us who believe that
the people cannot achieve further, that the transfer of
the countryside policies cannot be made to the cities.
They watch with scepticism as steps are taken to awaken
the slumbering giant, Shanghai, one of the industrial
hearts that pumps life-blood into the rest of the country.
However, let us look at the newly liberated Shanghai.
This center of corruption is being turned into a pillar
of production. The Shanghai Military Control Commission has already dealt effectively with the fearful
currency problem, the galloping inflation which had
caused such untold hardships to the people for twelve
years. The Military Control Commission always took
the needs of the people into consideration. As a result
of this, measures of safeguarding the people's savings
and their livelihood through commodity bank accounts
and other measures have won confidence in the newly
issued banknotes.

This confidence came partly from the manner in
which the Military Control Commission dealt with the
public. They made their policies clear and explained
with patience reasons for their every move, in language
everyone could understand. Above all, they exhibited
a sincere willingness to learn. Loss of face became at
once an anachronism. They frankly admitted every
mistake and they call for advice as to how they can
help the people to help themselves. They say: "You
industrialists, what must be done to start the wheels
of production spinning for the people?" To workers
and students: "What do you think of our proposals?" To

cultural workers and educators: "Release your thoughts that have been stifled and suppressed these many years. Tell us how you think the greatest benefit can go to the people." The total result of these policies has been the people's revolutionary support, and there can be only one further result—success.

The Chinese Communist Party has followed this method of handling its relations with the people in the political field also. Here are the delegates of democratic parties, people's organizations, minority races and groups, overseas Chinese as well as individuals prominent for their progressive outlook, who compose the Preparatory Commission of the People's Political Consultative Conference. For the first time in Chinese history there is such a wide representative group of the people, forming a real united front to carry out the joint program and to establish a genuine people's democratic government.

I would like to refer further to our cultural and educational workers. Their whole status in the community has been changed. Our teachers, writers, artists, musicians and dramatists no longer will be persecuted and exploited. Now they have the greatest audience of their lives. There is no fear of knowledge. Rather the cultural and educational workers are encouraged to live close to the people, so they can learn from them, so they can serve the people better.

That is the state of affairs on the national level. What does this victorious march mean on the international front? It means that the accomplishments of our people have changed the perspective of the entire world. No longer can reactionary forces think in terms other than their own extinction in the event they instigate a third world conflict. There is something which is non-fissionable, something more powerful than the atomic monster of imperialistic, military creation. This substance, the core of the world's future security, is the product of the world's peace coalition.

China's masses, in their revolutionary struggle, are welded to the people's governments and forces in every part of the globe. Together they have swung the balance of history. This is a mighty force in the hands of millions, and the units are workers, peasants and intellectuals. They are dedicated to prevent the destruction of civilization. They will exert every ounce of energy to assure that the common people everywhere get their due from life.

This is to say that the struggle does not end until every hovel has been rebuilt into a decent house; until the products of the earth will be within easy purchase; until profits from the factories will be returned in equal amount to the work exerted; until every family can have complete medical care from the cradle to the grave. When these necessities are equally at hand for everyone, regardless of race, color, creed and residence in this world, then can we say we have reached our goal.

This, then, is a call to the colors of the New China, of the New World! Comrades, let us proceed with our tasks of establishing an independent, democratic, strong and prosperous New China, and together with the peoples of the world bring about everlasting peace!

ON SINO-SOVIET FRIENDSHIP

A speech delivered in Peking at the Preparatory Committee of the Sino-Soviet Friendship Association

September 6, 1949

Almost a quarter of a century ago, Sun Yat-sen bequeathed to us his cherished dream of close cooperation with China's only friend—the Soviet Union. We well remember how joyfully he greeted the October Revolution and how earnestly he desired the cooperation of the Chinese Communist Party. After a lapse of twenty-four years, this dream is at last becoming a reality. We can now look forward to tackling our tasks of reconstruction and rehabilitation, of building together a new world of the people's culture and of social progress, as comrades-in-arms of our mighty ally and friend—the Soviet people.

Now, at last, the promises of the 1911 Revolution in China are being fulfilled. And this time there will be no turning back, because the leadership does not shy away from facing realities squarely. Furthermore, this leadership has the full confidence and cooperation of the Chinese people in carrying out its revolutionary duties.

Sino-Soviet friendship moves in an entirely different plane from the Atlantic Pact and its Pacific counterpart. The Atlantic Pact moves on a cold, "high diplo-

matic level", where a militarily and economically strong
government imposes its will on weaker nations. It is
bent on destruction, on exploitation of economic advan-
tages, such as the Marshall Plan dumping unwanted
American surpluses on European economies and destroying their local production and industries in order
to alleviate the United States' own crisis.

Sino-Soviet friendship moves on the "lower level"
of close cooperation between the people themselves, one
individual joining hands with another in deep understanding of each other's similarities. This friendship
means construction and mutual aid in clearing the
wreckages of the last war and the building of a Socialist
economy. Both countries, the U.S.S.R. and China, suffered unspeakably through this holocaust. They can,
therefore, work to secure peace and unity without sus-
pecting each other's motives and trusting the people's
desire and ability to write the first chapter of history
as masters of their own fate. Sino-Soviet cooperation
is the sure guarantee of victory for peace and democracy. Together we shall be able to conquer all difficulties. Therefore, we must strengthen and consolidate
the friendship between the two peoples in order to defeat
the intrigues of the instigators of a new world war.

Long live Sino-Soviet friendship and cooperation!

SPEECH MADE AT THE INAUGURAL CONFERENCE OF THE SINO-SOVIET FRIENDSHIP ASSOCIATION

Peking

October 5, 1949

Thirty-two years ago, the October Revolution shook the whole world. When this greatest event in the history of mankind was slandered and vilified by all imperialists, it was Sun Yat-sen who first pointed out that "with the success of the Russian Revolution, a new hope for mankind is born." Yes, at last, this great hope born thirty years ago is being realized in our motherland. The October Revolution, led by the greatest revolutionary leaders of mankind, Lenin and Stalin, gave new life to the cause of the Chinese people's revolution, and enabled us to apply the correct orientation of relying on the masses of workers and peasants. Since then, the foundation for permanent close cooperation has been laid between the two great nations, China and the Soviet Union. In bidding farewell to the Central Executive Committee of the Communist Party of the Soviet Union, Sun Yat-sen stated that "in the struggle of the world oppressed for liberation, these two allies must march hand-in-hand towards victory." Today, I rejoice in witnessing the realization of Sun Yat-sen's ardent desire.

We recall the Soviet Union was the first to abrogate all unequal treaties with China. We recall also the assistance rendered by the Soviet Union to China during the great revolution of 1924-1927. Moreover, we recall her aid to us during the anti-Japanese aggression, especially her great assistance in sending troops to Manchuria in 1945, thus enabling us to finally liquidate the Japanese Kwantung Army. During the past thirty years of our hard struggle against enemies at home and abroad, the Soviet Union was our only steadfast and loyal friend. Today, this most reliable friend of the Chinese people is the first to recognize our new Central People's Government.

The Chinese people will aways bear in mind with gratitude this precious friendship and assistance. Through thirty years of revolutionary experiences, the Chinese people have realized the correctness of Chairman Mao Tse-tung's advocacy of allying with the Soviet Union and the new democracies. The victory of the Chinese people is an important contribution to world peace. This victory is indivisible from the assistance rendered us by the Soviet Union. To safeguard and extend this victory until all oppressed peoples in the world have also won freedom and liberation, we must unite more firmly than ever with the Soviet Union and consolidate the forces for people's democracy and lasting peace. We are convinced that so long as the 200,-000,000 people of the U.S.S.R. join with the 475,000,000 Chinese people in heroic struggle, all reactionary militarists and imperialists will certainly be annihilated by the united might of the people's forces.

"With the success of the Russian Revolution, a new hope for mankind is born." Today, with the victory of the Chinese people's revolution and the unity and co-operation between the two great nations, China and the Soviet Union, the hope of liberation for all mankind is nearer realization. Let us join hands more closely! Let us struggle more firmly! Our forces are mighty! The dawn of the whole world is in sight!

A SALUTE TO STALIN ON THE OCCASION OF THE CELEBRATION OF THE 32ND ANNIVERSARY OF THE OCTOBER REVOLUTION

Shanghai

November 6, 1949

I join the liberated Chinese people in sending you warmest greetings on the anniversary of the October Revolution. With Sun Yat-sen, we regard this event as the birth of hope of mankind. Our present successes are based on his and Chairman Mao Tse-tung's understanding that only the U.S.S.R. sincerely desired the liberation of the Chinese people. Now Sun Yat-sen's dream of close cooperation between our two great peoples is a reality. We are grateful for the expression of this cooperation in the presence of the Soviet cultural delegation which has benefited us much. It has aided us in our determination to follow the prime example of the U.S.S.R. in our national construction, in the elevation of our people's livelihood and cultural standard. Long live the friendship, unity and cooperation between the peoples of China and the U.S.S.R.

SPEECH TO THE ASIAN WOMEN'S CONFERENCE

Peking

December 11, 1949

Sisters—those of you on the free soil of liberated China, to whom I can shout these greetings; those of you at home in your own land or region of people's democracy, who likewise can openly receive respects from this historic conference; those of you in the darkness of oppression, to whom I must whisper these salutations; to Asia's women, one and all—hail to your courage; a salute to your accomplishments; warm wishes for your continued progress toward complete emancipation!

When we analyze conditions in present-day Asia, when we re-examine the marks that history has cut into our lands and peoples, we find that women have had common enemies, along with and as part of those peoples. These enemies are: foreign imperialism and the resulting colonialism, and home-grown feudalism with its advanced stage of compradorism.

These cruel forms of politico-economic development have visited upon us suppression and havoc. They have committed crimes against our lands and our peoples. These felonious acts are yet in evidence in those sectors still being ground beneath the heel, and even in newly liberated areas such as this one.

Imperialism and feudalism have reduced the great masses of people to poverty. These social tumors have caused human beings to live like the lowest animals, without food, in the shabbiest of dwellings, in the merest rags, without health care of any kind. In many cases it is deliberate debilitation, without frill or facade. And always, women and children are primary among the victims. They suffer the heaviest exploitation, both when they work or when they are kept from work. If they do toil, they always receive the absolute minimum wage.

Ignorance is the accomplice of poverty in the process of suppression. Therefore, in colonial and semi-colonial countries, the people are kept intellectually as fallow as possible. There are either no schools or pitifully few. The people are purposely separated from their culture or from the stimulation they may receive from progressive lands abroad. Once again, the women suffer the greatest, receiving no schooling in most countries, or in some places having a few facilities for the privileged class only.

Socially and politically, women are reduced to the position of slaves, or, at best, secondary citizens. This conforms to the typical feudal and fascist pattern, where main stress is laid on binding the wife to domestic service, where women are considered inferior and incapable of learning or doing.

We have apprehended long ago that the women of Asia cannot expect even sympathy from the imperialists in their fight to liberate themselves from this abysmal status. You have but to witness how they treat the women in their own countries. For those men who can afford it, the women are ornaments. For all others, women are either house servants or, as workers, they are considered a threat to the jobs that men hold. From this springs the economic, political and cultural subjugation of women. There is an abundance of documentation at hand.

During World War II, the women of the United States made progress in freeing themselves. The vast expansion of industry to meet the war needs required millions of more skilled workers than were available. The fact that millions of men were in the armed services opened the way for women to enter industrial jobs of all kinds. The industrialists of America found what has been known for many years in other countries where women have participated in technical work. It was discovered that women take better care of their machines; they not only assume responsibility, but they form a stable and reliable segment of the working force; in addition, they are capable of displaying greater enthusiasm for the job to be done. It was evident that they can do anything, from the most precise machine work to running factories.

The future looked good for the women of America. But the picture darkened as soon as the victory was in sight and men began to return from the services. There was activity generally, and most of the labor unions participated in coordination with the most reactionary forces, to get women out of industry and back into the kitchen. The propaganda, in its usual American high-pressure forms, went, "Thanks for the help, ladies. You did a grand job, but we can handle it from here on and you can go back to the kiddies." Or, "Your man coming back from the war will need you at home. It wouldn't be right to greet him in grimy overalls when he pictures you in fancy lace."

There were no honestly meant "Thanks" for the contribution women had made to the war effort. Nor was there any consideration for the economic freedom that many women had won for themselves as a result of their labor. The real thoughts behind this movement were never expressed. The essence was economic fear, a realization of the inadequacy of the whole economic system from which imperialism stems. There was much talk of "full employment" and how to achieve it, but in front of everybody's mind was "job fear". Add to this the well-founded anxiety of unemployment which further engenders the fear psychosis in capitalist countries, and you can more deeply understand why women are relegated to their present position.

The same treatment takes place in other spheres. In England, for example, woman teachers invariably receive from 10 to 15 per cent less wages than men. When you consider that the average salary of school-teachers in England is in the category of unskilled and semiskilled workers, you can visualize, first, the value they place on education, and second, the way in which woman teachers are regarded.

In France, they have gotten to the point where they arrest, prosecute and sentence women for activities in behalf of striking miners who demand more daily bread; or they are hounded for being politically active in the preservation of world peace.

These are but a few of the classic examples of how women fare in the root countries of imperialism. Therefore, how can we in Asia or women anywhere else under colonial domination expect understanding and support from such an atmosphere and situation? No, it is an impossibility.

Consequently, it is no surprise when we learn that in all colonial countries, child-care and maternity benefits are usually non-existent. Or, when they are written into the law, those who own the factories, the plantations, the mills and other economic forces, also own the courts. It is obvious, they have no fear of being called up for justice when they manhandle the law. The imperialists and their native lackeys have gone so far, we find, that they have made it an offence to bear a child. They force women off the job when they are pregnant in order to avoid paying maternity benefits. They can also simply withhold any maternity leave or payments they are supposed to make.

These flagrant abuses of court law and the law of human decency are the crimes of imperialism and feudalism. But they are only the outcroppings of still larger transgressions. For the question of treatment of women and children is not an isolated one. It involves all other questions.

It is closely interwoven with the idea that land belongs to the tiller. It is a corollary: that in those countries where the ownership of the land is concentrated in the hands of the few, where the landowners take one-half to two-thirds of the harvest from those who actually do the work, in those places women and children are treated in the worst feudalistic manner.

Pre-liberation China is the foremost example of this truth. It is similarly true that the landowners who attempt to perpetuate this system are in league with the foreign imperialists, who can base their entire operation only on the fact that feudalism exists.

It follows that the question of woman's position in society is gauged by the amount of foreign imperialistic control over the national resources and industrial development. For it is one and the same pair of greedy hands that chokes the riches of a land from its people and simultaneously stifles the freedom and equality of its womanhood. With the same selfishness, the imperialists exploit the natural resources of our countries and prevent the natural development of our women, thus providing cheap labor, thus precluding them from contributing to the advance of our peoples.

Yes, imperialism and feudalism have caused the writing of the same story into the history of every Asian land, with the blood of the people. The pages are filled with the bitterness that the people have had to eat. Their children have languished; they themselves have had to sweat away their lives hardly before they had begun life's experience; they have been oppressed and known no democracy. These are the crimes. They must be wiped out, every trace.

It is historically inevitable that this will be accomplished. For just as the people of Asia have their enemies, they also have their friends. These allies are strong and tested. They have proven, and are verifying daily, their ability to help the downtrodden to emancipate themselves, to aid women in their full liberation.

The first of these friends is true national independence. We must use the word "true" for there is a certain type of sham independence before us in the Far East. These are the countries which have had shouted for them so the whole world could hear that they are "free". Yet, in reality, it is the imperialist shouters who still control them. It is to the strongholds of the imperialists that the nominal heads go crawling, to roll in the plush surroundings and beg for support. The people won't support them, so they sell more and more of themselves and their people's wealth to maintain their temporary power.

In sharp contrast, there is the independence that is founded in the welfare of the people, which is the fertile soil from which grows a people's democracy with their full backing.

Our People's Republic of China is but one of the cases in point. The time has come for us at last, when the mighty force of New Democracy, united in all classes and parties, will fight to construct a true national independence, a real democratic China, part of which will be the release of women, equal in rights with men in all phases of activities.

It is so written into our basic law, the Common Program of the People's Political Consultative Conference. There, in the company of the provisions that enumerate all the efforts to be made by and in behalf of the working class in alliance with the peasants, other democratic classes and minority groups, is Article Six. It says: "The People's Republic of China abolishes the feudal system which holds women in bondage. Women shall enjoy equal rights with men in political, economic, cultural, educational and social life. Freedom of marriage for men and women shall be enforced."

This treatment of women has been in effect from the very beginning of our government. 10 per cent of the delegates to the P.P.C.C. which passed the Common Program were women. They are in positions dealing with the formulation of policy and the actual operation of our economic, educational and cultural life. They are active politically, among other things, carrying out the very foundation of New Democracy, the land reform. What is more, their children are receiving care while they are working for the people. Witness the extension by over three times the number of nurseries in Shanghai alone since its liberation last May. See the tremendous increase of schools of all kinds and the vastly enlarged enrolments of students in all parts of the liberated areas.

Further evidence of the attitude of the People's Republic of China to women is this very conference. It is indeed a historic occasion when leading women in the struggle for peace and democracy gather here to consider how to further these vital ingredients of mankind's progress, along with the specific problems women face today.

These are the signposts of true national independence and a government which functions in terms of its people.

The second friend to which the people in the colonial lands can look is the world proletarian movement, that is, their international friends headed by the great Soviet Union. It is from this sector that *any* people will receive recognition and treatment based on equality and mutual respect. It is here that all minorities, all militants for progress, 'all oppressed will find sympathy and support. It is here that we find the prime examples of the development of women and the part they are playing in the peaceful construction of their country.

These two friends, national independence and the world proletarian movement, have rendered invaluable assistance to the people and to women the world over. As pointed out previously, they write equality of womanhood into the law. It becomes a crime against the state to mistreat the bearers of the future. Also, as the rights of children are so closely linked with those of women, these too are given special attention in writing. For example, listen to part of the momentous document written in 1936, known as the Stalin Constitution. Here is how the question of education is cared for:

"Citizens of the U.S.S.R. have the right to education.

"This right is ensured by universal and compulsory elementary education; by free education up to and including the seventh grade; by a system of state stipends for students of higher educational establishments who excel in their studies; by instruction in schools being conducted in the native language, and by the organization in the factories, state farms, machine and tractor stations, collective farms of free vocational, technical and agronomic training for the working people."

Using this as a directive, the educational workers of the U.S.S.R. have accomplished the point where today over 34 million children study free of charge, where they are taught in the tongues of the 100 nationalities of the U.S.S.R. This is how socialism translates words into concrete facts.

From the educational and other sections of the Constitution, it is apparent that the entire governmental system is at the disposal of the common citizens, and especially the women and the children. This holds for all of the people's democracies or those countries already on the road to Socialism. They are regulated and planned to produce energetic and creative people for the eras to come.

The second assistance women receive from our friends is equal job opportunities. No field of endeavor is restricted. Women are welcomed to the heaviest physical labor or the most delicate research, according to their abilities. Brains and talents are used without discrimination.

Likewise, wherever women work, they receive equal pay for equal output. This is no small advance and is paramount to the economic security of women. The same applies to full maternity leave with pay, such as all forward-going countries afford their women.

Next, we find in lands where there is people's democracy and national independence, the women actually have political rights on a par with men, as the law provides. They can vote without question. They can hold office. They can take an active role in bettering conditions of their society . They do not have to batter their way into the political arena through an unwritten law, such as capitalistic countries place before their women. Our women are there from the very beginning, by right, by law, by universal acceptance.

The new type of existence also provides such essentials as medical care, as fast as the technical personnel and facilities can be expanded. The fight against infant mortality is carried out vigorously. This is one of the greatest scourges of mankind. It is always the result of oppression and forced ignorance. But people's governments recognize the criminality of infants being lost unnecessarily. They establish institutions to take care of youngsters—creches, nurseries, kindergartens and children's hospitals.

Lastly, the new society unquestionably results in a general lifting of the living standards. The latest experiments of the science of agronomy are applied, so that extraordinary yields are obtained from the fields. This, along with the fascinating afforestation plans for controlling the weather to the benefit of the crops, means food is more abundant and of better quality. Additionally, industrial methods are constantly enhanced and put into effect. This, plus the tremendous output of the workers who understand that the means of production belong to them, results in more of everything for everybody. Housing improves and reaches out to a greater number of people. Consumer items increase in availability. All of this comes to the people at no extra cost, but as part of their due reward. It is usually accompanied by price decreases and tremendous savings for the general population.

All of this is evident in the Soviet Union. There, as a result of their five year plan, several sweeping price reductions have taken place since the end of World War II. Further price drops took place just in March of this year. These ranged from bread, meat, fish and tobacco, which were reduced by 10 per cent, to clothing which declined an average of 12 per cent, to typewriters and radio and television sets and plastic goods which dropped 20 per cent, to watches which came down 30 per cent in price.

What these reductions would mean to the ordinary people of the Soviet Union was estimated by Mr. Georgi Malenkov in his speech on the 32nd Anniversary of the great October Revolution. He said that these price declines would increase the purchasing power of the Soviet workers and employees by 71 thousand million roubles. This will be in addition to the 86 thousand million roubles gained in 1947 through similar reductions.

Now, just compare this record with that of the leading capitalistic country in the world, the United States of America. Rather than institute new and better methods of production, the exact opposite is done. The situation in the steel industry can be used as an illustration because it is a key to the price structure in America. Steel is used in so many products, that it is the determinant for the rise and fall in the whole standard of living of the American people.

It is a fact, the demand for steel is far above the present output of the industry. Yet, this does not have to be the case. Using the improved methods developed during the war plus the increased plant capacity built in that period, the American steel industry could not only take care of its own people's requirements, but it could supply a larger share of the world demand, *and at lower prices*. We all have a right to ask, "Why isn't this supply forthcoming then?" The answer is that the steel industry in the United States is in the control of a mere handful of men, who through their unified manipulations create a scarcity market in steel, artificially

raise its price, and the price of everything into which it
goes as a result, and at the same time make profits for
themselves at a fantastic rate. This is a typical monopoly operation. This vicious combine refuses to put the
new manufacturing method into widespread use because
it threatens their present processing with the tag of
obsolete. Through their disproportionate pressure on
the government, they were able to buy up at ridiculously
low prices many of the plants constructed for the war
effort. And they effectively prevented these plants from
falling into other hands which might mean competition
for them, all of this in the land of "free enterprise", or
so the American people are told. Therefore, while the
profits soar for the few steel kings, the rest of the
Americans pay for it, and starve for steel.

This same restriction of the new is enforced in other
industrial fields, including the peaceful use of atomic
energy. Here the public utility moguls have placed their
heavy hand, because the domestic use of this gigantic
force would eventually wipe out their empires. As a
result, constructive use of nuclear energy, which would
lighten the burden of hundreds of millions of workers
and release them for other production or education and
recreation, is being purposely retarded in favor of military adventures which pay quick and big dividends.
Once again, the people of the United States are the
direct sufferers and the rest of the world feels the impact
indirectly.

This shows up in the figures concerning the American economic situation. According to the May 27th
issue of "United States News and World Report," a most
conservative business magazine, the wholesale prices in

May were 80 per cent over the 1939 level. This pushed the living costs to a height 65 per cent above the 1939 index. From another source, this time the "New York Sun", also a conservative organ, we learn that "25 out of every 100 families are spending more than they earn to meet the present living costs." This simply means prices keep going up. Labor unions are able to boost wages, but at a much slower rate of increase. Therefore, the people's living is made increasingly difficult and the amount of the price increases goes into the bulging bank accounts of the vested interests.

According to the issues of "Economic Outlook", corporation profits in the 1936-39 period annually averaged 3.9 billion dollars. The average rate earned in the war years, 1942-45, was 9.5 billions. The first peace year, 1946, saw this increased to 11.8 billions. In 1947, the profits of business jumped to 16.1 billion dollars. This gourmand feast at the expense of the American people and the world continued in 1948 when profits taken came to over 21 billions.

We can sum up this unhealthy condition briefly: the American people can afford to buy less to put on their backs and on their tables, the high prices enable American business to register huge sales records; however, there is an increasing restriction of commodity movement per unit, which results in warehouses stacked and stagnant with merchandise, this being known in capitalistic economy as "overproduction"; it all adds up to tremendous profits for the basic financial groups in the United States, part of which is being used in pure imperialism, to buy up or into industry in Europe, England, Japan, South America and Africa.

The facts speak. The socialist way has proven itself. It gains at no one's expense. It results in more care for the people, more food for the family at lower prices and a future for all that is secure for full personal development and contribution.

To the people of the Far East, all of this can only mean one thing. We must learn from the Soviet Union. We women must learn from the Soviet women as we advance our civilizations. At the same time, countries like the newly formed People's Republic of China, the Democratic People's Republic of Korea and the Democratic Republic of Viet-Nam can erect the standard of advance for those countries not yet able to liberate themselves and their women. We must make this volume of experience available for all as they struggle to the inevitable victory.

And struggle they can! The women of Asia have long fought side-by-side with their men, in the armed campaigns for national independence, against colonialism and imperialism, against the feudalism and compradorism of their own people. They have faced gunfire, the tortures of concentration camps, death by every conceivable means. Asia's women have joined and led strikes and demonstrations, have sacrificed their lives in armed revolt through incredible deeds of valor. The list of heroines of China, India, Viet-Nam, Korea, Indonesia and other lands is one of which all womanhood can be proud.

It is our history, then. Asia's women have registered their bravery. They have displayed their ability. They have shown their spirit. This is a spirit of mammoth proportions. In those places where the underground fight and the armed revolt continue and grow, this sacrifice and courage must be applauded, encouraged and spread. In those places where the people have won out, we must channel this bravery and energy into the task of construction.

We have seen that this is a common struggle. Therefore, let Asia's women unite for that struggle. Along with the realization of Asia's fundamental needs, national independence and self-development, let us strive for these rights:

1) Equal rights of women in marriage.
2) All rights in the family and in inheritance equal to men.
3) The rights of mothers to their children.
4) Child-care through increased creches, nurseries, kindergartens, sanitation facilities and education in personal hygiene.
5) Legislation providing equal pay for equal work, maternity leave with full pay and outlawing child labor.
6) Compulsory free education for all children and the spread of the "little teachers" movement to wipe out illiteracy.
7) Funds for higher education for women.

In those countries where these rights are already part of the law of the land, let us see that they are enforced. In those regions where they are neither law nor custom, we must fight to put them before everybody in black and white.

Next, we must struggle to instruct everyone of woman's heroic position in the new society. Women must be recognized and rewarded for their guidance of our future citizens, those for whom all struggle and effort are made. As part of this, we must develop an entirely new conception of the "family."

China and the other feudal-laden countries have a hard fight before them against the inertia of thousands of years of custom. The feudal idea of the family is deeply ingrained in our minds, as deep as the very roots of our existence. Yet, "family" as we know it, is not the best mode of living by far. It is obstructive to all but the head. It in no way prepares an outlook commensurate with the present situation in the world. In fact, this atmosphere makes its members always look "in," never "out." Consequently, it stifles imagination. It prevents the understanding of being active in the creation of a plentiful life for the whole community.

Ridding ourselves of these iron chains is no easy matter. But as Marx teaches us, it can be done. He put it this way:

"However terrible and disgusting the dissolution under the capitalist system of the old family ties may appear, nevertheless, modern industry, by assigning as it does an important part in the process of production, outside the domestic sphere, to women, to young persons and to children of both sexes, creates a new economic foundation for a higher form of family and of the relations between the sexes."

From this truth, which lucidly lays the future before us, there follows just as clearly what is woman's share of the responsibilities in the advancement of our undeveloped countries.

We must first strive to lift the political level of our sex. Without this we cannot understand the inevitableness of both the basic victory and our own. Neither can we understand the methods which must be employed to obtain these victories. But if we are politically alert and we do comprehend the world situation and our own conditions, then we can contribute fully to our emancipation. It will not be handed to us on a silver platter. We must secure it ourselves and this is impossible without political understanding.

Secondly, from the Marx quote you have just heard, from the rest of his and other revolutionary writings, from our own experience, we know that industrialization for our backward countries is imperative. Without this factor, we cannot free ourselves from either foreign imperialism or our feudal yoke, as a nation and as the women of that nation. Therefore, we must lift our knowledge of science and our technical level of work. We must take our part of the assignment in the building of factories, in the elevation of all science to the point where it serves the people. We must participate in all fields which will result in the industrialization of our countries. We must learn these elements of construction in unison with men. Otherwise, we will only retard our own development and liberation. As Engels wrote: "The emancipation of women and their equality with men are impossible, and remain so, as long as women are excluded from social production and restricted to domestic labor. The emancipation of women becomes feasible only when women are enabled to take part extensively in social production."

This leads to the third responsibility which the women of Asia must assume. Since we will be entering productive work and political activities, we must take an enterprising part in the organizations which lead in these spheres. We have to accept seriously the fact that we can enter trade unions, for example, or women's associations or peasant organizational movements. These are the elements which are of the masses of the people, the prime movers of society.

In order to make trade unions, women's associations and farmers' associations fulfill their historic roles, we must take our life experience into them. To apply our hard-won knowledge, and also to make these organizations effective, we have to take up part of the leadership. This will require intensive study of organization and administration. And these, in turn, require a closeness with the masses. We must keep their needs always before us. We must find answers to those needs.

We must make the mass organizations expand until they affect all the people. Consider our women's organization in China. We must build on the fine work already accomplished. Our efforts must filter down to every small cluster of farm houses. The women of farm and factory, of school and home must realize the importance of this work. They must understand that the women of China are affiliated with the Women's International Democratic Federation and that means we have friends and co-workers in practically every country in the world. When the women of China recognize this fact, when they become more active in even greater numbers, we can then contribute that much more to China, to international womanhood and its objectives. What applies to China stands for all countries of the Far East.

There is another consideration to make. Whether it is in this field of woman's work or trade unions or farmers' associations, progress is possible only through collective effort. This has an importance all its own. For collective effort develops an understanding of the future, and understanding of the validity of the socialist form of living. Women have a definite part in both its materialization and its furtherance. Therefore, we must prepare ourselves for the acceptance of a share of the building and maintenance of the new way of life.

An important group in this advance of our peoples will be woman intellectuals of Asia. But experience has shown us that their effectiveness is measured by the ratio of their closeness with the masses. It is for this broad group that the work of creation and instruction must be produced, for it is only the strength of the people that will liberate all of Asia. It is to this end that woman intellectuals must work and for this purpose that they must take up their responsibilities.

I have said much on the task we women have to shoulder in the emancipation of our countries and ourselves. I would like to heavily emphasize at this point what responsibilities our men have to assume.

There are those, of course, which men and women share alike, involving the fight for democracy and freedom, for country and for people. However, there is one duty which men alone owe to themselves and the womanfolk.

The law of equality can be written into the historical documents for all to read. The fact of its existence can be widely publicized. There can even be some advancement on the part of women toward this equalization. But all of this will be voided unless the doctrine of equality is thoroughly thought out by the men and held in their firm grip. We women have evidence of many men who are progressive in other matters, even to the extent of risking their lives for the people's cause, but who persist in clutching to their antiquated ideas regarding women. This has an unwholesome and repressive effect and must be completely exposed.

Habit is always difficult to pull clean from ourselves. But the importance of men ridding themselves of this line of thinking can best be indicated by the message Lenin gave the men of the Soviet Union:

"A woman's domestic life is one in which she is sacrificed every day amidst a thousand petty details. The ancient right of man to be lord survives secretly. Our political work among the masses of women involves a considerable effort to educate the man. We must root out the ancient outlook of the lord and master to the last fibre in the party and among the masses."

In Asia, therefore, we should make it a cardinal principle, to have our men rid themselves of the "ancient outlook," to have our women assume their obligations in their new freedom, to have both march shoulder to shoulder to the victory which will be the people's.

This victory is vital to the entire globe. As each Asian nation achieves its supreme triumph, it represents another link of steel forged into the prospects for world peace. These two concepts, world peace and national independence, are inseparable. They can be obtained only together, and they must be had at all costs.

On the road to peace, the women of the world are the most potent force. It was they, represented by the Women's International Democratic Federation, who took the initiative for the World Peace Congress held in April of this year, in Paris and Prague. We must tell our opponents again and again. That Congress represented the desires of over 600 million people on this earth. They were represented through 561 national organizations and 12 international bodies, and they all meant to secure the same thing—world peace.

This was only the beginning. Every nation which participated in the World Peace Congress has since had other meetings to promote this precious idea. In China alone, in but two cities, Peking and Shanghai, over two million people demonstrated to show the world their intentions in the direction of peace. Demonstrations are still taking place all over the world and they will continue to appear.

We must make it clear for those whose minds are misty with war clouds. When the common people of the world say they want world peace, it does not mean they will take it at any price, nor will they be merely passive in their quest. They will not beg for it. They will *struggle* for it.

Neither does the struggle for world peace mean reducing any of our demands for national independence and the complete freedom to select and erect any form of government we deem best for our situation and our people.

At first, to the uninitiated, this conflict appears as if it is an irresistible force (the people's will for peace) meeting an immovable object (the monopoly capitalists' drive for war). However, this is an idea ill-founded. It has for backing neither fact nor historical recognition. We have before us at this exact moment the very solid fact that the people eventually win their struggle. In the past 32 years, no less than eight hundred million people have liberated themselves and established people's governments. This great collection of partisans for peace, plus the vast multitudes of restive people in the colonial countries of the Far East, the Middle East and Africa, plus the forces of resistance in their own countries, indicates just how isolated are the warmongers of the military and financial interests in the United States and Great Britain. We can thwart their desperate and frantic stabs towards world destruction. We can stop them entirely. And we women of Asia, cooperating with our sisters all over the world, will be the leading spearhead of peace.

In order to forward this struggle and let the world know the position of the free women meeting in Peking, I propose this conference send two messages of militancy. The first should be to the women of Asia. Let us say:

"Women of Asia!

"The chain reaction of freedom started in 1917 with the great October Socialist Revolution and resulted in the founding of the mighty U.S.S.R. This impetus of liberation has freed tens of millions of oppressed. Ifs momentum will not stop until the people in all lands are free. Take heart! Redouble your vigilance and your fight! Your contemporaries have met here in Peking, the capital of the People's Republic of China. We have rediscovered your strength. Here are our hands and spirit as we extend the world-wide struggle for peace and self-determination to you wherever you may be. If you are in liberated land and territory, we say improve your country and your position in it. If you are still counted among the oppressed, we say struggle to organize, and then ARISE!"

The second message should be addressed to the women of the United States, Great Britain and other western countries.

"Women of the West!

"The ranks of free people are daily swelling. This frightens those who would rule the world, who through their commercial and military might would rule as masters over slaves. These are the vested interests, the privileged few in your countries. In their ill-omened position, they have attempted to erect a blockade to the progress of mankind. Events of the past years have proven the futility of such paper-like obstacles. The liberation of all mankind has dawned and nothing can stop it.

"The monopoly capitalists in your midst wear fascist clothes at home and abroad they wear the robes of imperialists. They will refrain from no tactic, from no calamity in their attempt to preserve their holdings. A third world war is on their agenda.

"The women of Asia know that you recognize this state of affairs. We want you to know further that we support you in your struggle against the suppression you face as you fight to preserve your human rights and the world peace. We have faith in your strength and in your courage. The women of Asia salute you!"

I propose this conference of Asian women make certain these messages reach all hands for whom they are intended. Further, let us give these slogans to this mighty rally to elevate the position of women and children, to save the civilization of the world:

"Women of the world, protect the peace!"

"Women of the world, unite for the struggle until all mankind is liberated!"

"Women of the world, assure that all women and children receive their due rights, their just rewards!"

FOR STALIN'S BIRTHDAY

Appeared in a special magazine published in Peking
on the occasion of Stalin's 70th birthday

December 21, 1949

On this day, December 21, 1949, millions upon
millions of people the world over will celebrate the
seventieth birthday of one man—Joseph Vissarionovich
Stalin. Their joy will be in consonance with the importance of the occasion. For most of these seventy
years have been filled with labor for the advancement
of the common people. Each toast to Stalin's continued
health will be attended by the knowledge that his struggles have borne fruit. Already we know that history
has conferred upon him the honor of "Great Man of
the People."

On this day, we should carefully examine what
makes Stalin great. Is it that all of the wisdom of the
ages is concentrated in this one mortal's mind? No,
that is not the answer. Others can claim wisdom yet
display but shallow achievements. Stalin's greatness
has wisdom and still another vital component. His is
an all-encompassing discernment coupled with humility.
He counts not his own strength, but rather the might
of the working people of his country, of the world. He
sees their plight and their potential. Both have taught

him. Both have guided his every decision. The first he has always maintained as his own. The second he has constantly fought to materialize.

The life of this man, Joseph Vissarionovich Stalin, the continuer of Lenin's cause, the teacher of the people as well as their pupil, is something we must earnestly study. It is instruction in overcoming hardships. It is valuable lessons in making practical edifices of the word, the idea that labor is creative and those that labor have their right to the world. It is basic truth concerning the need for a party of the people, founded in the doctrines of Marx and Engels as they were advanced by another "Great Man of the People," Lenin.

Let us learn from Stalin, then. Let us learn from his people and his party, as we, the People's Republic of China, mould our own future of construction and point the way to emancipation for all those still under oppression.

Long live Stalin, born of the people!

Long live Stalin's leadership of all mankind's liberation!

THE DIFFERENCE BETWEEN SOVIET AND AMERICAN FOREIGN POLICIES

Appeared in the magazine "People's China" Vol. II

January 16, 1950

Chairman Mao Tse-tung, in his now-historic speech on July 1, 1949, pronounced that the new China, the People's Republic of China, would lean to one side in all matters, foreign and domestic. That is the side led by the great Soviet Union under the leadership of the mighty Stalin. That is the side of peace and construction. That is the path joyously followed and ardently studied by the overwhelming masses of the Chinese people.

Events in the world have proven, and are every day verifying, that this is the only side to which progressive countries can lean. For there are merely two choices at hand. One is the Soviet Union. The other is represented mainly by the United States, Great Britain and France. As we have contact with these two sides, through their foreign policies, we quickly see that they are as different as day is from night. One has all the brightness of day and all the warmth of the sun. That is the Socialist Soviet Union. The other is as forbidding as a wintry night with all its coldness. That is the imperialist band led by the United States.

By comparing these two choices, it is easy to see why in actuality, survival and revival of oppressed nations necessitates leaning to the side of the Soviet Union.

What do the imperialists offer?

First, they offer Marshall Plan "aid." Their method is to "educate" you on how good it will be for you. This is done in typical, high-pressure, American advertising style. The sales talk is directed to all those who are floundering in the high seas of unplanned economies and who fear changes which use the strength of the people. The American Wall Streeters hold up their concoction as the newest thing in life-savers. "It is streamlined," they say. "It will pull you through any situation." Some governments have fallen for this line and have had the "life-saver" tossed at them. From their experience, it is now history that this highly publicized contraption turns out to be but a strait-jacket. It is filled with lead and bound to sink anyone who attempts to use it.

The U.S.A. expects to enslave the countries of Southeast Asia by means of Marshall Plan "aid." The peoples of these countries, however, are against this "aid" as it has an aggressive purpose and has certain political conditions attached. American "aid" will mean further and intensified exploitation of the country which receives it, to the detriment of the people's present welfare and their future constructive efforts. Witness Western Germany today as it serves Wall Street in full colonial capacity. Coal, timber, scrap metal and other raw and semi-finished materials are pouring out of the country into British and American factories. In return, this highly industrialized part of Germany' is being made into an importer of finished products. The result is that their manufacturing industry is rapidly deteriorating and they have accumulated a debt of over three billion dollars to the United States.

Marshall Plan "aid" will further mean then, long lines of unemployed workers and shrinking standards of living for their families as factory after factory suffers the smothering of home markets by American goods. Witness Italy, where 2,500,000 workers sit idle, while the Italian Government statistical institute informs us that nearly half of the families are living on a standard below the necessary minimum. Witness France, where the purchasing power of the people has dropped more than 20 per cent in the past year and devaluation of the franc further cut into their livelihood. Witness Britain, where the people suffer because the critically affected foreign export trade is diverted to the west, which does not want it, instead of being allowed to exchange goods and services with the vast expanse from Czechoslovakia to China.

Finally, this gracious "aid" will mean continued harassment by nature. Witness China's case once again, where the important bulk of the funds and energies were used to fight the people instead of preventing natural disasters. That is why floods once ruined millions of acres of land and millions of tons of food, and the number of famine-sufferers ran into the tens of millions.

The record is clear. Marshall plans will not help any country. They are not instigated for that purpose. There is another intent.

It has become clear once again that America's capitalistic system is a humpty-dumpty which has fallen off the wall of history. It is cracked, and severely so. Therefore, the monopolists on Wall Street try to put it together again. They use the very expensive Marshall Plan, while the American people, and all peoples upon whom it is imposed, are made to pay for it. But even this astronomical expenditure is not enough to mend the broken egg. The situation gets urgent, later it degenerates to the frantic stage. Measures of fear are then applied.

These measures are the preparations for war, as expressed in terms of the Atlantic Pact, the promised Southeast Asia Alliance and similar malicious attempts. These are strait-jackets of another sort for those who participate. They are in addition to the Marshall Plan and entail further obligations, this time the entirely non-productive, non-creative spending of money on arms and munitions, according to American standards, from American factories, at American prices, paid for in American dollars. Not one of the contracting parties, including the United States, can afford such waste. But economic and political pressure of every variety is exerted by the American Government and its Wall Street jockeys until their objectives are reached: super-profits at home, control of the markets abroad. The national sovereignty of others means nothing to them. They tread upon the people's livelihood with arrogance.

It is a truism: those who keep freedom from others, they themselves are not free. It follows: those who cause impoverishment, they themselves will soon be reduced to that state. It is precisely to this position that the American people are being steadily pushed.

Unemployment in the United States is reaching into figures like six million, with ten million workers only partially employed. This occurs when the cost of living rises to 180 (with the year 1939 as 100) and real wages actually drop below the 1939 level. According to the Chief of Reports and Analysis of the United States Bureau of Employment Security, there is no relief in sight for this situation. In fact, according to this official organization's calculation, there are 600,000 more people looking for jobs every year. The casual remark at the end of this report was, that if this condition continues, it will mean something is wrong with the economy.

We can say now that something is wrong, for the people of the United States. But for the few financial groupings operating out of the darkness of Wall Street, things are quite right. Their profits are bursting out all over. In 1947 they hit the record of 17 billion dollars. Through further exploitation of the world, in 1948 they gathered unto themselves the gigantic sum of 21 billions. It is plain for all to see. Into these greedy hands falls the Marshall Plan money. The funds required for the execution of the Atlantic Pact also find their way here. And lo and woe to anything or anyone who tries to stop this game of gamble and garner.

The bigger the profits get, the more the people in the United States are suppressed. Civil rights are beaten down and discarded. The police actively show they are mere tools of the vested interests. They protect only the hand that feeds them sop, rather than the people, as was demonstrated in the Peekshill Incident.* Educational standards are constantly attacked through the intimidation and firing of teachers and professors who object to the fascisation that is taking place. Science is closeted and put under lock and key, the latter in the hands of the financial wizards who control everything else. They do not even allow their imperialist partners to take a peek, as we have seen from the recent breakdown of atomic energy conferences held in Canada between the United States and Great Britain.

This brought out into the open but one of the contradictions which exist between imperialist countries. The American Government attempted to put all research and development of the important source of atomic energy into their own hands and exclude Britain and Canada from this field. They failed in this case, just as they met with a rebuff in the bargaining concerning the delivery of arms for the Atlantic Pact requirements. Historical analysis proves that such contradictions will ever be present and will become increasingly important. However, the American Government in due time will treat its satellites as it treats its own people. For

---

* This incident refers to the attempt by fascist elements in the United States to prevent the famous progressive, Paul Robeson, from performing at a concert in Peekshill, New York. The police did nothing to prevent the hoodlums from beating the members of the audience.

how long can Britain, for example, keep up her resistance when she is so dependent upon United States funds to keep herself from the brink of bankruptcy? The answer is, if Britain continues her present anti-Soviet policies, she cannot last very much longer, and sooner or later, the United States will have its way completely.

That is the picture the imperialist group presents.

Now, let us examine the policies and practices of the Soviet Union as they appear on the world scene.

To date, this socialist land has made trade arrangements with the following People's Democracies: Czechoslovakia, Rumania, Bulgaria, Albania, Hungary, Poland, Mongolia and China. All of these agreements were made with one, and only one, purpose in mind—to sincerely aid in the development of these countries. There was no pretence, no bait, no "education". There was only one question asked: "What do you need?" Here are a few practical examples of how this worked out.

China, in its liberation, was faced with tremendous problems concerning rail transportation. The reactionary Kuomintang armies had destroyed bridges by the hundreds. The equally reactionary administrations had allowed equipment to be wasted and ill-used, and the roadbeds were in urgent need of maintenance. This had to be remedied immediately, since so much depended on moving supplies from the countryside to the newly liberated cities, and in moving the People's Liberation Army to positions for the final strike against the American-supported Chiang Kai-shek.

Among the very first arrivals in China from the Soviet Union were railway technicians. They worked at the complicated questions and rendered support that put the restoration of our rail system months ahead of schedule. They came without benefit of fanfare. They did their job and not one single thing was asked in return.

Likewise, this past summer, the Northeastern provinces of China suffered an epidemic of the plague. We did not have enough doctors and technicians to stem this dangerous disease, so we called on our great neighbor. The medical teams we required were soon on the scene. They came, they gave their help and when they were finished, they went home. There were not even thoughts of repayment or concessions to be sought. They did not ask the right to do anything, except to serve the Chinese people.

Bulgaria offers another example. This country chronically suffers from drought. Inspired by the Stalin plan for remaking nature through afforestation and forming bodies of water, Bulgarian organs made a plan of their own. To implement this plan, the Soviet Union has given technical assistance, machinery, equipment for power stations, transmission lines to carry the power, made locks for irrigation dams and provided other essential materials, just to assure success in this vital project.

This spirit of cooperation is now the working principle among all the People's Democracies. Before, as an example, the countries of Czechoslovakia and Poland were always bitter enemies, as a result of imperialist intrigues. However, since 1947, they have been working together under a five-year agreement on mutual economic policies and a series of detailed protocols. The result is that they have increased the exchange of goods and assistance five times over the figures for 1938. Further, Poland has set aside part of its own territory on the Baltic sea for the construction of ports, so Czechoslovakia can have an outlet to the sea for commercial purposes. Cooperation is also evidenced in the joint development and use of natural resources in their border areas and the joint construction of power facilities.

There is no cut-throat competition here; no strangulation of the smaller or weaker by the stronger. This mode of operation has grown out of the foreign policy of the Soviet Union, which functions through pacts of friendship, sincerely implemented mutual assistance pacts, and pacts of non-aggression. Is it not clear then that we lean to one side because only the Soviet Union advocates and practises such a fair and honest policy? Only the socialist system allows for such an outlook and at the same time maintains constant upward development of the home economy.

Yes, we also lean to one side as a result of appraisal of the Soviet Union's domestic scene. We envy the fact that there is no unemployment, and rush to learn how it is done. We rejoice that in such a short time, they have liquidated illiteracy in their expansive country, and once again we ask to be shown how it was done. We like to see, for instance, that the post-war five-year plan calls for increasing living space by the tremendous amount of 84 million square meters, this including tens

of thousands of individually-built homes. We are joyful
when the news comes that this goal is almost reached.
We think it is significant that in the last thirty years
over 27,000 rural power stations have been erected in
the Soviet Union. In undeveloped China, we are marked-
ly impressed when we learn that in formerly backward
Turkmenia, heavy industry has increased 111 times between 1913 and 1941; in the Uzbek Republic, industrial
output jumped 75 times in 27 years; in the Kirghiz
Republic it has risen 153 fold in that same period.

There is no question that without the fullest application of science, these accomplishments could never
be realized. We quickly learn that the whole conception of science is different from that which is
practised in capitalistic countries. In the Soviet Union
it is freed for practical use and expedited to the
maximum degree. Instead of allowing nature to run
her own unchartered course, Soviet scientists harness
her to work for mankind. The progressive and constructive use of atomic energy is the most vivid illustration of this method. Atomic energy is being used
to move mountains, to change the course of rivers, to
make arid deserts fertile. It is not kept beneath a
cellophane cloak and made a pawn in some nefarious
international game. It is used for the benefit of the
people.

Education and culture are treated with the same
respect. This accounts for the fact that the Soviet Union
today has over 220,000 schools with 34 million pupils
and 837 higher educational institutions with over one
million students. In ten pre-war years alone, these

institutions turned out over one million engineers, agronomists, teachers, doctors and other experts.

Thus, our comparison is complete. The imperialist band led by the United States financial groups is a hindering clod in the way of man's progress, both at home and abroad. The Soviet Union, however, lends a helping hand to struggling young nations both within her borders and without, until they can navigate their own way. Therefore, the conclusion remains. The People's Republic of China leans to one side. We appreciate the principle of "working with" friends. We especially admire friends who have such a constructive way of living and know tolerance in their treatment of other people. We think that all such friends should correlate their efforts to construct a new society, to protect world peace so that that society can prosper Consequently, China will continue to follow the policy of leaning to one side, to "work with" all those who earnestly strive for honest cooperation. And in this period of history, China is pointing the way for the whole Far East.

CHINA'S CHILDREN IN THE LIBERATION STRUGGLE

Written for Young Pioneer Newspaper, Moscow

May 8, 1950

It can be said that China's revolution has stirred even the smallest grain of sand. This tells you the heaviness of the oppression our people have undergone. It indicates how every segment of our population rose in struggle against that oppression. It explains that the children of China were a part of this great battle and they too contributed to the victory over feudalism and imperialism.

In many ways, the historic period of revolutionary activity compiled by our youngsters parallels the past deeds of the valiant Soviet youth. Recounting the exploits of daring and self-sacrifice on the firing line, behind it and in the organization of resistance in the midst of reactionary circumstances, brings to mind the stories of "Timur and His Squad" and "The Young Guard". We have our "Timurs" and our "Young Guards" also, demonstrating the internationalism of courage in the fight to win for the people what is rightfully theirs.

The children of China took up their revolution with zest. They acted upon their convictions with maturity. And today they have a steadfast confidence in their future. A few illustrations from the history of the program among working class children of Shanghai conducted by my organization, the China Welfare Institute, will explain how our youngsters have arrived at this point.

Three years ago, thousands of young people in the factory districts of Shanghai were an inert mass. They wallowed in poverty and were blinded by ignorance. They existed under the reactionary Kuomintang government that feared to give them knowledge and lived by exploiting them and their families. Into this situation strode the organizers of the China Welfare Institute.

The purpose of the program we started was to mobilize the children of the working class, teach them the value and use of their mass strength and on the foundation of this strength to penetrate the whole community with the revolutionary truth.

The wall of ignorance that surrounded these children was so great that we decided first to wipe the areas clean of illiteracy. But just teaching these young people to read and write was not enough. We had to teach them responsibility to their class and to themselves. This was accomplished by working on the principle of "what you learn, you must teach others", known as the "little teacher" system. The idea was eagerly grasped and spread like a forest fire. In short order, the China Welfare Institute had literacy classes, conducted by the awakened children themselves, operating in every conceivable nook and corner of the Shanghai slums.

The textbooks they used were especially written. These told of the value of labor, a dangerous idea to know in those days. They explained the strength of the masses, a criminal offence in the eyes of the reactionaries. They predicted the brightness of the future which the people themselves would win and build, a thought that could land you in prison or worse. But these were the ideas that aroused young people took home with them, took to their classes, took to their jobs in the factories and mills. These were the lessons they first learned themselves and then taught others. To do so and survive they had to learn quickly how to exist in the middle of fascist oppression, and this came from their own organization.

"Little teachers" in every part of Shanghai had their own democratic groups. They practised the use of criticism and self-criticism. They organized for self-protection and for all possibilities. These working class youngsters learned how to help themselves, as was proven in one emergency after another. They once saved the homes of 1,400 of their own people from the flames of fire. Just prior to the freeing of the city by the People's Liberation Army, they had a secret network through which the underground forces could learn the situation in any part of the district where these youngsters lived. After the liberation, these joyous young people immediately recognized the people's victory that had been achieved and quickly organized teams to explain it to one and all.

It should be added here that this program involved thousands of youngsters and there were only ten adult supervisors, which shows the extent of organization and responsibility these young people carried and the amount of tempering they went through.

Another part of this program which the China Welfare Institute operated was a Children's Theater. This was the first of its kind in all of China. It was a theater for and by the working class children, with a revolutionary purpose. It took education through song, dance and drama to hundreds of thousands of children and adults who never knew such wonderful things existed before. The theater was made up of young people, many of them homeless, who wanted to devote their entire lives to serving and becoming artists of the people.

They received their revolutionary training under the toughest of conditions. Beneath the very noses of the Kuomintang secret police, defying arrest and possible death at every turn, and long before Shanghai's liberation, these youngsters were explaining to their audiences what was wrong with their society. They told how it was possible to make a world in which the working class was honored and all-powerful. Many of the songs, dances and plays were composed by the children themselves. They also took many of the forbidden folk dances and songs to the workers and the students with the word that these had come from the regions which were already liberated, under the guidance and leadership of the Chinese Communist Party.

As the hour of liberation neared and the reactionaries became desperate in their arrests and executions, these young people had to run for their lives. But even in their seclusion, they hid in teams and prepared for the fast-arriving liberation day. When it came, the Children's Theater gathered and burst upon the Shanghai streets. They sang and danced for days on end, for factory workers, for the People's Liberation Army and for the people themselves. They explained that a new day had dawned in China's life and that all should learn and take part. This spirit so endeared them to the public that today hardly a function of the government or the labor unions takes place where these children are not called upon to perform.

These are but a few of the incidents that were lived through by the city children of China. They were duplicated a hundredfold by the youngsters in the countryside and in the People's Liberation Army. There the young people acted as road guards, for example. Many are the stories of travellers finding themselves looking right smack into the point of a red-tasselled spear wielded by a "Small Red Devil", who demanded your road pass or you could not proceed. Just as numerous are the stories of children acting as messengers of important information as they crossed the enemy lines back and forth. Some were caught, but they invariably acted with the courage of the now famous Liu Hu-lan, a young Communist organizer, who faced torture and met death at the hands of a warlord rather than betray her comrades.

At this time, the liberation struggle continues. China has to shake loose every last remnant of our former backward customs. We must take up the revolutionary way, the way that leads to Socialism. Then we have to defend that decision for our future from the onslaughts of the raging imperialists. In this new struggle, the young people are vitally important, for the future is in their hands. It is for the future that they are daily preparing themselves.

This is an intense preparation. The leadership for it comes from the Young Pioneers and the Youth League, comparable to your Young Pioneers and your Young Communist League. It is a preparation that all of China's youth is taking part in, drawing from our own past and learning the valuable lessons from our great neighbour, the U.S.S.R.

Our children realize that their progressive advance is felt not only in China, but by the youth in all nations which are still oppressed. China's children today join those of the Soviet Union and the other People's Democracies in leading the way to liberation, in leading the way down the road to life for all of mankind.

SHANGHAI'S NEW DAY HAS DAWNED

Issued to the Shanghai newspapers on the first
anniversary of the city's liberation

May 26, 1950

It has been an event-packed, fast-moving year since
Shanghai awoke from a nightmare of oppression and
took up its new life as part of liberated China. For
this we owe undiminishing gratitude to our People's
Liberation Army.

This has been a year of learning. We have learned
about ourselves. We have learned about our city. We
have learned about our future.

What have we learned about ourselves? We have
discovered that the Chinese people have a mountain of
strength, bursting vitality and a genius that can com-
petently meet any problem and overcome any difficulty.
These are exactly what we need, for the task before us is
not easy. No revolutionary accomplishments are easy.
And it is a real revolution to turn our economy so that
it works for the broad masses of the people, and at
the same time defeats the reactionaries. Yet, after one
year, we can see that both are possible. We can see our
daily necessities at stabilized prices. We can see our
skies cleared of enemy bombers and the People's Liberation Army on Hainan and Chusan Islands. We can see

that there is not one reconstruction problem which we cannot solve. Not one. What is more, it is plain that we are going to drive far past our present obstacles. We are going to bring prosperity to our city and to China, the likes of which our long history has never recorded. We will accomplish this because our people have strength. We will accomplish this because our government is founded on that strength and is rooted in the people. That is what we have learned about ourselves after one year of liberation.

What have we learned of our city?

We have found that the eyes of the nation are on Shanghai. We have become a symbol of the struggle against the dead weight of imperialism and the cynicism of bureaucratic capitalist speculation. These blights have ridden the backs of our workers and citizens almost from the very first day of Shanghai's existence. The rest of the country knows how deeply embedded is the rot of these blights. Therefore, they encourage us as we struggle to make this a people's city, to make its factories and mills work for our country.

The workers of the Northeast shout to us: You will soon be like us, not one unemployed person. Keep up the fight! They back their faith in Shanghai by solidly contributing funds to the workers rendered jobless by the enemy bombing and blockade, both imperialist inspired and supported.

The farmers of the interior send us grain in quantities which account for stockpiles adequate to care for all the food needs of the city. This is an expression of their faith in the people of Shanghai. This is to let our merchants and industrialists know that there is going to be an ever increasing market for them, as the land reform proves its effectiveness, as the farmers' purchasing power steadily rises. All of this begins to have results.

The business people of Shanghai, who misunderstood and moaned at the people's government six months ago, now begin to comprehend and cooperate. Now they realize that overcoming the evil effects of imperialism, compradorism and bombing is not a one-day task. At first they expected miracles from the People's Liberation Army and the Communist Party. Now they have learned that nothing is accomplished if you wait for or expect such unrealities. Victories are nurtured with hard work, self-sacrifice and resourcefulness. This is the lesson we have learned.

With this new attitude becoming widespread, more and more people have come to believe in the new Shanghai to be. They have come to believe in the plans of the people's government. For it becomes clear that we can defeat imperialism and reaction. It becomes clear that Shanghai can belong to China and to our people. That is what we have learned about our city after one year of liberation.

What have we learned of our future?

We have found that our People's Republic of China is like an unusually strong and healthy newborn baby. While we are experiencing many of the illnesses of childhood, we have the resiliency of childhood. There is no question that we are going to grow up and be vigorous, with the power to pay our own way in the world and with plenty to spare.

One of our sicknesses, which came to us by inheritance, was the degeneration of our water conservancy works. This caused flood and famine in many parts of our country. But, with speedy despatch, we have put the People's Liberation Army on the job, building dykes, moving rivers, planting millions of trees. We have put the very people afflicted with flood and famine on the same work. We have put our revitalized transportation system into effect to move grain.

The result is that we have brought both flood and famine under control. This proves how we can bounce back when adversity strikes at us.

The only people who do not like this idea are the phony philanthropists from the American halls of monopoly capital. They want to play doctor to our baby illnesses, so that they can cure us once and for all, of everything, including life itself. Let them keep their lethal pills. China will make its own solutions, through the principles of production and self-help.

The manner in which China has handled its relief problems indicates how we will mould our future. However, there are other important signposts. Deputy Premier Chen Yun, in his report to the seventh session of the Central People's Government, explained how for the first time in China's history, our finances are centralized. He explained the centralization of food distribution and how both of these, along with other factors, have stabilized our economy. This was accomplished within one year of the liberation of most of the mainland. Previous governments have been trying in vain for tens of decades to do the same thing.

Still further evidence of our future prospects is contained in Vice Chairman Liu Shao-chi's May 1 address. He told the world of the advances made in the Northeast in one year. Agricultural production increased by 37 per cent; workers in public enterprises increased by 240,000, the average real wages of workers increased by 27 per cent; private industry in Shenyang (Mukden) alone increased by 23 per cent. All of this has been achieved under the people's government. All of this points the way for Shanghai and the rest of the country.

If we need help on the way, we can get it. What we lack, our good neighbour, the Soviet Union, will help us make up in the development of our natural resources, in trade, in scientific knowledge and in communications. We can rejoice that this is help based on cooperation, mutual respect and mutual help.

Add it all up. The sum is a healthy baby, overcoming all illnesses and getting bigger and better all the time. Add it up again and again, for the sum total of China's future is unlimited. Under the wise leadership of Chairman Mao Tse-tung and the Communist Party, we have the era of New Democracy. On the horizon looms the sunlight of Socialism and a new and bountiful land. This is what we have learned of our future after one year of liberation. The challenge has been flung before us, citizens of Shanghai. We have learned from the liberation. We have our future well defined. Let us go to work with full strength to build a new city, to build our new China.

CHINA SIGNS FOR WORLD PEACE

Written for "Pravda"

June 8, 1950

The Chinese people are signing up for world peace. Szechuan rice farmers, newly liberated from oppression and illiteracy, pause from their toil and proudly affix their names to peace petitions. The factory workers of Shanghai and the Northeast gather at the end of their shift to pen their ardent desire for world tranquillity. The commercial circles, the artists and writers, the youth and students—all are anxious to add their weight. From every village, from every city, the tens of millions are crying out through these petitions which demand that the peace be kept and treasured. It is a mighty stream of voices that grows to a river, and gathers other rivers to empty finally into an ocean, where the roar for peace leaves no doubt what the Chinese people want.

The uncertain scrawls of farmers, the accomplished flourish of the intellectuals, the heavy strokes of the workers—these signatures are but one manifestation of what the Chinese people are doing and will do for peace. There are certain concrete things taking place, or about to take place, which fight against the possibility of peace slipping through our fingers, as if it were sand.

For one thing, we are determined to render every support to our People's Liberation Army so that it can terminate the liberation war as quickly as possible, to expel imperialism from China once and for all, and to stamp out the last impeding relics of feudalism. Every shot fired to bring Taiwan back to its rightful owner— the Chinese people—every step taken to liberate Tibet, means that much more security for the world. For upon the completion of these tasks, the people can devote full time and energy to the reconstruction of this country. Thus, the result of this armed conflict is in the interest of peace. A strong China, completely unified and in coalition with other peace-loving powers, places an obstacle before the warmongers of the United States and Great Britain. It seriously reduces any chances of victory if they actually begin their Hitlerian adventure to rule the world with force.

The second thing taking place in China today, which is a link in the struggle for world peace, is the stabilization of our economy. For tens of decades, previous governments have tried to effect this. All have failed. Why? Because in reality stabilization was not their purpose. Fleecing the people was. But within this year of the complete liberation of the China mainland, under the people's republic, finances have been centralized, food distribution has been nationally regulated, statistics can be gathered and economic planning can be accomplished.

These measures have had a healthy effect upon the psychology of the people. They see the prices of their daily commodities remaining stable for protracted periods. They have come to understand that their own strength can control the economic life under the guidance of their people's government. There is less and less hoarding of goods in preparation for inflation, such as had to be done in the past.

The people have come to have faith. Now they understand what Chairman Mao Tse-tung meant when he said that China had obstacles, but that it also had solutions. Investments in China will increase in future. A closer unity of labor and national capitalists is growing in order to accelerate the industrialization of the country. Trade and development pacts have been signed with our great neighbour and ally, the U.S.S.R., to increase even more rapidly our growing strength. And the stronger we get, the more prosperous our people are, the less chance there is for war.

The Chinese people are making a third contribution to the maintenance of peace. This is the unwavering stand they have taken against the so-called "European Recovery Program", the "Atlantic Pact" and their offspring in other parts of the world. Correlated with this is the fact that we are making a clear distinction between the reactionary governments which promulgate these historic failures and the people of the United States, Great Britain, France, Italy and others who have to bear the consequences.

We have made it quite plain, and will continue to do so, that we want none of the destruction or choking of home industry that accompanies such "recovery" programs. We want none of the long lines of unemployment. Nor do we want any of the attacks upon the democratic groups, which are part of the price to be extracted for arms and ammunitions received or for unnecessary luxuries, cigarettes and soft drinks. We will do without all of that. We will do what we have to do with our own strength and with whatever fraternal assistance we require, whether it is building up our country's industry, taking care of famine or revitalizing our agriculture. In other words, we recognize such vicious "aid" programs and arms pacts for what they are—imperialist manoeuvres and preparations for war. We will never submit to the handful of Wall Streeters and their satellites who attempt to shove them down the throats of the people.

It should be emphasized, neither will we stop encouraging, assisting to the fullest, and in every possible way, the people of the United States, Great Britain, Italy and other countries as they resist these crimes against humanity. The peace front knows no barriers, national or otherwise. The struggle for civil liberties, for a press and radio which honestly reflect the thinking of the broad masses, for full employment, for equal opportunities, for productive and peaceful relations with the rest of the world—all of these are the battles of the common men and women the world over. Therefore, the struggle is one and the same. If one element for a peaceful life is missing in any of the countries on the globe, that element is threatened in all others. Conversely, a victory such as that of the Chinese people's is a victory for all others. It weakens the imperialists, while it infuses strength into the people's front.

These, then, are the means which the Chinese people are mobilizing for the peace movement in the world today. The mass of signatures that is being obtained for the peace petitions indicates how widespread is our determination to struggle. We have known war in this land almost continuously for one hundred years. We are more than ready for peace. We demand it. The Chinese people want to make themselves a bigger bowl for more rice, and they want to contribute to the world's well-being at the same time. This we can do by implementing the measures of our People's Republic of China. This we can do by following the leadership of Chairman Mao Tse-tung and the Chinese Communist Party. This we can do by standing steadfast by that indestructible rock of peace, the U.S.S.R., as led by the mighty J. V. Stalin.

Millions are daily making our government a living and growing instrument. Millions are following our determined leadership. Millions are standing by that rock. And these 475 million awakened Chinese people are leading the whole of Asia to the goal of world peace You can be certain we will stop at no point short of our objective.

NEW CHINA'S FIRST YEAR

Statement issued on the first anniversary
of the People's Republic of China

October 1, 1950

October 1, 1949, was a memorial day, a historic day, a happy day. It marked the beginning of an emancipated people, a revived China. It was the threshold of a new era, over which we stepped into the future, the epoch of the people.

October 1, 1950, is a signal day, a day of ending and yet beginning. It marks the completion of the first year of our People's Republic of China, and the commencement of the second. It is a period of summing up our accomplishments and preparing to spring off to even more magnificent ones.

October 1, 1950, is a day of peace. It denotes that, in this year of New China, the whole strength of our 475 million people has been thrown behind the cause of world peace. We have shaken a mighty fist in the faces of the war-mongers. "We demand peace! We demand construction, not destruction! We demand genuine international cooperation, not imperialism!" These have been the mandates of the liberated Chinese people in coordination with peace-lovers throughout the world. Therefore, on this anniversary day of the People's Republic of China, let us lift our voices to proclaim, "The people will have peace! Long live world peace!"

Thus, we will indelibly write New China's first year into history.

FRIENDSHIP IS UNITY

Speech delivered in Peking
upon the first anniversary of the
founding of the Sino-Soviet Friendship Association

October 1, 1950

"Sino-Soviet Friendship"—These are sounds with a
world of meaning. This is a phrase which makes an
imprint on history 10,000 li wide and deep. These are
three words that secure the present and cast the
future.

This friendship is evidenced in a myriad ways.
Some are the simple, very human expressions—full
hearts bursting out through comradely smiles, hearty
handshakes and fraternal embraces. Others are the
mutual appreciation of cultures, the exchange of admiration for courage displayed and feats accomplished.
There are the acts of fraternal assistance, and the keen
respect for national self-determination. Above all, there
is the unity which springs from the oneness of cause—
to advance mankind.

To the Chinese people, the Soviet Union is the land
of creation, prizing labor as if it were a precious jewel.
It is a land which incessantly inspires, prizing the people
as the essential element of existence. It is the land
of multiple experimentation, always in step with tomorrow.

To the Chinese people, the Soviet Union is the land of Stakhanovites, the new type of human, ever-advancing, selfless, and steeled in battle against adversity. It is the land of science, which is applied in its highest forms, never allowed to rest but pushed onward for man's benefit. It is the land of Socialism, the hope of the world's working class.

To the Soviet people, China is a nation newly awakened. We have risen in our wrath to crush feudalism. They see in us an aroused people, ousting imperialism for all time. They see in us a nation that has caused the glow from the flames of liberation to light the way for the whole of Asia.

The Soviet people know us as a land of immense potential, with our national genius released full force for the first time in our history. They see our earth abounding in virgin resources and know we will use these gifts to the maximum. They know us as a people teeming with energy, capable of moving mountains, building factories and controlling nature.

The Soviet Union and the People's China, these are two great masses of land and people. Arm-in-arm they march, their strength fused to smash the chains of reaction wherever they bind and oppress, thrusting fear into the black hearts of those who would unleash war and attempt to destroy man for a few pinches of gold. Arm-in-arm they march, holding aloft the banner of peace and forging the world-to-be.

Long live Sino-Soviet Friendship!

WHAT THE KOREAN PEOPLE'S STRUGGLE MEANS TO ASIA

First appeared in "Kwangming Daily", organ of the Democratic League of China.

October 11, 1950

There is a broad and absolute truth that permeates Asia today. It is an aged but still virile fact taken from the history of man. Lenin stated it by saying that a people that has taken the power into its own hands is invincible.

Embodied in that one sentence is the knowledge that the armed masses eventually win all revolutions and gain all independence struggles over imperialist aggressors. Contained therein is the data which demonstrates that the armed masses win and keep their victories when their additional weapon is revolutionary thought founded in the science of dialectical materialism.

The heroic struggles of Korea's patriots and their brilliant achievements provide now, and their eventual victory will in the future provide proof of this truth and all of the irreducible lessons written within it.

MacArthur, his generals and the "violet-picking" diplomats of the U.S. State Department, in chorus loudly proclaimed that South Korea was an "impregnable bulwark", meaning "invasion spearhead", against the

People's Korea, against the People's China, against the Soviet Union. The United States created, equipped and trained the South Korean army for this purpose. The world was told that one of its regiments could vanquish a whole North Korean brigade. But what was the truth of that boast? Events have filtered it down to an inaudible squeak. The South Korean forces were routed almost immediately after their attempt at aggression and have all but disintegrated. Why is that?

The military might of the capitalistic world is being thrown against the Korean people—planes, ships, tanks, artillery and other devices of devastation. The Americans first sent a battalion of their troops to rescue the encircled South Koreans. Then a regiment was sent to rescue the battalion. Next a division was dispatched to rescue the regiment. In fact, Americans now have more combat soldiers in Korea than they had in the North African invasion in 1942. In order to meet this difficult situation, America has had to further increase her forces for new manoeuvering, hoping to attain her objectives. But the iron determination of the Korean patriots to liberate themselves will cause the foreign aggressors to be drowned in total rout.

America's allies in Asia, America's own armed forces, despite modern weapons, special training and mountains of money have been unable to and will never defeat Korean revolutionaries! Again we ask, why is that?

The first part of the answer is another historical fact, a section of the broader truth. It is not the gun but the ideological makeup of the man behind the gun that determines the outcome of any conflict. In other words, the Korean masses have something to fight for, whereas the imperialists, both the local and the imported products, have nothing. The Korean war is not one of firepower and logistics, but one of ideologies.

Kim Il Sung, the leader of the Korean revolution, puts it thus: "The American imperialists still fail to understand that today the people of Korea are not what they were yesterday, that our people are not a docile flock of sheep meekly allowing themselves to be devoured by hungry wolves".

The Korean masses are imbued with an idea—they have taken the power into their own hands, and they are going to liberate their country from foreign aggressors and their puppets. They know the mockery that imperialists make of the principle of national self-determination. They know from bitter experience that imperialists would never leave them alone to work out their own destinies, but would remain to perpetuate the shackles of the feudal order and to bind them to misery and endless exploitation. Therefore, in their fighting, they are determined, they are resolute, because they are struggling for their own good earth.

This is borne out on the battlefield. The politically illiterate American army is opposed by a revolutionary army. One American officer described the fighting this way: "They came at us in swarms, each with a do-or-die mission of his own. They acted like every group was assigned a certain place to take, and they didn't give up until they took it".

This tenacity in battle is characteristic of all Koreans who have become politically liberated. The reason is this. The North Koreans, with the aid of the

Soviet Union, are working out a plan for life's better-ment. The South Koreans, under American oppression, easily recognized the vast differences between their bare existence and the full life their Northern brothers and sisters have attained. They want the very same things —the land and industry in their own hands, democratic rights, processes and representation. They long for the power of the People's Committees that had been theirs after the defeat of the Japanese, but which was ripped from their hands by the Americans and the Rhee gang. They want on top of all this that the Japanese collaborators and the American puppets be given their due for all of the misery they have wreaked on the people. Consequently, the Korean masses as a whole, the Northerners to keep their victories, the Southerners to win them, fight with a ferocity that overcomes all odds against them. They fight in the Stalingrad tradition. They fight only to lose their chains.

The second and equally important part of the answer to the Korean people's triumph deals with the imperialists themselves. It involves their whole out-look on the world and war.

The imperialist strategy and action on the battle-field are likewise an extension of their daily thinking and living. They reflect the short-sightedness of avarice and sterility of capitalistic thought. Like their political and economic theories and attempts at philosophy, their war techniques and tactics retrogress and become warped from reality.

Politically, the imperialists drive for fascism at home—the few rulers separated from and against the masses. Economically, they drive for monopoly—the few rich against the impoverished people. Philosophically, they drive to idealism and mysticism—the few content in a "never-never" world, the masses discontent in the face of hard, tangible facts. Strategically, they worship the weapon and forget the man—the few, afraid of the new and daring in all other fields, cannot alter their methods of war and order the masses into indefensible positions.

How does all of this affect the imperialist camp itself? There, in place of hope sits depression; in place of certainty lurks fear; in place of cause stands self. This can be the only result, because in order for the few to retain control, the people must be constantly deceived. Their governments lie to them. They lie to them about their standard of living. They lie to them about their present and future. Above all, they lie to them about war and peace.

The United States provides the typical example. The Wall Street rulers of this country are now engaged in a planned, concerted attack against the popular movement to secure signatures for peace. They mark this vital campaign as a Soviet instrument. What they do not tell their people is that the Soviet Union certainly does use peace to mobilize its people. Factories, mines and mills over that vast Socialist country are working "peace shifts", in honor of peace, to forward the concept of peace. On the opposite side, the United States is using war to mobilize its people, to rearm, to destroy innocent millions, to reduce to rubble whole cities and industries. Since this is such an unpopular road to travel, the American people are being led down it blindfolded, their rulers using every possible camouflage and deceit.

The plan of the American imperialists is quite obvious. Their Defence and State Departments instigated the aggression in Korea. This provided Wall Street's political arm with the incident it needed to "demand preparations for any eventuality". In the first weeks of the Korean war, the officials issued statement after statement. The American people were told this was a "police action", it would not disturb the national economy, would not require additional manpower, would not cause a reduction in the people's livelihood. Yet subsequent announcements, step by step, led industry to war production, forced peaceful citizens into the armed services by the tens of thousands, increased taxation and thereby reduced the people's means of living.

Not content with clubbing their own people into a state of war, the American rulers have taken over the United Nations. This international tribunal is also used for purposes of legality based on lies. But open pressure, such as threatening to withhold economic aid, is applied and outright orders to rearm at the expense of the people are issued to the Western European countries, to force them to provide cannon fodder for the war Truman, Wall Street and Company want to provoke on the entire world.

All of these measures are directly antithetical to the people's welfare and desires, in America, in Europe, anywhere on earth. In the last analysis, they represent fear of the people, for they must be accompanied by complete destruction of civil liberties, the hounding, persecution and assassination of progressive leaders and the use of terror to foster a fear psychosis. The last analysis shows something else. All of these are measures of defeat in advance of the fact. The people of the world just do not want war, as evidenced by the hundreds of millions of signatures affixed to the Stockholm Peace Appeal. There is even more forceful evidence on the very battlefields of Korea. In addition to the strength which the Korean people have displayed, there are the testimonies of American prisoners of war, who not understanding why they had to wage such a fight in the first place, upon seeing the unjustness of the United States policy, broadcast to their fellow-countrymen, telling them to stop the war and leave the Koreans to settle their own affairs.

Thus, we have two of the reasons—the purity of a people's revolution and the rottenness of imperialist reaction—why the masses persist in struggle, overcome obstacles and achieve final victory on the battlefield, politically and economically. This is the way it happened in China. This is the way it is happening in Viet-Nam and Korea. It plots on the graph of history a growing shift of power and becomes a politico-military fact of extreme importance for Asia today. It heralds the emergence of a new politico-military strength in this expanse where over half of the world's population lives. Formerly, for example, Chinese soldiers were caricatured marching to war shouldering an umbrella. Now, the picture has radically changed. The new Asian soldier, armed with revolutionary political thought stands up and fights the Western imperialist man-to-man, unafraid and ready to face any material disadvantage. This is the keystone of the people's military upsurge in Asia. Upon it rests the ability to adapt either or both positional and guerrilla tactics, allowing for modernization of armies and still giving them flexibility. It is the idea of whole armed peoples taking the power into their own hands. It is an idea which can only be accepted and enforced by people's democracies.

This concept of armed struggle gains hold at a time when Asia is at the boiling point. Its peoples are quickly learning the imperialist causes of their poverty and ignorance. They are straining for independence and eager for freedom from exploitation. They see how victories are accomplished against incredible odds —man has to blow up tanks, animals have to be used instead of trucks, ingenuity and infiltration tactics are employed to overcome the threat of planes and artillery. They see all of this, and the sacrifice too. But they also see the end result—victory for the masses. It cannot but inspire all of those still oppressed to struggle for their own triumphs, until the whole of Asia is liberated.

THIRTY-THREE YEARS OF PROGRESS

An article in "People's China". Vol. I (Russian edition)

November 1, 1950

The Thirty-Third Anniversary of the great October Socialist Revolution signifies thirty-three years of constant progress, for the Soviet peoples and for the people of the entire world. Such progress belongs equally to all working men and women. The Revolution's beginning was a manifestation of their upsurge to rid themselves of their chains. Its consolidation through the years was in the name of the world working-class unity. And to this day, the Soviet Union continues as the shining light which leads all workers to their future.

The October Socialist Revolution and the thirty-three years of progress that followed in its wake have been monumental to laboring people for many reasons. Principal among these has been the death blow they have dealt many of the basic concepts, many of the fallible "infallibilities" of bourgeois-imperialist thought.

For example: "There cannot be any production without capitalists or their managers." Long had this been dinned into our ears. It was meant to keep the workers subjugated to the whims of financiers for eternity. It was used to create in workers' minds the belief that they could not possibly expect to make industry move on their own, that they could not learn techniques, engineering and innovation. Such complicated "brain-work" was not for simple people who labored with their hands. It was reserved for a special breed of human, who by divinity, heredity, thievery or connivance gained control of the means of production. Workers were not supposed to oppose that control, lest they wreck production.

Upon the establishment of the Soviet Union, this idea was wiped out in short order. The Soviet workers proved that the people can do wonders without exploiting bosses or war-bearing cartelists and monopolists. By the millions, they have risen from the rank and file to verify that workers can superbly manage industrial projects of any size, can plan, can build, and above all, can fairly distribute the full measure of their productivity. This has been a drastic defeat for capitalistic thought and a glorious achievement for all workers to behold.

Another example: "Socialism is an impractical dream." This one was used to defend the chronic unemployment and the cyclical crises which fester capitalistic economy. Its purpose was to have you believe that there was no use to battle against uneven development and excessive working of resources, or attempt to gainfully employ every able-bodied person. These kinds of ideas were for dreamers of utopia. If you penetrated too close to the truth and exposed this lie, you were even called insane. In other words, nothing should attempt to disturb the control of the bosses.

The thirty-three years of progress of the Soviet Union have made this idea a relic of history. Socialism is here! There is the Soviet land with the people in power right before our eyes. Socialism is a living thing, a growing thing. It is a mountain of facts on production. It is repeatedly lowering prices on consumer commodities. It is a steadily rising standard of living and a labor enthusiasm that cannot be duplicated anywhere but in a socialist atmosphere. The Soviet Union proved that socialism is far from a dream. It is the concrete, pulsating present and the future as well, right in the palm of every worker's hand. Thus, another of the bourgeois' ideas was knocked into a cocked hat.

Still another hoax: "Large-scale industrialization of undeveloped areas depends solely on outside capitalists." This was to mean that unless the opportunity was presented to take out more than a normal profit, the imperialists would not bring their capital into a country. Therefore, unless you gave them concessions of every sort, unless you put the control of the economy and political organization in their hands or the hands of their accomplices, your land would languish in the backwardness of feudal times.

If any thought has been disproven without any doubt whatsoever, it has been this one. The Soviet Union has proven, and all colonial countries will add their own testimony in due time, that the imperialists in the long run do not aid industrialization, but actually impede it. Their concept of industry is narrow and detrimental to national development. Therefore, if a backward country is to industrialize, if it is to lift its agriculture to the mechanized and socialized level, this must be done by relying on the people's own efforts. During the early Soviet times, this imposed the entire burden on the Soviet people, since they were surrounded only by enemies. But in these times, due to thirty-three years of progress, the former retarded countries which are now liberated have, in addition to their own strength, the fraternal assistance of the Soviet Union. This means there is even less necessity for reliance upon foreign capital. This buries even further into the folds of antiquity the idea of depending on outside, self-seeking "help" to modernize a nation.

Yet another lie: "It is natural for people of different race, color and customs to fight each other. They need a strong hand to control and save them from themselves." Under this foul piece of "philosophy", the imperialist nations appointed themselves as the "strong controlling hands". In the process they enslaved hundreds of millions of people, extracted billions in wealth for their own use, built empires and for a time ruled the world. They did this by pitting one group against the other on flimsy pretexts while blinding the combatants to the fact that they had more to gain from unity than from conflict. The imperialists followed this policy between nations and within their own precincts, all for the purpose of facilitating their rule and exploitation.

Now, this too has been successfully assailed and is tumbling down amidst the crumbling of economic kingdoms. The experiences of the Soviet Union since 1917 have displayed this idea in all its maliciousness.

In that great land, where there are a multitude of nations and ethnic groups, there, under the formulations of Stalin in his "National Question", nations for the first time in history started living side by side, in peace, on equal terms, cooperatively for constructive purposes, exchanging culture and genuine brotherly love. No more can race, color or customs stand between men, since the example of true equality is in full view of every man on earth.

When you consider these and the many other victories won by the Soviet Union, how great loom the contributions to mankind of the great October Socialist Revolution and the thirty-three years of progress! They expose the fact that bourgeois thought is founded in fable, whereas Socialist thought is rooted in science. They explain how capitalism exists merely for the few to profit, whereas people's states operate only in terms of the welfare of the masses. They finally resolve to the conclusion that capitalism leads to war, whereas Socialism works only for peace.

Just make a comparison. Witness the invasion of Korea by the military forces of the United States. Mark its economic penetration into Western Europe and Southeast Asia. Witness the sending of technicians and industrial help from the Soviet Union to the Eastern European democracies and People's Asia. Mark the constant flow of cultural groups and professors from the great Soviet land to its friends. Compare the decadent economy of the United States and its frantic preparations for war with the blooming life in the Soviet Union and its breath-taking construction of dams, huge irrigational canals, plantings

of whole forests, controlling nature at every turn for
the benefit of man.

There is no question. Working men and women
all over the world see the results of this comparison in
all its forms. Thus, they deeply appreciate the significance and meaning of the Thirty-Third Anniversary
of the October Socialist Revolution. That is why on
this occasion, in every language used on the globe, we
will hear:

Long live World Peace!
Long live the Soviet Union!
Long live the Soviet Peoples!
Long live Stalin!

A MESSAGE FROM NEW CHINA

A speech recorded for the China Welfare Appeal,
New York.

November 18, 1950

Greetings, friends of the Chinese people. This is a most propitious moment to send you a message. The People's Republic of China has just concluded its first glorious year. It is a period of summing up our accomplishments, for taking into focus the great changes that have come about, and for preparing even more magnificent ones. It is a time which thrills and inspires 475 million people.

In my opinion, the greatest change in China since the historic date of October 1, 1949, is that for the first time in our entire existence, the title by which our country is known has the word "people" in it. That word is not there for mere display, since also for the first time the emphasis and essence of our government is contained in that massive force—the people.

This makes itself evident in every phase of our daily lives. I would like to tell you each detail of the complete picture, but time does not permit. Therefore, on this occasion, I will restrict my report to the ways in which the new situation this past year has affected emergency relief work and my own organization, the China Welfare Institute. This means I am reluctantly bypassing the tremendous progress that has been made in such vital sectors as land reform, the reconstruction of industry and commerce, the strengthening of national defence, the development of China's minority nationalities' first freedom and many other facets.

In conformity with its surroundings, the whole concept of relief and welfare work has changed. It is no longer considered as some purely humanitarian and endless process. Rather, it is looked upon as an important segment of the entire economic reconstruction program of the People's Government. It is still humanitarian, but it is positive in approach and strives for concrete results that eliminate the need for relief in the future. Welfare services are considered a fundamental right and privilege of every person, for all time, but where emergency relief is specifically concerned, it has a definite beginning, a definite method and a definite ending.

Its beginning is now, necessitated by the misery of flood, famine and unemployment. Its method is salvation through self-help, and self-help through production. Its ending is to coincide with the achievement of national economic well-being, or when we have achieved what Chairman Mao Tse-tung termed, "The struggle for the fundamental turn for the better in our financial and economic situation." We have set the goal of three years to reach that point.

Let us examine how some of these relief problems are met. First let us consider the question of flood.

China has for centuries been afflicted with this menace. However, it became exceedingly destructive this past year due to the criminal measures the warlord troops took as they were routed by the valiant People's Liberation Army. In their frenzy, these reactionary forces weakened and wrecked thousands of vital dyke areas. Consequently, last summer, when the rains were heavy, the water came flowing over the land, inundating tens of millions of *mou,* destroying houses and crippling the livelihood of millions of people.

Previously, under the Kuomintang and U.S. "aid" programs, flood was met with giant talk of what was to be done, but the actions were those of a pigmy. On this occasion, the deeds exceeded the announced plans because the situation was realistically met with the full strength of the People's Government. The Ministry of Water Conservancy was called into action and attacked the problem as if it were a nation-wide military campaign. They set up a massive operational system of 334 work and observation stations throughout the country, linked directly to a flood-fighting headquarters in Peking by tele-communications. They mobilized 4,690,000 men and women as well as members of the People's Liberation Army. During special periods, they further mobilized millions more. On each occasion they especially drew workers from among those hardest hit by the flood. These masses of people were used to effect a short-run and a long-run plan simultaneously. It meant curbing the raging waters immediately, and at the same time working toward strongly harnessing them for the future, so they would benefit the people, not destroy them.

The army of flood-fighters were paid for their labor by the government. At the same time, they were educated as to the meaning of their work. Meetings were held on every level, from small village groups to huge area mass gatherings. Every detail was carefully explained—the job to be accomplished, why they were mobilized, how they would get paid, what their work would mean to their future and the future of the country. The result was inspired, creative labor.

These workers shifted in one year's time 365 million cubic meters of earth. To give you some idea of the size and weight of this shift, that is enough dirt to build a wall one meter high and one meter wide around the equator eight times. In practical terms, our people repaired more than 25,000 kilometers of dykes, in addition to working toward permanently controlling such rivers as the Yangtze, Huai, Yellow, Yi, Pearl, Han, Liao and the sea dykes of East China.

This strenuous effort enables me to report at this time that seven out of every ten hectares which were under water last year, this year are under cultivation. In addition, vital and vast irrigation projects were accomplished. For example, in the dry Northwest alone, 300,000 hectares were newly irrigated and work has already started to reach a further 2,000,000 hectares. As a side result, from this particular project will come 3 million kilowatts of electric power from the drainage.

This gives you some idea of how we met the threat of flood, how we met the problem of beneficial distribution of water, how our People's Government has the power of the masses and how we used it.

Next, let us consider the question of famine. This is a favourite topic for your newspapers as well as for certain political philanthropists. Yes, we had famine in China. We never denied it. We made it quite plain that such disaster had been visited upon our people. We also made it quite plain that the famine was the result of the floods and the floods were the result of Kuomintang destruction. At the same time, however, we also told the world we had a way out of our troubles.

China has its own strength and through using this efficiently, the suffering was reduced to a minimum. Due to the faith which the farmers have in our government, because of land reform and other beneficial measures, the deliveries of tax grain have been on time and well over 90 percent fulfilled. Due to the foresight and energy of our People's Government, we were able to materialize a movement of that grain within our country on such a scale that every food deficiency area was reached. There was not one mode of transportation that was not organized and put into play— the newly reconstructed railroads, river-boats, wagons, wheelbarrows and the very backs of our courageous people. The slogan was "None Shall Starve". To meet that slogan here are the figures of the grain moves:

> From Manchuria—1 million tons and more if it was needed
> From Szechuan—110,000 tons
> From Central and South China—740,000 tons

This life-giving grain was used in the famine areas for public works programs such as water conservancy, for production programs to reclaim the land, for loans to stimulate home and part-time industry. In a minority of cases, it was distributed as outright relief. And there was still enough to go around elsewhere. Shanghai, for example, usually dependent upon foreign rice, could now make its way with ease on homegrown grain.

This unprecedented and decisive action on the part of the government not only defeated famine, but it also had a most salutary effect on the whole economy. Prices of the basic foods were stabilized. This made all other commodities level off and remain relatively constant. To many it seemed as if a miracle had taken place. No other government had been able to do this. But it was no miracle. It was the result of a People's Government that has the support of the people, and that moves with dispatch after thorough preparation for that move.

The final effect of the price stabilization was that universal confidence was established in our people's currency. This, in actuality, was the best of all possible "relief" programs for the nation as a whole. People's minds were at ease for the first time in years. They could fully concentrate on their jobs and strive for increased production. Also from this sprung renewed and unswerving faith in Chairman Mao's statement that while our country has difficulties, it also has the solutions.

I wish to show how this thinking was applied to other relief matters, that of unemployment in some cities. First I must point out that this problem was confined to those cities which were most burdened with compradore-imperialist influence and which have only recently been liberated. It must also be made clear that this problem settled on cities which were severely bombed by the American-supported Kuomintang air-force. I have brought these factors up for the following reasons:

1. In the case of the compradore-imperialist influence, unemployment is a special problem arising out of internal conditions. There is now taking place an adjustment of industry and commerce so that it produces for the Chinese people and not mainly for export, which was exploitation pure and simple. This is no easy task, to turn industry so that it faces inward, particularly since it was set up and developed in the directly opposite direction. This takes time, careful calculation and analysis, education of workers and industrialists as to its meaning to the country. This calls for a transition period, and during this time there is bound to be some dislocation. From this stems the unemployment. But it, like all other problems, can be met with the same technique—the mobilization of the people.

2. In the case of the bombing, unemployment arises from strictly external causes resulting in the destruction of power plants, mills and factories and the disruption of shipping, preventing the importation of raw materials. This

too can be met and is being met by the same technique—the mobilization of the people.

Unemployment is handled through the joint efforts of the trade unions and the government. The labor organizations work this way: they mobilize the workers themselves, both the employed and the unemployed. They conduct campaigns for the collection of funds and supplies and are entrusted with the funds turned over by the government and other organizations.

It should be pointed out here that help has come from every sector and section of the land, in response to the slogan of "Unity; those with jobs and means, help those without". The workers of Manchuria, since there is no unemployment there, especially were liberal in their contributions.

These funds were once again mainly used to put the unemployed workers to productive tasks. Public work programs have been instituted, vital construction jobs undertaken and technical training projects established. Workers are paid for both work and study.

At the same time, the government takes other positive and energetic steps. Every attempt is made to revive production, both in the publicly-owned and the privately-owned plants. Loans are issued by the People's Bank to start the wheels moving when there is no other capital available. Large orders are placed by the government purchasing agencies to keep the factories producing and at the same time to stimulate trade between the city and the country by satisfying the needs of the people in the rural areas. Another way the government steps into the breach is by procuring the necessary raw materials and allocating these to the deficient plants. This is accomplished by financing the purchasing of supplies abroad and their shipment by rail within the country, and also by sponsoring the extensive planting of agricultural industrial products, such as cotton. The workers with jobs, for their part and as a result of labor union education, conduct raw material economy drives and constantly improve their techniques so as to raise the level of production. The total result is an increasingly improving business situation, using the government policy of benefiting both labor and capital, both public and private enterprises.

Now there is one other field where this mass technique is applied with signal success. That is, in the realm of medicine.

As you know, how to take modern medical practice to the Chinese people has always been one of our prime problems. Epidemics have swept our land endlessly. But the time has come when the end is in sight for such catastrophies. The reason is that the People's Government has taken measures to control the forces of nature and has mobilized the great masses of people in this mammoth battle. For the immediate enemies, such as plague, cholera and others, teams consisting of hundreds of medical workers have been assigned to do combat. In Manchuria, on two occasions, they have stopped epidemics in their first stages, these, incidentally, being remnants of Japanese bacteriological war preparations. In other areas, medical workers have saved hundreds of thousands of livestock from various animal diseases. In Shanghai, after inoculating almost four million people there were only some ten cases of proven cholera this past summer. This indeed, is a new record.

How can these miracles of medicine be accomplished? There is only one way: to educate the broad masses to participate along with technical personnel in the fight against disease. Workers, farmers and soldiers, all are part of this great medical army. In the main cities, in the regional centers, in the district centers, exhibitions, lectures, demonstrations and training are given to lift the level of medical and sanitation knowledge of the people. Such expansive programs have been outlined and talked about for years and years. But in this past year, the plans have been implemented with vigor over the entire country, even in the newly liberated areas.

This is not just a temporary measure. It will be years before China will have enough trained personnel in the field. This means that the emphasis in medicine must continue to be along preventive lines. For this to succeed, it must be founded in the masses and their education and training must be even further deepened and intensified.

In the meantime, the government is undertaking a most ambitious program. Within three to five years, we hope to establish on every governmental level a medical organization with qualified personnel. This plan calls for medical units in regions, districts and villages, all linked and cooperating. To implement this program, China in the following five years will train twenty thousand doctors, over thirty thousand medical workers and thousands of technicians and dentists. In addition, as part of China's industrialization, we will strive to erect factories and laboratories to produce our own supplies and equipment to the greatest extent possible. This plan can only succeed with full participation of the masses.

With this illustration, you have four examples of how the masses of people fight calamity in the New China. The technique, whether implementing relief or projects in the welfare field, is mass in character, in orientation and in backing.

The agency to foster and guide this work and to lead all of the organizations functioning in the relief and welfare fields was formed just this past April. It is the People's Relief Administration of China (PRAC). It was formed upon the call of people from all over the country and under the auspices of the People's Government.

The purposes of PRAC are as follows:

1. To unify relief and welfare plans throughout the country.
2. To determine the spheres of work.
3. To control the allocation of personnel, funds and materials according to the plan.
4. To see that publicity conforms with action.

The principles of PRAC are derived from the experiences of the people and are as follows:

1. The Chinese people have won military victories over all odds and liberated themselves. With this same strength they will liberate themselves from misery of any and every source.
2. To help people to help themselves so they can make the land secure, so they can increase

production, so they can heighten their standard of living.

3. To cooperate with all individuals and organizations that are engaged in genuine relief and welfare work as long as they conform to the principles of PRAC and are willing to follow the lead of the People's Government.

4. Not to refuse, but to welcome well-intentioned international assistance and in turn to aid international friends wherever and whenever possible, since now our basic position has changed with the people's victory.

Armed with these purposes and principles, the People's Relief Administration of China joins forces with our government and with all other people's organizations to meet the trials which are the result of victory and to help push on with the transition from the semi-feudal, semi-colonial society, to the new people's society.

I am sure that many of you are asking how all of these new conditions of the past year have affected my own organization, the China Welfare Institute (CWI). The fact is that we have just recently undergone a reorganization which started with our name and worked its way down into every corner of our work. Satisfied that the big relief problems are being handled expeditiously by the government, the conference which initiated PRAC gave us new objectives for our work. We have now entered an advanced phase of our history, to assume one of the positions of leadership in the planning and developing of techniques in the welfare field.

From this point forward, the China Welfare Institute will concentrate its efforts on the women and children of workers, farmers and soldiers. The emphasis will be on the establishment of model and experimental projects in medicine and health, culture and education. The results of our work will be published and will be broadcast throughout the nation by PRAC and other people's organizations.

This emphasis on women and children is in keeping with the new, elevated status they enjoy under the People's Republic of China. In the Common Program, which is our fundamental law, Article 6 gives women full equality with men in every phase of life. In Article 48, the children of the nation are provided for. Women, in addition, are aided by the promulgation of the Marriage Law, which obliterates for all time the feudal prerogatives of husbands.

The purpose of the CWI is to help make the emancipation of women and children as complete as possible, as quickly as possible. That is why we operate a maternity, health and child-care network in the textile factory districts of Shanghai, where over 80 percent of the workers are women. That is why we have a model nursery and creche for over 250 children. That is why we are ardently striving to perfect our program, in order that it may be duplicated all over China, thereby freeing millions of women for work in the government, in industry, in the fields and in our People's Liberation Army.

The China Welfare Institute is similarly attacking problems related to the enhancement of our children's lives. Take the field of education as an example. Our government is doing a magnificent job. Already there are 20 million youngsters in primary schools and another one and a half million in secondary schools. In addition, the Ministry of Education plans to eliminate illiteracy in the near future. This is a tremendous program, but it is still not enough to meet all of the educational needs of this country. Every person and organization which can lend a hand must do so. Since the CWI has broad and deep experience in mass education and cultural activities, since we know how to link these activities with the economic and national reconstruction requirements of China, it was natural that we should establish a children's cultural center in the middle of a worker's district. From there we are able to carry on our mass literacy classes, the after-school cultural mobilization and other works. Once again, we use this project to point the way, so it can be duplicated a thousand times over, until there are a thousand children's cultural palaces in China.

It is the same story in dramatics and people's art. Our country has become a singing, dancing, acting country since the liberation. Cultural groups and dramatic troupes spring up everywhere. In Shenyang for example, there are 350 amateur theatrical troupes, with over 12,000 members, most of them factory workers.

China has never seen such far-reaching cultural activity, and the CWI is part of the whole movement. Our Children's Theater is the first of its kind in this country. It is dedicated to the children and is run by them. We have 100 talented youngsters in our Theater. They have their own dramatic troupe, their own playwrights, set designers and stage managers, their own dance ensembles and their own orchestra. As in all of our work, this is a pioneer project and we won't be satisfied until there are hundreds of such theaters in every part of our country.

As time goes on, the China Welfare Institute will also participate in scientific research. For example, we have already begun a project for the gathering of statistics on the development of Chinese children, using control groups. This is the first time that such work is being carried out on a large scale and using the latest scientific methods. There are other similar projects under consideration.

To summarize, all of the work of the CWI has the same purpose—to serve the people by spreading the results of our experience as far and as wide as possible.

Thus, through this brief report on how we are handling relief questions and what the outlook of the China Welfare Institute is, you are able to obtain a general idea of how the New China is functioning. First, we do things in step with the people. Second, we face our difficulties squarely and we are a nation hard at work to erase them. Third, we are willing to receive honest, fraternal help from all sides, but at the same time we are capable of using our own resources and genius to the maximum.

There is one other characteristic of the New China. We are a nation for peace and construction. No people appreciates the meaning of peace more than do the Chinese people. We have known war for over 100 years, so to us, peace is a treasure. We will struggle to maintain it. We will protect it at all costs.

It disturbs us to see the club-swinging measures which some circles in your country have taken against peace. It angers us to witness your finest sons and daughters imprisoned for advocating the making of peace into a living condition. We condemn the "summer-time peace patriots" in high place and low, who at this juncture turn their backs on the people. But at the same time, we possess steady and root-deep faith in the masses of the American people. We know they have the strength to resist and overcome the pressure and intimidation of those who seek a profit-grabbing war. You once gave us a sample of that strength when the Chinese people faced their darkest days. You were a constant source of encouragement to those of us who were fighting for the birth of this New China. Now we would like to reciprocate. Please accept the inspiration of the Chinese people, a people in control of their own destiny. To us it is a rule of life that the struggles of the common men and women all over the world are the same and inseparable. Our difficulties are equally shared, but so are our victories. The liberated Chinese people extend their hands across the sea to firmly grasp yours, so that with unified ranks we may hold the peace. This is the message we want relayed to the American people.

STATEMENT ON WINNING THE STALIN PEACE PRIZE AWARD

Shanghai

April 11, 1951

It is a most profound honor of my life to be named among the winners of the Stalin Peace Prize. It is a privilege to be associated in the fight for peace, with the name of Stalin. For peace is what the people of the world want most. And Stalin is the name which most personifies peace.

In accepting this most valued honor, I do so as a representative of the Chinese people. It has been their unrelenting revolutionary struggle which has placed the might of our nation on the side of peace. It has been their victory, in conjunction with the Socialist strides of the Soviet people and the courageous advances and stands of all other progressive elements, which has re-aligned the world for all time in favor of peace and people's rule.

The united front of all people today continues at a most intensified pace the fight to maintain the peace. The moneyed moguls of the United States and its satellites, befouling the word "Peace" by claiming to act in its behalf, are sustaining serious defeats. As a result they have become mad. They would mercilessly destroy all peaceful construction, as they have trampled into dust the achievements of the valiant Korean people. They would fiendishly tear child from mother or destroy both, as they are doing in Korea, Malaya and other parts of the world. They would strap all mankind to their exploitive service, to be reduced to slaves and cannon fodder, as they are attempting to do at home, in Western Europe and Japan. But they will never succeed in accomplishing their wicked ends, for the people's united front has its own special strength. Our hundreds of millions are pitted against their few, and as the World Peace Council demonstrates, there is not one sector of this earth where there is not representation and struggle for the aim of "consolidating peace among the nations."

Therefore, let us use this occasion of the awarding of the Stalin Peace Prizes to re-dedicate ourselves in the cause of world peace. Let us gather new power and inspiration to defeat the enemies of man, to open the unparalleled vistas of peaceful work and joyful play that are man's due. Let us join in one voice to shout:

Long live Stalin, leader of the peoples for peace!
Long live the world peace forces!
Long live world peace!

NEW CHINA FORGES AHEAD

"Some Impressions from a Trip to the Northeast"
Published in 'People's Daily' and
'People's China', Peking

May 1, 1951

Along with Comrade Lin Po-chu and others, I have
recently completed an investigation of New China's
Northeast (Manchuria). We travelled its length and
breadth, penetrating deeply into the changes which have
come about in the people's lives. What we experienced
so inspired me, that I want to report my impressions
to the nation and the world, to report that New China's
future is in the making and our Northeast is leading
the way.

This will not be an attempt at an overall and detailed analysis of the Northeast. Rather it will be a brief
summary of those sights and subjects which impressed
me most as we covered over 4,260 kilometers of Northeast territory. A total of 54 different places and projects were visited, including seven main cities of the
Northeast, as well as four villages where land reform
had been completed. We inspected eleven industrial
plants and one mine and innumerable welfare and cultural establishments. In each place we either heard or
were handed reports. In addition, we conducted personal inspections, talking with the ordinary farmers

and workers as well as the heads of industrial and governmental administrations.

Thus, we were able to make an intense, factual and comprehensive study of the gigantic strides being made by the Northeast. We saw the tremendous improvement in the economic life, the elevation of cultural activities and the improvement of hygienic conditions in the lives of the peasants after land reform. We saw how these advances favorably affected the lives of the city working class and with what enthusiasm they have set out to revive and reconstruct industry. We also witnessed how thoroughly our government and the Chinese Communist Party work, how they attack each mistake in search of the truth, how they fully understand the strength of the workers and peasants and how they mobilize this strength to move on to even greater accomplishments.

The Villages and Land Reform

Even while the fighting of the Liberation War was at its most furious stage in the Northeast, the land reform was begun. In fact, it was at the very time of the Kuomintang's peak strength when the people's forces were strategically withdrawing, from July to December 1946, that 12,000 cadres were assigned to this duty and sent to the countryside. Their mission was to start the struggle against the feudal and bandit elements, to establish the fundamental territory from which the revolution would be consolidated over the entire land.

It was not an easy task, since the reactionary elements were strong. But gradually the peasant masses understood the significance of the land reform movement and, by the end of 1947, the enemy was routed in the social and economic sectors of rural life, just as he had begun to suffer devastating defeats on the battlefronts. By the end of 1948, the Kuomintang military remnants had been cleared from the Northeast, liberating all ten provinces. Thus, the way was paved for the consolidation of the land reform and the new life which was to follow.

The farmers of the Northeast showed their enthusiasm for the new life by reaching in 1949 a total volume of agricultural production equal to 14,500,000 tons of grain (not including two million tons from sideline production). In 1950 approximately 18,000,000 tons were produced. The 1950 production was 93 per cent of the 1943 figure, the best year of production under the Japanese imperialists. However the average yield per hectare was much greater than in 1943, and in some sections, Paicheng Hsien of Heilungkiang Province for example, production reached the 1943 figure.

From my observations, the reasons for this unprecedented upsurge in agricultural output are as follows:

A. The farmers are now the masters of the land.
B. Improved farming methods.
C. Good organization of labor on the farm.
D. The examples set by the model workers, the members of the Communist Party and the New Democratic Youth League.
E. Government aid to the people in time of adversity.
F. The funds and grain left over after taxes and expenses, encouraging the farmers to produce more.

I would like to deal more or less with each of these reasons.

Peasants Are Masters of the Land

When you first enter a village where the land reform has been a long accepted fact, you can tell this immediately, by the looks of self-confidence on the faces of the people, by their proud, erect bearing. Their new approach to life shows all over. The whole atmosphere is one of purposefulness. The villages are busy places, with the peasants and the family members either at work or studying. The homes and village streets are clean and neat. It all stems from the fact that the farmer can point out to the fields and say in his measured way, "It's mine". It seems such a simple way of expressing such an important piece of information!

A more graphic way of expressing the same information is by using a chart. One of the villages we visited is called Yung Kwei. It is located in Hulan Hsien of Sungkiang Province and you can tell its history in recent years from the figures below:

DISTRIBUTION OF PROPERTIES IN YUNG KWEI VILLAGE, HULAN HSIEN DURING THE LAND REFORM

Kind of Class*	Average land for each person (in Shang)		Average housing per person	
	Before	After	Before	After
	the land reform		the land reform	
Hired Peasant	—	0.66	—	0.33
Poor Peasant	—	0.66	0.12	0.31
Middle Peasant	0.55	0.67	0.24	0.38
Rich Peasant	2.41	0.66	0.70	0.22
Landlord	3.30	0.66	1.62	0.15

* Owing to the number of new families moving into the village during and after the land reform, the population of Yung Kwei Village has been increased from 676 to 772.

	Average horses per person		Average carts per person	
	Before	After	Before	After
	the land reform		the land reform	
Hired Peasant	—	0.16	—	0.04
Poor Peasant	0.08	0.13	0.01	0.02
Middle Peasant	0.35	0.18	0.05	0.05
Rich Peasant	0.42	0.11	0.06	—
Landlord	0.70	0.06	0.06	—

By this you can see that in the village of Yung Kwei the land has certainly gone to the tiller. The result has been that in 1949, production was increased on the average of one picul* for every shang** over the production before the land reform. Similar conditions and similar results were found everywhere we went in the Northeast.

Improved Farming Methods

With the basic step of land reform completed, the next step was to improve the methods of production. This means that in addition to reclaiming unused land and irrigating the fields, long-term and seasonal planning and the day to day work had to be elevated to a scientific level. This has already assumed the proportions of a wide-spread movement in the Northeast. Deep plowing, generous use of fertilizer, frequent cultivations and harrowing, level planting and many other new methods have now become standard farming procedure. There is also a healthy appreciation among the peasants of the Northeast for modern implements, seed selection

* A picul is roughly equivalent to 133 lbs.
** Shang as used here refers to a "small" shang which is equal to 10 mou. A mou is equal to approximately one-sixth of an acre.

and protection and scientific care for the farm animals. Some examples from one of the villages we visited will make clear the reasons for this mass movement to apply science to agriculture.

Pao An Tung is a village in the Chiao Ho Hsien of Kirin Province. Before the liberation of the Northeast it was known for its poverty. Now it is renowned throughout the territory, not only for its wealth, but also for its advanced farming techniques. Here are some statistics concerning Pao An Tung Village:

In 1947 it had 30 animals
In 1950 it had 42 animals
In 1947 it used 10 implements
In 1950 it used 27 (including foreign-style plows and one combine-cultivator given as a prize by the Department of Agriculture)
In 1947 it cultivated 38.8 shang
In 1950 it cultivated 53.06 shang
In 1947 it applied fertilizer to 66% of the land
In 1950 it applied fertilizer to 90.5% of the land
In 1947 its total production was 240 piculs
In 1950 its total production was 700 piculs

The application of new farming methods and new implements has proved to the peasants of the Northeast that they provide greater yields by far, as we see by the above. We were also given a practical example of this fact by the villagers of Pao An Tung.

Farmer Chang compared his millet crop with his neighbor Yeh King. Much to his chagrin he found he was only getting 1.5 piculs per crop, whereas Yeh was obtaining 4 piculs and 50 per cent more stalks for feeding the animals. Upon exchanging work experiences, it was discovered that Farmer Yeh had prepared his land with the foreign-style plow and Chang had relied on his old rakes. When Yeh could go into his field and be completely lost from sight due to the tall, rich millet crop, this became too much for Chang. In a fit of anger he burned his rakes, swearing never to use such out-moded tools again.

The farmers of Pao An Tung have also learned another valuable lesson. The new methods mean less man-labor and more animal-labor. For example, from spring plowing through summer cultivation, for every 10 mou of land, using old-styled implements, they would require $24\frac{1}{2}$ units of man-labor. However, using the new tools, only 10 units man-labour are needed for the job, shifting more work to the animals. Thus, introducing the use of new implements into all of their work, the farmers of Pao An Tung were able to save 372 units of labor last spring and summer. This released many of the villagers for other jobs. As a result, they increased their earnings by ¥5,580,000 for the season.

This does not mean that all of the problems regarding new farming methods have been solved in the Northeast. Far from it. There is still a great need and demand for technical knowledge and experience. The important fact is that the farmers realize the great strides that can be made with science as an ally. This is also constantly demonstrated to them by the activities of the Department of Agriculture. For example, in a recent wheat harvest, with the help of the Department's technicians, one village was able to thrash 4,000 bundles a day. The very best record the farmers had been able to accomplish previous to this was 300 a day, and that was only with the greatest of effort. Such practical proofs have had a telling effect on the peasants' thinking and they are willing to incorporate into their planning and daily work the results of such exhibits.

There is another important effect that this advanced thinking has. I am referring to its influence on the people's livelihood.

The head of Yung Kwei Village, King Chen-ling, told my party, "Before the land reform, there were only 11 middle peasants and 72 homes of poor and hired peasants. Now almost 90 per cent of the village is in the middle peasant class. Some farmers, though they cannot afford to own a horse, yet they have plenty to eat and wear. Their living conditions vary very little from those of the others. They are called poor peasants only because they have no horses."

The figures on Yung Kwei Village, as seen in the chart, prove King Chen-ling to be correct. Furthermore, we found that the resources of the village have increased 40 per cent since land reform and the use of new techniques, and the peasants' income from auxiliary occupations has increased by approximately 45 per cent.

When you multiply the progress made by Pao An Tung and Yung Kwei by the thousands of villages in the Northeast, you can be rightfully impressed with what liberation means to our nation's farmers, what prosperity new ways and new tools bring to them.

Good Organization of Farm Labor

The organization of labor on the Northeast farms we found to be an application of both science and democracy according to the principle expressed by Vice-Chairman Kao Kang in March 1950. At that time he said in a speech, "While nothing should be done to frustrate the initiative of individual economy, attention would need be paid to the development of cooperation and mutual aid, in order to develop village economy."

This means that there is an emphasis on the formation of cooperative work groups based on voluntary participation and mutual help. They are founded and operate according to the conditions prevailing in each particular district. But also taken into consideration are the planned regional requirements of agriculture and supplementary production, the demands of the peasant masses and the ability of the organizing cadres. Since this organization work is rather complicated, the greatest attention is paid to the actual working of these mutual aid groups rather than how they appear superficially. What is more, they are promoted with the idea of long-term functioning and linked with such vital segments of rural economy as the ever-extending use of new implements and consumer cooperatives. The central aims of these groups are to increase production and to prove to the peasants that working together is always better than working alone.

Every village that we visited had these cooperative work groups. We found them operating with a scientific division of the labor to be done on the farms and with a rational allocation of labor power. The cadres are most careful in calculating just how much work can be done by the various implements, by the animals and by the peasants themselves. Everything is reduced to work units and the number of hours required to complete a definite task.

The job assignments are made in a most democratic manner. The small group system is used, with each group responsible for certain work and each group having a leader. Every person in the cooperative is paid for his work according to labor units and according to the labor appraisal made each day in the group. Their principle is "More work, more reward". This whole set-up seems to satisfy everybody and raises the morale of the peasants, giving them confidence to tackle all sorts of difficult jobs.

The mutual aid teams enable efficient use of labor and thus the land is more intensively cultivated. An example of this is shown in the following table which traces the production in Pao An Tung Village in recent years.

A COMPARISON OF THE RATE OF PRODUCTION
(IN PICULS) SINCE 1947

	Total Production	Average Production Per Shang	Remarks
1947	240 piculs	6.5	
1948	380 piculs	8.0	
1949	490 piculs	8.4	The increase was not significant due to drought in 1949
1950	700 piculs	11.5	

We also found that while the small type of work group is prevalent at this time throughout the Northeast, there are also those activists who want to leap further ahead into the future. These leaders have organized larger work cooperatives and brigades. It is worth while to briefly recount the story of one of these to show the advancement some Northeast farmers are making.

The spring of 1947 saw the preliminary conclusions of the land reform of Pao An Tung Village, and out of this struggle came a good cadre named Han En. He took the lead, with several others of his comrades, in the production emulation which followed. Therefore, it was like planting an especially selected seed in the most fertile soil to suggest to such a man that cooperative work groups be formed. This idea had been put forth by the Communist Party District Committee. Immediately after, Han En called a mass meeting of Pao An Tung to explain to the farmers how they could get rich through organizing themselves.

At first this idea did not go over too well, for all of Han En's enthusiasm and eloquence. One peasant said that he had two cows and could manage all alone, without mutual help. Others voiced their fears about the land really belonging to them and the recriminations they could expect for participating in such groups if the landlords should ever return to power. Others merely shrugged their shoulders at the idea of cooperation, saying, "The heavens will never let a blind sparrow starve," or in other words, "I'll get help if I ever need it."

Despite these objections, Han En went from house to house and gradually convinced some of the peasants to try the idea. He finally got three small groups functioning. Naturally, their production results soon had everybody else's eyes popping out. After that, practically all of the farmers joined the work cooperative movement.

At the beginning of Han En's drive to make the cooperatives succeed, the form of each small cooperating

unit was fixed. There was no exchange of labor between groups. All sorts of work were done within each
group, whether they had enough talent and numbers to
handle the job or more than enough of each. This turned out to be more efficient than individual farming, but
it by no means reached the top efficiency. For example,
not every job required all of the labor power contained
in each group. In some cases, though perhaps only
five units of labor were required, yet just because there
were seven members in the group, all seven would do
the work. This was an obvious waste of labor. It was
also a disruptive influence at times since among the
villagers the same type of work received different labor
credits, depending on the number of group members,
the time spent and the individual amount of work accomplished. This caused dissatisfaction.

Han En studied the whole problem and thought out
a new way of allocating labor. He suggested the assignment of labor power according to the actual needs
of the job. In order to do this it was necessary to
break the rigidity of the group form, making it possible
to exchange labor between groups. The villagers of
Pao An Tung tried this new method and it worked out
quite satisfactorily. Based on their experience, they
decided to continue the practice of what they call the
"Joint Group" system. In effect, it is a small labor
collective which allows for even more scientific planning and direction of the village work. The results?
You will recall I have already mentioned that Pao An
Tung received a combine-cultivator as a prize from the
Department of Agriculture, that the villagers have risen
from poverty to wealth.

Thus, the farmers of the Northeast have learned the importance and the science of cooperation and good labor organization. They have seen how it makes for the most effective use of the latest farming methods, how it allows the individual farmer to exercise the full extent of his creativeness as the member of a group, what a great part it plays in giving them a better life.

Model Farmers, Communist Party and Youth League Members

It is difficult to emphasize enough the importance of model farmers, Communist Party and New Democratic Youth League members when analyzing the successes of the rural areas in the Northeast. They have had a most profound influence on every sphere of village life. All of the factors mentioned previously—the land reform, use of new implements, cooperation, the rise in production and the standard of living—all have been possible because there were those villagers who could mobilize the masses for action, who could set the example for the others to study and follow. Such people, through the guidance of the Communist Party and our People's Government, have been nurtured into self-sacrificing cadres, men and women who put the revolution above all else, who look past their present successes to the future task of building an agricultural base for industrializing China and giving its people the joys of Socialism.

There are certain marks of distinction which I found among the cadres of the Northeast. It is best perhaps to express these in the words of one of these advanced people, someone of whom you already know something, Comrade Han En. As he put it, "A good cadre first should not be feared by the villagers. Second, the villagers should believe in his words. Third, he must actually work for the villagers. In order to lead the production work well, he must go into the small cooperative groups personally and show others that he can work better than anybody else."

Han En is someone from whom we can learn, and the words he expresses about what a cadre should be are worth thinking over. The reason I say this is not only that he has successfully started cooperative work groups and was elected a delegate to the National Conference of Labor Models. I say this on the basis of what his fellow-villagers think of him.

One said, "Han En is the kind of man who won't let you walk on a bridge which does not have supports." Another said, "Everybody is willing to become wealthy under his leadership." Still another spoke up with, "Han En knows how to run meetings democratically. He discusses everything with the masses and never makes a long speech beforehand. He is apt to express himself last, summarizing all of the villagers' opinions, picking out the correct ones, explaining what is wrong with the incorrect ones. Finally he lays out the plan for action. Since Han En's ideas contain all the best ones in the village, they are usually the decisions of our meetings."

These are the most valuable appraisals of a cadre's work, the words of the people. In this case there is no question of the people's appreciation of Han En's service. But then generally speaking, he typified the kind of model farm workers, Communist Party and Youth League members we met in the Northeast. They were wide-awake people, capable of accepting new ideas and methods of work easily, taking into consideration all details and working them into their plans, carefully and patiently explaining everything to their co-workers, taking the lead in learning as well as in working. It is no wonder one villager remarked, "We know in advance that our plans will never turn out to be failures."

The people are thankful for such leadership. I recall a speech made by an old farmer of Yung Kwei Village. His name is Feng Wan-shan. First he told of his hardships in the greater part of his life and what the liberation meant to him and his family. Then he concluded with, "I have lived to such an old age, but I have never seen such a day of blessing as this. I am determined that I will exert every ounce of my strength to make the next crop a good one so I can collect all of the grain possible. This will be my share in the economic reconstruction of New China. This will be my repayment to Chairman Mao and the People's Republic of China."

Such a statement is a tribute to the leadership of the Northeast, to the model farmers, the Communist Party and New Democratic Youth League and the government cadre members who labor for the people.

Government Aid In Time of Adversity

Another reason the peasants of the Northeast throw their whole hearts into the production work is because they know the government will come to their aid in time of adversity. It has been at these times in the past that the People's Government has demonstrated it is one with the people.

My party found several examples of this fact in the Northeast. For one, there is the history of the rehabilitation of Hu Chia Tien Tze, a village on the outskirts of Changchun.

This village was virtually wiped off the map by the puppet and Kuomintang regimes. Over 500 houses were destroyed. At the time of liberation, the only assets were seven lean cows and other animals plus one broken cart. The peasants themselves were naked and on the verge of starvation.

Immediately upon liberation, the People's Government rushed 30,000 catties* of relief food to the villagers and extended them a loan of 65 animals. Later the land reform took place in this village.

How has Hu Chia Tien Tze fared since? Although in 1949 toward harvest time there was a shortage of food, yet every villager was able to afford a new padded winter coat. By 1950 we found all of the houses rebuilt and now their animals consist of the following: 141 donkeys and asses, 20 cows, 600 pigs. In addition there are 61 carts in the village. The food supply improves constantly and by 1951 every person in the village had a new suit of clothes.

There is another example. Since our national development has not yet reached the point where measures to control nature are advanced, on occasion calamity strikes at our farmers. This was the case

---

* Catty — one catty is equivalent to ½ kilogram.

with Ming Ho, a village in the fifth district of Shuang Cheng Hsien in Sungkiang Province.

When we saw it, the village streets were a colorful sight, with golden ears of corn and brilliant red peppers dangling from the eaves of the houses and the cords of firewood neatly stacked alongside the walks. It made a happy scene. Only recently, however, the mood of the Ming Ho villagers was not so happy. In 1947 their land had been hit by drought. They were just about recovering from this when last year they suffered a hailstorm which seriously damaged the crops. The yield was only 30 per cent of the average. Consequently, when the summer cultivation of 1950 approached, the village was short of both food for the people and the animals. But the government was watching the situation closely and came to the aid of the Ming Ho people. Through the consumer cooperative in the village, it placed 66,540 catties of foodstuffs at their disposal. A rural credit committee was set up by the peasants for investigation and allocation of the grant. It was through this help that Ming Ho was able to pass through a most anxious period and concentrate on its production, so that the fields would produce their normal quotas.

We found that similar concern is exercised by the government of the Northeast districts for the families of soldiers and revolutionary martyrs. These people have their own houses, plenty of food, new clothes and animals. As the economic level of the villages rises, so does the status of these families. For example, in Yung Kwei Village there are 25 soldiers' families. Of these, 21 families were hired farmers before land reform. After land reform, one family has reached the rich peasant class and the remaining 20 have become middle peasants. The others retained their previous status of middle peasants, or they have moved up into the rich peasant group. In all cases where sending members of the family into the armed forces causes a shortage of labor or hardship of any kind, the government and Communist Party are ready to step in and ease the burdens.

Thus, the peasants of the Northeast realize that they have support from every side, in normal times and in times of trouble. This has a direct and invigorating effect upon the level of production.

Funds Left Over After Taxes and Expenses

It is a most pleasant fact that nowhere in the rural Northeast are there to be found hungry, frozen or sad-faced people. On the contrary, it is the normal situation to find beaming farmers and their families with three-layer new clothing—new surface material, new padding and new lining. It also is normal to have peasants tell you that for the first time in their lives they have surplus grain and other supplies on hand and cash in the bank. This means that the elevation of the standard of living is practically taking place right before our eyes, that the peasants have their own wealth after paying taxes and providing for their daily living and that of their animals. It proves that by working for the New China, the peasants also are working for themselves.

After the bumper autumn harvest of 1950 and due to the fair sales and purchasing policies of the cooperatives and state trading organs, the estimates place the grain surplus in the hands of the peasants at 4 million tons. This is double their 1949 surplus. In addition, it is reported that the savings deposits in the Northeast increased 7.5 times in 1950 over 1949, these including the deposits of the farmers. All of this indicates the progressively increasing purchasing power of the peasants and their families. According to preliminary estimates of the Northeast General Cooperative Office, the prospects for 1951 are that this will increase 60 per cent above the 1950 mark.

The record of how the peasants use their rising purchasing power in regard to cloth is interesting. In 1949 they bought 4,000,000 bolts. But in 1950 the sales jumped 125 per cent as they purchased a total of 9,020,000 bolts. Not only that, but the peasants' buying habits changed.

The time has come in the Northeast when the demand is not merely for cloth. Before, either blue or black would satisfy, just as long as it was cloth. But now the farmers feel prosperous. They want to dress up, so they demand cloth with designs and color.

One of them said, "Color is life and we have just begun to learn what life is."

It is obvious that the increased purchasing power is a vital stimulant for further advances in farm production. It is also obvious that this situation is responsible for stimulating industrial production. The demands of the peasants extend beyond their personal needs. For example, government economic organs in the Northeast have placed orders for tens of thousands of farm implement sets to satisfy the peasants' requirements. The demand for all sorts of goods is on the rise and this focuses attention on the consumer co-operatives. Therefore it is necessary to understand the role of consumer cooperatives in the rural economy.

The Role of Consumer Cooperatives

Liu Yin-lan, manager of the Ming Ho Village Cooperative Society said, "The Cooperative Society must rely upon the demands and will of the people, these being linked with production."

This is a lesson derived from experience. Liu Yin-lan and many other cooperative managers had to learn it the hard way, since previous to the liberation they had had practically no contact with such organizations. When many of the cooperatives started, they operated merely for quick turnover of goods, for short duration and for profit only. They handled commodities such as superstitious goods, cosmetics and other luxury merchandise. Some cooperative societies did not even have shares. The village people merely pooled their money obtained as the fruits of their struggle with the landlords. They felt this was money above what they would ordinarily expect, therefore, it could be used as a sort of "gamble" on the cooperative. This shows they had no correct conception of cooperatives and therefore no attachment to them. They were thought of as mere passing fancies. In some cases the peasants had the idea that since they were members of the cooperative, they did not have to pay their bills on time, that it was something like a family debt that could wait a bit longer.

It was only after much education and help from the Communist Party and district cooperative bureaux that these misunderstandings were eliminated. District leaders had to start from the very beginning of the cooperative lesson, teaching what the responsibilities of a board of directors are, how to hold meetings, what to discuss and decide in those meetings, how to investigate accounts and so forth.

After such help, the cooperatives began to stock the basic necessities of the peasants. This aroused interest in them and the farmers began to join in great numbers. Then the managements began to understand that their societies were not only stores, but also centers for solving problems of production and livelihood. When this took place, the people really moved to become associated, so that hardly a person in the village was outside of the cooperative.

An example of how this actually works out can be seen in the experience of the Ming Ho Village Cooperative Society.

This cooperative was completely rebuilt. After they learned the correct principles of operation, they sold shares, allowing the poor peasants to pay for theirs in installments. Then responsible officials were elected and regular meeting, examination and auditing systems established. The staff was paid by loaning them labor to work their land while they attended to the cooperative business, and providing them clothing and food according to a definite monthly budget. All of this was teaching the peasants modern business methods. As well, it provided another lesson in democratic administration since practically the whole village parti-cipated in the decisions of the cooperative.

After these reforms, the Ming Ho Cooperative prospered and developed. It eventually became strong enough to buy and sell the farmers' produce. This saved the farmers so much trouble and the results were so satisfactory, that it solidified their faith in the co-operative. In addition, the cooperative made a profit and in June 1950, when the accounts were closed and settled, the shareholders received dividends equal to 25 per cent of the total capital.

Under Liu Yin-lan's able direction, the Ming Ho Cooperative Society began to thoroughly integrate it-self into the life and economy of the village. To illustrate, in the spring of 1950 there were not enough seeds for the planting. Liu called a meeting of the executive committee immediately. They calculated the amount of seeds required. They then sold some of their stock to purchase seeds and these they distributed on a short term loan basis, on the very easiest of terms. This saved the whole planting schedule.

Still other ways in which the cooperative society helped the Ming Ho peasants were by anticipating their needs and stocking the correct farm implements ahead of time, or by providing food on loan against a harvest, to protect the harvest when the farmers ran short of food and were faced with the prospect of having to eat the unripe crop.

With the absolute backing of the people, now the Ming Ho Cooperative Society has taken an advanced step. In addition to its other services, it has begun to participate in the rural economy as a financial organization. It has set up a deposit and loan section. On the one hand, the society will supply the needs of the peasants. On the other hand, through this new section, it will help the peasants to loan out their surplus funds and grain at interest. This will promote production, which in turn will stimulate trade, thus solving many of the village's economic difficulties with its own resources.

This is a new trend, a mass credit organization which will move otherwise stagnant capital under the auspices and protection of the larger financial organizations, such as the Northeast People's Bank. To date it has had initial success, with the Communist Party members once again taking the lead by depositing their grain and funds with the society, and the deposit and loan section solving all sorts of problems, including personal ones, which would otherwise impede production.

Thus, the consumer cooperatives by adding banking to their other duties have further cemented their relationship with the people. They have enhanced their contribution to the reconstruction of the rural economy and New China.

Cooperatives have become a great power in the life of the Northeast peasants. In 1950 their membership increased by 127 per cent. Their retail trade increased by 494 per cent, exceeding their plan by 25.8 per cent. Their purchases increased by 394 per cent over 1949, exceeding their plan by 7.4 per cent. We can see by these figures that consumer cooperatives not only aid the peasants, but they also are a momentous factor in urban-rural trade exchange, an essential factor in reconstruction of our country.

The Villages and Political Advancement

With the basic economic situation changed by land reform, the way was opened for the peasants of the Northeast villages to change the entire political environment and structure. In place of the oppression of former times, there is freedom for the masses. In the place of tyranny centralized in the hands of the landlords and their bullies, there is power in the hands of the masses. These changes are no less impressive than the advances made in production and are, of course, inseparably linked with them.

Perhaps the most outstanding single fact in this connection is the broadness of participation in the village political life, the fact that all segments, with the exception of the former landlords, are actively engaged in running the government. Most villages were divided into sections, with a definite number of families in each section. These nominated candidates for the election to the village people's representatives' conference. After the elections, the representatives' conference elected a smaller committee.

The village committee is the operational level of the government. Within it, the division of labor is clearly defined, with each member in charge of one section. While it varies from village to village, these are usually the sections: Office of the Village Head; Office of the Village Deputy Head; Civil Affairs; People's Court or Mediation Office; Production Office;

Militia; Public Security; Education and Culture; Public Health; Finance and Food. Usually the Village Committee also has a secretary attached to it.

The village people's representatives' conference usually meets three times a year, but more frequently if it is necessary. Often special meetings are called to mobilize the farmers to attack certain problems. For example, in September 1950 many of the village people's representatives' conferences were expanded into general meetings to plan an efficient wheat harvest. From these mass meetings, a Wheat-Harvesting Committee was elected and charged with responsibility for the harvest, inspection of the work, keeping of the accounts, storage, delivery and other work.

People's delegates' conferences are also called to make concrete plans for the season's and the year's work. These conferences inspect the progress of the plans decided upon and they report directly to the villagers on the results. Still other meetings are called to exchange experiences of production and government as well as to make awards of honor or to criticize and issue penalties in connection with the production effort.

The most valuable weapon of criticism and self-criticism is greatly developed in village government. It is responsible for uncovering many defects and deviations from the government's policies. For example, in some villages it was found that certain farmers had been deprived of their citizenship on the basis of misjudgments as to their class background. In other instances it was found that the policy of protecting the middle peasants was abused and landlords escaped the people's judgment. Both of these mistakes, and many others, have been vigorously attacked and corrected through criticism and self-criticism.

The convention of the village government representatives elects district representatives, while these elect the hsien governments. The process is continued up to and including provincial government. On each level the main characteristic of the government is consultation with the masses. This has most gratifying results, not only where it concerns domestic and local issues, but also where international problems are concerned. For example, the villagers have a clear conception of the world struggle for peace and they demand to be declared as part of that struggle. 80 per cent of Yung Kwei Village signed the Stockholm Peace Appeal, and out of 1,470 people in Ming Ho Village, 1,101 put their names down for peace, just to indicate the results in two villages.

Each village has its own armed force, organized by the peasants themselves and controlled by them through the Village Committee. Both men and women participate. The duties of this militia are to protect the harvests and the fields, to guard against fires and the intrigues of landlords, or the sabotage of imperialist agents and Kuomintang remnants.

Another indication of the political development of the Northeast peasants is their record of voluntary enlistments in the People's Liberation Army. Thousands upon thousands have entered its ranks. There is probably not a village in the Northeast which is not represented in the P.L.A.

Since production and politics cannot be separated, neither can you separate the participation of the members of the Communist Party and the Youth League in them. It is these progressive elements who on every occasion in both spheres exert the greatest effort, make the biggest sacrifice and deliver the severest self-criticism. Their proportion to the village population is small, but their influence is great.

I have already illustrated how the Northeast peasant masses follow and are thankful for their leadership. Now I would like to relate a story which demonstrates that they also treasure this leadership.

Before the liberation, it was the practice to name villages after the biggest and most powerful landlord. Now that practice has been changed. Today villages are named after people's heroes.

All through this report I have been mentioning the name of Yung Kwei Village. There once was a man by that name, Man Yung-kwei. He was a hired laborer from the time he was 12 years old, but from his earliest days he knew there must be a better life than the one he was leading. Yung-kwei was an inquisitive person and he found that way, with the guidance of the Communist Party. Before the liberation of his village he organized the farmers, and after, he was elected the head of the Liberated Peasants' Association. In that position he led the struggle against the landlords and to put the fallow fields to cultivation so the poor could eat.

Yung-kwei labored tirelessly for his village, encouraging the peasants to produce more, associating this with their fight to uproot feudalism from every aspect of their lives. He became one of the leaders of his village and then he became the head of the whole district. At that time he also became a member of the Communist Party.

This most selfless man lived as frugally when he was a district head as when he was chairman of his local peasants' association. And he worked just as hard. When the harvest time came, he was taken ill, but Yung-kwei refused to accept sick leave. He worked on and on, fighting off his tiredness and the pain which racked him. His disease went from bad to worse until finally his spirit could keep him going no longer. He died after having given his all for the people.

Later at a mass meeting, peasants Liu King-shan, Yang Kun and others made a proposal. It is recorded that they said, "Our village is known as Hwang Yu. Before, the landlords could exercise their might and authority over us. But with the arrival of the Communist Party, our late district head, Man Yung-kwei, led us to destroy feudalism and he provided us with a foundation, a foundation of "how to become rich". It is he who has led us to the road of liberation. He was of our class and we must do something to remember him. We suggest, therefore, that the name of Hwang-Yu be changed to Yung Kwei Village in honor of our beloved Comrade Man Yung-kwei." This resolution met with the unanimous approval of all the villagers, who valued Man Yung-kwei for himself and for the party he represented.

*   *   *

Another indication of the advancement of the Northeast peasants politically is the way the women of the villages have risen in status. They now take an active part in every walk of life. For their labor in production, they receive the same credit and equal money with the men. Their representation on the village councils ranges as high as 45 per cent of the total members, as we found it in Yung Kwei Village. They hold responsible positions in economic circles, culture and health. Generally we found the Northeast peasant women developing into the new type of Chinese person, ridding themselves of all feudal holdovers, and helping their menfolk and the older people to do the same.

Advances in Welfare and Culture

We thus see that the land reform has transformed the rural life of the Northeast economically and politically. This has, of course, been reflected in the welfare and cultural activities in the villages.

In the field of health, great progress has been made. Most of the villages have three inoculation campaigns each year, against typhoid, cholera and bubonic plague, and one vaccination drive against smallpox. Not only are all of these services free, but in most villages they in themselves represent a 100 per cent increase in medical service for the people. Previously, under the Japanese imperialists and the Kuomintang, the villagers had no contact whatsoever with modern medicine.

All of the medical work is carried out from the clinics in the district centers. The clinics themselves give free medical service or charge nominal fees in special cases. In addition, many places have medical cooperatives set up by the peasants. These supply medicines at low prices and help promote the rural medical work generally. Sungkiang Province already has 100 of these cooperatives in operation.

The question of village midwives has been dealt with excellently. In order for them to practise, they have to undergo training in modern methods at the district centers. In this way, the old-fashioned midwives are retrained and the new ones are trained in the correct procedure from the very beginning.

The policy in most villages is to allow mothers one month's rest after the delivery of their babies. During this period they are given special provisions of rice, white flour, eggs and sugar.

The result of the training and retraining of midwives and the special treatment for mothers is a most heartening drop in the infant mortality rate. In Yung Kwei Village, for instance, within 1950, forty-four babies were born. Three of these infants died, yet in looking back to the past for comparison, this death rate is negligible. Now the health authorities in Yung Kwei and its district are striving to reduce infant deaths to the minimum. This they propose to do by exercising even greater care for infants and continuing to insist that all midwives adhere to the policy of not making deliveries without the basic equipment of umbilical scissors, alcohol and sterilized raw cotton.

As for other medical practitioners, the health authorities in the Northeast allow old-style Chinese doctors to continue practising, but they are constantly encouraging them to obtain more medical knowledge and training. In the meantime, as more qualified personnel become available, they are assigned to work for the peasants.

We found that the peasants as a whole are taking up the advice given to them regarding sanitation and are applying it to their daily lives, and to their cooking methods. Also, due to their improved livelihood, they can afford better food, clothing and shelter. Consequently, the whole standard of health has noticeably risen. The people of the Northeast have become a robust people, flushed with the looks of good health and bursting with energy.

* * *

The same progress has been registered in cultural and educational activities. In the past, practically all villagers were illiterate. Mail was either unheard of or the cause of a great occasion. To get a letter read or written was a major task. Now, almost every village in the Northeast has its own primary school, serving the children of the farmers and the farmers themselves. Last year, 2,673 more of these schools were established.

The peasants of Hu Chia Tien Tze, at the same time they rebuilt their village from the ruins, also built the first school-house they had ever had. 70 per cent of the school-age children attend, and this figure is increasing every year. The fact is that in all of the Northeast, practically all of the children of school-age can obtain proper education at this time.

As in every village, the adults of Hu Chia Tien Tze also make extensive use of the school. During winter sessions, over 700 adult pupils are registered, and of these 300 are women. Several of the adults who before did not know how to write their names, at present recognize as many as 1,000 characters. Most of the people in the village can also do simple sums and simple writing. The progress of the youngsters is marked by the fact that some of them have begun to advance to senior primary and middle school.

The village of Yung Kwei has a similar story to tell. They have 100 per cent of their youngsters in school. Just as important, upon the demand of the peasant masses, they have raised the school age to 17 years, so as to spread the benefit of the school further. For those over 17, they attend the winter literacy sessions.

From these illustrations, we can see that the peasants of the Northeast have been liberated mentally and are thirsting for knowledge and culture. This has become an era of enlightenment and advancement. As it proceeds, sharp inroads are made against the old, retarding customs of life and thinking. A prime example of this is the fact that the old superstitions have lost their hold on the people. In Yung Kwei Village we found that the custom of worshipping the various gods had been completely abolished. What is more, there is no longer the waste of money on buying incense and other superstitious goods, nor the waste of time worshipping idols during the New Year festival. The peasants of the Northeast have put these things where they belong, in the history books and museums They realize there is only one power, and that is the power of the people. Such is the progress of the peasants of our Northeast.

The Cities and Reconstruction

Founded on the increasing agricultural production of the countryside, the cities of the Northeast are being rapidly developed as the base of New China. For it is in these cities, located in the midst of the country's richest resources, that we find a comparatively modern industrial concentration. It is from this foundation of heavy industry—the iron and steel mills, the power plants and the factories which make machines to build other machines—that you derive the real importance of the Northeast. It is when you see the new masters of China, the aroused industrial working class, on the job, overcoming difficulties and utilizing the Northeast plant capacity, that you understand nothing will prevent the Chinese people from realizing our cherished dream of industrialization.

The recent history of Northeast China's industrial plant is one of remodeling and rebuilding. It had to be remodeled from its colonial character under Japanese and puppet rule to one that served first the Liberation War and then to improve the people's livelihood, to make the cities aid in the economic reconstruction of the villages.

It had to be rebuilt from the destruction wrought by the Japanese and the Kuomintang as each saw the mark of defeat on their vile plans. According to Kao Tsung--min, Vice-Chairman of the Northeast People's Government, during the Kuomintang control alone, from 50 to 70 per cent of the machinery and equipment was destroyed and there were attacks upon and killings of skilled technical personnel to intimidate and scatter them. Furthermore, not a single major railway bridge was left intact.

It is due to the increased productivity resulting from land reform, and the reliance upon the working

class in the cities that the industrial capacity of the
Northeast has been gradually restored and put on the
road to complete rehabilitation and further development.
Northeast industry has not only fulfilled its duties
toward our People's Liberation Army and the peasants,
but it has also accumulated both funds for economic
construction and experience in large-scale production.
Since 1949, it has developed in a series of great leaps.
In 1950 alone, the total investment of the Northeast
People's Government in industrial construction amounted to 40 per cent of its budget, 3.6 per cent above the
plan. This investment resulted in equipment expansion
which ranged from 10 to 60 per cent, and in some individual plants reached as high as 800 per cent. The total
floor space of new factory buildings and warehouses
constructed or repaired in 1950 amounted to 870,000
square meters. At the same time, workers' dwellings,
hospitals, sanatoria, nurseries, clubs and other institutions increased by 1,560,000 square meters.

The total value of 1950 industrial output by the
state-owned factories was 117.3 per cent of the 1949
figure, while the number of workers on the job over the
entire Northeast increased by 35.2 per cent. In the
meantime, the purchasing power of the city people increased 20.5 per cent last year over 1949, giving further
impetus to both trade and industrial expansion.

The People's Plants

In this report I will comment only on several of
the state-owned plants of the Northeast and give a
few of my impressions as my party inspected them.

The Harbin Railroad Repair Factory has a history of 47 years and now consists of 19 branch factories in addition to the main headquarters. Its regular work is to repair and inspect trains. Not only have the workers carried out their appointed tasks, always over-fulfilling their plan, but they have retrieved many locomotives from the junk pile, some of which have become famous for their endurance. One of these was named after Vice-Chairman Chu Teh.

The Harbin Factory in addition has been called upon by our country to do work over and above its regular duties. In fact, these extra duties exceed the ordinary work by one-third. For instance, when the bridges over the Chiamusze, Sungari and Laling Rivers were being replaced, the factory was given the task of making the bridge frames. This required the reinstallation of a three-ton electric furnace for making steel. After five nights and days of intense work, the workers, technicians and engineers completed the job, several days ahead of schedule. Later the Harbin Factory completed an 80-ton double-armed bridge-layer, which will be a great help to the future bridge-building and repairing in China.

*　　*　　*

It can be truthfully said that the Hsiao Fung Man Power Plant was built with the blood of the Chinese people. Its construction was begun in 1937 by the Japanese. They forced thousands of workers to do this job and mercilessly oppressed them. The result was that by 1945 only 29 per cent of the work was finished. However, the cost in lives to complete even that much was tremendous. Some estimates place the death rate as high as ten thousand Chinese workers.

Just before the liberation, the Kuomintang sent a group of soldiers to destroy the power plant. However, due to the dexterity of the workers, the marauders were fooled into destroying only some minor parts, leaving the main equipment intact

After the liberation, the workers adopted the slogan, "No Stoppage of the Electricity Supply". To make a fact out of the words, the workers and cadres have been laboring without a let-up, repairing machinery, rebuilding dykes and maintaining a "no major accident" record. Now Hsiao Fung Man produces electricity for the people, for the New China.

*   *   *

Perhaps the industrial enterprise with the longest history and best known in the Northeast is the Anshan Iron and Steel Corporation. We learned that as early as 1,300 years ago, the Koreans smelted iron at Anshan. At that time the Kao Chu Li Kingdom of the Koreans occupied what is today the Liaotung Peninsula.

In 1933, the Japanese invaders took over the works that had grown up in Anshan and expanded the equipment and production for their imperialist purposes. However, they used manpower instead of machinery, because it was cheaper to exploit the Chinese workers. Therefore, they had a laboring force as large as 170,000.

When the Kuomintang took the plant over in 1945, it had been seriously damaged. They did manage to get one furnace producing steel, however, and had about 10,000 workers on the job. At the time of liberation, though, in February 1948, most of the workers were scattered.

The People's Government set about reviving this wounded giant. The cadres called the workers back, using as a basic force those activists who had previously withdrawn with the people's army, or those who were organized and left behind to try and protect the plant. From this group was born a great labor enthusiasm which resulted in many sensational accomplishments, including the raising of steel production to over 136 per cent of the scheduled output.

There are now thousands of workers at the plant and many of the most complicated jobs are in the hands of Chinese technicians and engineers, positions they were once forbidden to hold by the Japanese.

While going through the giant steelworks, the unending thrills of organized, social production made me speechless. I could only keep in my mind the future of the Chinese people, as represented by the making of that iron and steel.

I saw the immense open hearths where the hardworking steelmen were tapping the furnaces. Peering through special glasses, I witnessed steel being made. Cranes rumbled overhead, shrill whistles shut out all other sound, and engines thundered past. The steel furnace door was opened and its one brilliant light reminded me of the story of Cyclops, the one-eyed demon. The steel was poured from huge buckets and this caused mammoth fireworks which lit the whole sky. "There go China's sinews," passed through my mind.

Inspecting Anshan gave me other thoughts. Many times I have heard that China needed outside technicians and could not do anything for herself. Of course, in our undeveloped condition, we do need technical help. But as this problem came to mind, the solution also came. It was spoken quietly and with firm confidence. Comrade Wen Liang-hsien, head of the iron-smelting plant and formerly an iron-worker in the old liberated areas, said, "If only we fully rely upon the workers and learn modestly, I am certain that we can properly operate modern plants."

As I left the Anshan Iron and Steel Corporation, there was no doubt in my mind at all that Chinese workers will one day run that plant completely and the many others like it that New China will erect.

I could go on giving the history and descriptions of the Kirin Paper Mill, the Dairen Dockyards and of the other industrial projects which we saw, but these examples should prove sufficient to demonstrate that our Northeast is a budding industrial power, and that the workers have taken control in a manner which befits the masters of the land.

The Importance of Soviet Help

Until now, in recording the industrial progress of the Northeast, I have not made mention of the part which was played in this advancement by the technicians and workers of the Soviet Union. This was done with a purpose. In the first place, our Soviet friends have so generously given us the benefit of their experience, this display of internationalism deserves a special section. In the second place, their role in our reconstruction has been so great and vital on all levels of production, that it should be set down in some detail.

The Soviet technicians and workers have brought to China a treasure of know-how in solving practical problems of all sizes. They have brought with them a great knowledge in the application of the highest science. They have brought with them a rich experience of working in behalf of the people. Many of them participated in the early days of reconstruction after the October Socialist Revolution. All of them have done valiant work in the building of Socialism and the preparation for Communism in the U.S.S.R. Therefore, the conditions we meet in China and the obstacles we have to face, they have met and overcome before. Their assignment and greatest joy is to help the Chinese people use this experience to build the New China.

Everywhere in the Northeast where Soviet technicians and workers are on the job, we found the work progressing in close harmony between them and the Chinese workers. Our people call them "Big Brother". I recall when inspecting the Harbin Factory, the Director of the plant, Comrade Chang Hung-shu, earnestly remarked that he wanted to be a primary school student in learning from the Soviet comrades. Vice Director of the factory, Khilgevich, pleasantly smiled and spoke glowingly of the progress that his co-worker was making. This mutual respect is a universal characteristic of Sino-Soviet cooperation.

There is no question that a great deal of the desire to learn from the Soviet workers is due to their attitude toward work. In the Harbin Factory, we were introduced to a Soviet worker who had been elected a labor model. His name is Polokin, a 75-year-old man who is head of the Steam-Hammer Department. What he told us can best express this attitude. He said, "Everybody has his good friend. Mine is the steam-hammer. The most important thing for a worker is to love and take care of his tools. Because if the tools don't work, we have to stop work too. This would be a loss to our country. All these years, therefore, I have loved my steam-hammer as my best friend."

This love of labor and the tools which create wealth for the people is accompanied by a passion for accuracy and science in both management and operation. "Every little detail is important to our Soviet Comrades", the Chinese workers commented. "Nothing is done unless it is accurately calculated first," they added.

An example was cited in the Anshan plant. Plans were drawn up in September 1949 to completely restore a large furnace by August 1950. However, upon meticulously inspecting both the plans and the conditions of the furnace, the Soviet technicians recommended that repairs be begun immediately and predicted that it would be ready for use within the year. This was met with skepticism by the old engineers, but the Soviet technicians countered with their experience of making repairs in the far worse weather conditions of Siberia. With this assurance to back them, the workers pitched in and completed the job a few days before 1949 ran out on them.

The way the Soviet workers make every possible use of science was illustrated in connection with an incident which occurred at the Hsiao Fung Man Power Plant.

One of the important pieces of work in connection with the rehabilitation of the plant was the reconstruction of the dykes, which form a lake and from which the electricity is eventually derived. This work was scheduled to last well into 1951. However, the Soviet technicians assigned to the plant recommended that the work be completed by July 15, 1950. The reason given was that the meteorological observations showed in the autumn of 1950 there would be an increase of rainfall. If the dykes were not prepared for the extra load, they would most likely sustain heavy damage and render all previous work useless.

This advice was accepted. The Sungari River rose higher last autumn than in previous years, but the dykes were ready and the work of the power plant continued in its normal course.

The examples of the help rendered by these international friends could be endlessly enumerated. So could their warm-hearted regard for the livelihood of the workers, their living quarters, their medical and sanitation conditions and their study.

Even as this is being written, I think back on the genuineness of those Soviet friends, of the self-sacrifice of people like Port Master Novikov of Dairen, who was head of the Leningrad port during the last war and whose only son was killed liberating Berlin. We visited several of these comrades in their simple but neat quarters and learned their life stories. After getting to know them, I could see why production records are constantly being broken. When I read that efficiency for steel refining was upped 35 per cent, that the time for coke refining was reduced from 21 to 16.5

hours, that in all Northeast coalmines production went up from 20 to 30 per cent after Soviet methods were introduced, I have a good idea of the efforts the Soviet technicians put into their work, side by side with their Chinese comrades.

The New Chinese Worker

The same application of Soviet science to industrial operation has been made to management systems in the Northeast.   This has made it possible to institute reasonable wage systems based on "piece work". Along with the guidance of the labor unions and the Communist Party, the new system has stimulated a most vital innovation movement among the workers. This movement has produced a new type of Chinese worker, a working class vanguard which thinks only in terms of our country's advancement. In the cities they parallel the labor heroes in the villages. Together they forge our New China.

Just to take one industrial project as an example, I will cite some figures concerning the Harbin Factory. On its honor rolls you will find the name Pang Hsi-hsun. This worker invented an iron mould that not only increased production from 350 to 1,500 units daily, but lifted the quality from 50 per cent perfects to 90 per cent.

Take a look a little further along the list and you will come to the name of Tuan Shang-chien. He invented two new methods, one connected with the rolling of metals which increased efficiency six times, and the other was an iron-pressing machine which released 15 workers for other labor and increased production in the shop by 280 per cent.

In the whole Harbin Factory, 1950 saw the adoption of 320 innovations suggested by workers. Through these, ¥368,400,000 was saved from January through September 1950 alone. By utilizing waste materials, ¥5,260,000,000 more was saved. In addition, waste steel is being used to build 1,000 square meters of office space, a small hospital, a nursery and 2,000 square meters of new workshops. In the first six months of 1950, production was increased throughout the entire factory by 30 per cent while the management staff was greatly reduced through using Soviet management systems and a more scientific division of labor.

These are all explanations why the Harbin Factory had 387 model workers, 64 honored heroes of labor, 658 superior workers and 398 advanced workers, all elected by the workers themselves. These are all explanations why 28 first-class cadres were selected from among section heads or chiefs of branch factories and sent to other more important jobs and why the present section heads and branch chiefs have risen from the workers' ranks.

This is emancipated labor, following and learning from the Soviet example. This is an atmosphere which produces workers like Chao Kuo-yu and his record-breaking movement, which spreads into every segment of industry until 21,740 new records have been established and workers by the tens of thousands have participated, individually and collectively.

The Effect on Private Industry

The land reform, the great revival of Northeast state industry and the workers' enthusiasm have been a great stimulant for the entire Northeast economy. This includes private industry. During the time of the Japanese invaders and the Kuomintang marauders, private industry was either allowed to decline or purposely pushed out of the market. The People's Government has reversed this condition. Private industry is now encouraged to revive itself by facing toward the rural areas and thereby aiding the economic reconstruction of village economy. Industrialists are helped in the following ways:

A.   Solving the problem of finding a market for their goods. The government organs place orders for manufactured goods, or give the private factories semi-finished goods to process.

B.   Solving the problems of both labor and capital. The government encourages the signing of labor-capital contracts which take into consideration the interests of both, and also encourages the establishment of labor-capital consultation committees on production. The experience to date has been that this policy has increased production and motivated "cut-down waste" movements among the workers of Northeast China's private industry.

C.   The government has systematically aided in obtaining raw materials, power and capital.

D.   The government has constantly improved the taxation system of appraisal and levy.

E. The government has strengthened the work of the industrial-commercial associations in the Northeast.

The result of these policies has been that private industry has begun to move ahead in its development, especially those plants which are directly connected with the state economy, such as machine building, iron and steel works and so forth. In Shenyang (Mukden), for instance, in January, 1950, there were only 596 ironwork shops. But by the middle of the year, they had increased to 1,014 shops and the number of workers had doubled. In this same period, Shenyang's private industry saw its capital investment increase from ¥94.6 billion to ¥171.4 billion. The value of its output during the third quarter of 1950 rose by 23.2 per cent compared to the first quarter. To grasp the complete picture, according to Vice-Chairman Kao Kang's recent report, Shenyang's private industrial enterprises, between December, 1949, and November, 1950, increased by 30.2 per cent and the number of workers increased by 32.4 per cent. Since this is the situation in the key industrial city of the Northeast, we can see that private industry over the entire territory has revived in step with the reconstruction of state industry, as fostered by the government's policies of linking both the rural and the city economies.

The Cities and Political Advancement

After the liberation of the Northeast cities, they had to be entirely reorganized politically. The basic government before had been the vicious "pao chia" system* which hung like a yoke on the necks of the people. This burden was lifted for all time with the institution of the district government system. This method puts the responsibility of governing into the hands of the people. They participate directly in the selection of their representatives through their lane and street associations, or as members of organizations. For the first time in the history of Northeast cities, they are receiving direction which guides their development in favor of the masses.

The district government elects representatives who then attend the city people's representatives' conference. The city governments are elected by these meetings. They forward the opinions of the masses, discuss and pass the laws and elect the officials.

In studying the history of these conferences, the interesting fact to note is that as they meet more and more frequently, they become more and more representative of the people. The number of delegates increases and the proportion of delegates from the various circles is gradually adjusted so that representation accurately reflects the composition of the city's population. In Changchun, for instance, the first city-wide conference had seventy delegates in attendance. By the time the fifth session was held, the number had grown to 310 representatives.

The role of the Communist Party and the New Democratic Youth League members in the cities has

---

* Pao Chia System, was used by the Japanese and the Kuomintang. It made families in a certain street or district responsible for each other's actions and all responsible to the local Japanese and Kuomintang officials.

been as important as it has been in the villages. In production, the Party and League members have constantly been in the forefront, fearing no sacrifice. There is the example of Chao Kwei-lan, the woman Communist who lost her arm protecting a Dairen factory from an explosion.

The actions of the Party and League members have been guided by the directives issued by Chairman Mao, the Communist Party and the Central People's Government. These have been: to preserve the means of production when taking them over; to revive them by overcoming difficulties; to make every possible dollar available for production; to train cadres; and finally, to struggle for the realization of China's economic rehabilitation and industrial construction.

The Communist Party and the New Democratic Youth League have also taken the lead in awakening the people politically. The result: Northeast masses have stood at the head of the nation in expressing our wrath at the American aggressors for bombing our cities. They have the gains of our new life in their hands. The future advances are within their grasp. Therefore, they have been the first to let the Americans know our determination to resist and defeat their imperialist attack on Korea, China and world peace.

This unequivocal stand of the Northeast city masses in the lead of the nation attests to their rapid political development.

Welfare and Culture in the Cities

One of the developments of the Northeast which impressed me most was the great strides that have been made in the fields of welfare, culture and education for the city working class.

Closest to the workers' lives are the measures which have been taken relative to the safety and sanitary conditions in the factories, mines and mills. These have recently been very much extended and improved. The Shenyang factories can be used as an illustration of these advances.

Although there are in Shenyang (Mukden) 204 factories under government and public ownership alone, safety and sanitation had not been very satisfactorily developed in preceding years. When the time came for the People's Government to take action in this connection, two factories were first singled out for experimentation. The results from these were gradually expanded to the other plants and eventually, in 1950, the Factory Security and Health Committee was formed. With the support of the city administration, and in conjunction with the Bureaux of Labor and Health, the trade unions, the police and medical specialists, the work was made to penetrate deeply into the entire industrial structure of Shenyang, both public and private. As the work progressed, the interest of the working masses of the city was aroused and the struggle for safety and sanitation on the job became a regular movement.

The chief mission of the Security and Health Committee was to study and improve the machinery, and to delve into all the problems related to security and sanitation installations. It was also to make statistical studies, promote education within the plants, and to take preventive measures to avoid industrial accidents.

Based on this, the committee began a thorough inspection of the factories and plants so as to understand them completely. At the same time, a medical examination of the workers and a health card system was started. Simultaneous with this, the establishment of clinics began in those plants which did not have them. While this was underway, the most important questions were attacked. These dealt with poor ventilation in most of the plants, improper lighting, high temperature and high humidity, dust and other occupational hazards injurious to the workers. Suggestions have been forwarded and tried out in many of the plants, and as the solutions to the problems are found to be reliable, they will be applied on an extended scale. Additionally, work is advancing in taking sanitary conditions to factory kitchens and dining halls, to the dormitories, bathrooms and latrines. In those places where these welfare facilities do not exist, steps are being taken to install them as early as possible.

As far as safety measures are concerned, these have been enhanced through a new system of responsibility. Under this system groups of workers have specific responsibilities for their machines. Such responsibility may even extend to entire sections of a factory, mine or mill, depending on the industry and the layout of the plant. It is the duty of the workers to eliminate defects that might lead to accidents. The management, in turn, is responsible for ensuring that the defective machine parts are replaced or repaired or other action taken to remove the danger. Contracts are signed between labor and management specifying in detail the responsibility of each party. In addition, safety committees are set up and regular campaigns are held in safety education. Every new safety measure is usually submitted to the workers for discussion before being implemented. This system has been a great success in the plants which have used it.

Safety and sanitation work is complicated in a big industrial city and must proceed carefully. The Factory Security and Health Committee of Shenyang is, therefore, progressing according to a definite program, first concentrating on the bigger factories where it will obtain experience, and then gradually pushing the work into the smaller plants. The greatest gains are still ahead but, in any event, this entire program is an indication that the People's Government recognizes the necessity for such efforts.

In other Northeast cities, there have been advances which extend health measures for workers much beyond the plant. In Dairen, our party visited the sanitorium for the workers of the Far East Electricity Company, one of the industrial installations just completely turned over by the Soviet Union. The sanitorium is a modern construction, nestling at the foot of a mountain and facing the sea. It makes a beautiful picture, surrounded by green pines, red maples and cherry trees. Before, it was a villa for Japanese militarists, but now it belongs to China's working people.

This sanitorium draws its expenses from the labor insurance fund of the company. Each worker who rests there continues to draw his salary but he also gets a regular daily allowance. Model workers, those with good production records and factory cadres rest here in the soothing surroundings, enjoying the good food and the recreational facilities. Every two weeks 100 new workers arrive to take advantage of this opportunity to build up their health. After the two week stay, they generally register gains in weight.

Taking the Northeast as a whole, such health measures in behalf of workers have spread to the point where at present there are several hundred hospitals, clinics and sanitoria for their use in the territory. This is a sign of the times, the time when the workers are the masters of our land and the new society enables them to make every possible advance on the road to good life.

In order to accomplish the production tasks set for the Northeast, and to elevate the health of the people generally, the same care and attention is given to the public health programs. Despite the shortage of health personnel and lack of material facilities, the Northeast health workers have succeeded in carrying out the policy of "Prevention First, Treatment Second". This success is due to the method of fostering cooperation between the government and individuals, organizing the medical workers in the cities and mobilizing the masses to join the campaign for health.

Great reliance is placed on the rank and file people of the cities. In Shenyang, for example, over eleven thousand health activists were cultivated. They led the campaigns to clean up garbage dumps, kill flies and to do other cleaning jobs in the city.

Also important was the work done to activate the medical workers upon the principles of "Take the Medicine to the people", and make each medical worker be responsible for certain health activities in his district.

Another vital measure was to set up women and children's health centers to bring down the infant mortality rate and improve the well-being of both women and the youngsters. When I saw this work, it reminded me of the projects my own organization, the China Welfare Institute, has undertaken among the women workers of Shanghai, conducting health publicity and education, giving training in the care of children, ante- and post-natal examinations and deliveries.

When the health work in the Northeast was summarized as to the lessons learned, this was what was presented:

A. To start mass-scale health work, cooperation between the health institutions and the public security organizations is indispensable.

B. In setting up basic health organizations, training beforehand is effective and mobilizing the rank and file is essential.

C. The doctors who participate are the pillars of the health structure as they serve as the bridge between the health institutions and the activated rank and file.

D. Once the people see the significance of health work, they will demand more and carry on some of it themselves. However, guidance from all levels and constant encouragement are necessary.

We found the city people in the Northeast with the same interest as in other parts of China when it came to child-care work. They too understand the necessity for nurturing the future of China by training our youngsters from early in life. There are many nurseries in operation and their number is increasing constantly. Many of these obtain their support directly from the People's Government as well as from the labor unions and the women's organizations.

As a result of conferences on nursery work, the child-care cadres in the Northeast aim at the following goals:

A. To help the children obtain a correct conception of labor, that labor is the creation of all wealth and that they should love labor;

B. To cultivate the children's wisdom through an interesting educational program;

C. To help the children develop new morals, which consist of love for our country, for our leaders, for our people, for labor and for the property of the people;

D. To help the children obtain and maintain the best of health through education in good habits and good preventive work.

*   *   *

The advances made by the Northeast in cultural and educational work demonstrate how these fields can develop when the people come to power.

Primary schools have now grown to 34,000 and they have a student body of 4,576,111. This figure includes village youngsters. Middle schools increased 21 per cent in 1950 over 1949, and the number of students increased 38 per cent to reach 155,748 in that same period. In addition, there are 61 technical schools and there are many of what are known as "short-term" schools which especially cater to cadres from the peasant and worker class. In the Northeast there are also 16 new style higher education institutions for training technical workers and including departments or courses in finance and economics. At present there are 17,978 students in these universities and colleges.

Coinciding with the formal schooling is the massive campaign to wipe out illiteracy among the working people of the Northeast. Hundreds of thousands of workers study in the night schools, adding their numbers to the 4,500,000 peasants who attended winter school.

Naturally, all the educational activity creates a demand for printed materials. In 1950, more than 40 million volumes of new books were printed by the Hsinhua (New China) Book Store. In addition, there operates in the Northeast a far-reaching network of distributing centers for books, magazines, newspapers and other publications.

What are the results of such a promotion of knowledge and education? Take Dairen-Port Arthur as an example. Before the liberation, one-third of the population was illiterate. By 1949, at the start of the program to erase illiteracy, there were 200,000 people enrolled in the courses. Already over 50,000 have graduated. The standard for workers is to know 1,200 characters, 1,000 for ordinary citizens and for the peasants, 800 characters.

Among the children, middle school students increased 266.5 per cent over Japanese times, primary school students, 217.9 per cent. In addition, these cities now have a university with a complete course of subjects. There are also technical schools which function right in the factories and plants. The workers have a cultural palace, nine cultural institutes, 92 cultural clubs and 332 cultural centers.

A typical cultural installation is the one we visited in Dairen known as "The Workers' Home". This was in reality the home school and cultural palace of the workers of the Dairen Transporation Company, half of whom are women.

The slogan of the company is "The Factory Is the School", and this spirit of constantly promoting the work is carried into their workers' home. As the work is split into three shifts, the home is full of people all of the time. There they have their spare-time study and their technical school. They proudly tell you that both the manager of the Dairen Transportation Company and the headmaster of the school are graduates of the workers' home and from the workers' ranks.

The workers' home was set up out of the profits of their cooperative. They bought an old, dilapidated school, and with their own voluntary labor turned it into a palace. There are club rooms and recreation rooms, a playground, library, classrooms, bathrooms and a dining room. They also have a fine auditorium which can seat 800 people.

We saw many of these installations throughout our visit to the Northeast, in addition to such cultural institutes as the Oriental Culture Museum and War Historical Museum in Port Arthur. In each place the workers had taken an active part in actually constructing some section or all of the building, or were running the organization. In each place, we saw the people of New China learning and enjoying a life that just a few short years ago they could not even dream about. It made them eager to contribute more to our country's growth and prosperity. It made them determined to protect it with all the valor and love they possess.

* * *

Conclusions

To sum up the substance of the impressions I gathered from the Northeast:

The state power of imperialism, bureaucratic capital, warlordism and Kuomintang corruption has been thoroughly smashed. This has been replaced with a power that is in every respect a people's state.

This has enabled the land reform to be accomplished and consolidated. Never again will the peasants of the Northeast return to the oppressive, feudal, poverty-ridden past. They have strode out onto the road of collective effort, onto the road of New Democracy which leads to the Socialist epoch.

This has enabled the working class in the cities to release all of their creative genius. Together with the Soviet technicians, who help us in the true spirit of internationalism, they are rapidly reconstructing industry and providing a base for its future growth in the era of New Democracy, the preparatory period for the completely organized, ultra-efficient industry of the Socialist epoch.

This has enabled both peasants and workers to enjoy a constantly rising standard of living, gaining materially and in the realm of culture with giant strides. This is remoulding our alert, inventive people into the citizens of New Democracy, on their way to becoming the advanced type of person of the Socialist epoch.

As evidenced by the Northeast, New China is truly forging ahead to its glorious future.

STATEMENT ON THE FOUNDING OF THE INDIA-CHINA FRIENDSHIP ASSOCIATION

Cabled to the Founding Meeting in Bombay

May 1951

The founding of the India-China Friendship Association is an event of great importance, one which can have far-reaching effects on our two mighty lands, on Asia and the world. You are to be heartily congratulated, therefore, on taking this significant step. I wish you all possible success in fostering the growth of your organization and the growth of the exchange in culture, commerce, information and inspiration between India and People's China.

It is natural that there should be such an organization as yours. In the first instance, relationships between India and China in all phases of international life are rooted back in times of antiquity. In the second instance, not only should these relationships continue, but they take on even more significance today. Our young Republics face a world situation marked by the dying stages of imperialism and the upsurge of people's rule. In such a situation, our countries will come under attack from the imperialists, this taking many forms and shapes, from outright physical aggression to diplomatic baiting. How successfully we parry and thwart these attacks, how much of our weight we can throw on the side of peace, will mean much to the final and full-fledged emergence of people's rule in Asia and the rest of the world. Consequently, we must draw the Indian and Chinese peoples together, so that they can obtain strength from each other, so that they can defeat any enemy of the Asian peoples, so that they can contribute their full measure to the cause of world peace.

Long live the friendship of the Indian and Chinese peoples!

ON PEACEFUL COEXISTENCE

Written for "In Defence of Peace",
Journal of the World Peace Council

June 1, 1951

There is a heavy pall of international tension which hangs over us today, a tension that threatens every person on earth. Many solutions have been offered to remedy this situation, but there is only one worth consideration. That is the proposal for peaceful coexistence. This idea rules out the thought of war from the very beginning. It calls for the different economic and political systems existing side by side and competing on a peaceful basis, to let history judge which system satisfies the masses of people most efficiently and effectively.

On What Grounds Is This Concept Brought Forward?

This concept of peaceful coexistence is brought forward by all partisans of peace with the recognition that differences do exist between the various systems. It further notes that not all of these differences can be solved at once. But it is an honest offer "to meet the other fellow half-way", to work out the differences together and thereby strangle war before it ever gets started. It is an offer jointly to isolate the warmongers, to consolidate the ranks of all those who favor peace so that it may be nurtured to full-grown strength.

Therefore, the concept of peaceful coexistence is not a mere slogan or tactic, premeditatedly tossed out to dupe the unwary. It is a precious principle meant for energetic promotion and sincere implementation, a policy with which the people of the world can advance to everlasting peace and the satisfaction of all their welfare and cultural needs. Peaceful coexistence means a call for unity of action on all levels for world tranquillity.

Is Championing Peaceful Coexistence A Sign of Weakness or Strength?

In understanding the concept of peaceful coexistence, it is fundamental to recognize that it is not advocated from a position of weakness, that it is not a plea to gain some concession or time advantage. On the contrary, the idea of peaceful coexistence springs from unparalleled confidence and unswerving faith in the strength and abilities of the masses of people. This confidence in the advantage of people's rule is such that we are fully prepared to put it into peaceful competition with all others at any time. This confidence is founded in fact. There is, for example, the overwhelming success of the Soviet Union's postwar Stalin Five Year Plan, the stabilization of China's economy and her great leaps forward in reconstruction, the obvious advances that are being made in every nation, in every factory and on every farm where the people are in control.

A second indication of the strength behind the concept of peaceful coexistence is the fact that the great majority of mankind wants peace. Thus, this idea has world-wide support. Even in those places where the term "Peaceful Coexistence" is slandered along with all efforts for peace, the masses in their hearts know that war and its preparation can only profit a few, that for the people, war's only promise is poverty and sorrow. "Peaceful Coexistence" may have been kept from their sight and they may never have been allowed to hear the term, but they arrive at the same conclusion as a result of their experiences. The people associate their own struggle for a decent life with the fight for peace. They soon come to know that it is better for their government to peacefully compete and benefit the masses than to wage war and plunder them.

We see then that the concept of peaceful coexistence is based on fact and is the will of the majority of mankind. There is no other position of strength which can match this combination.

Is Peaceful Coexistence Possible Under the Present Circumstances?

Since it represents the will of the majority of mankind, there is no question that peaceful coexistence can be successfully carried out. Not only is it possible for the nations of the earth to exist and compete peacefully side-by-side, but it is also possible for them to construct an era of great cooperation. We have but to look back to the anti-fascist coalition of the last war to see the validity of this. That coalition demonstrated, for all of the differences in systems and governments, that the people of the Soviet Union, China, the United States, Great Britain and the other allies all had identical interests—to defeat imperialist reaction and to liberate the masses in every country from the fear of want. Those interests are the very same today for the same people. Thus, if it could be accomplished to win a war, it is certainly possible to form a coalition against war, based on peaceful coexistence, to settle all present-day differences in behalf of universal harmony and cooperation.

Since Peaceful Coexistence Is Possible Who Is Preventing Its Implementation?

There are certain segments of the American and British ruling circles who simply refuse to recognize this truth, who just cannot live peacefully. They have blood in their eyes and are always spoiling for a fight. Even the mildest mention of the Soviet Union, People's China or other people's countries and organizations causes them to rave in the wildest manner. These are the handful of monopolists and cartelists of Wall Street and the City, with their mouthpieces, such as the Trumans and Attlees, and their "men in the field", such as the bloodthirsty MacArthurs and Montgomeries. These are the "bosses" of the American and British people, the would-be exploiters of all mankind. These are the only ones who profit from war. These are the enemies of peaceful coexistence.

These enemies would have the world look the other way while they rip out the pages of history that detail the rape of Nanking, six million European Jews slaughtered, Seoul bombed off the map. They shout "Peace" to the high heavens and would have us believe that unceasing shiploads of arms to Europe, Western Germany and Japan are for peace, that airbases in Africa and Turkey, naval bases in Taiwan and Trieste also are for peace.

All of us know, it takes two sides to improve international relations, to ease the tensions and enhance the peace. But from the above we can see the warmongers are doing everything possible in the opposite direction. If we look to the city of Paris these days, we can observe similar indications. There the deputy foreign ministers of the Soviet Union, the United States, Great Britain and France are discussing an agenda for a proposed meeting of the four foreign ministers of those countries. We can see that one side, the side led by the United States, constantly thwarts the efforts of the conference so as to delay any decision, even to the point of refusing to accept its own proposals when the Soviet delegate agrees. In the meantime, this side effects its rearmament policy at increased speed. In this conference, and on all other fronts, the three western powers are seeking to blunt the attempts to achieve real peace. They would drive from our heads the very thought of peaceful coexistence. This makes the task of all peace partisans more difficult and doubly urgent. As the enemy strikes one blow for war, we must strike two for peace.

How Can We Defeat the Warmongers and Assure the Victory for Peaceful Coexistence?

In mobilizing the campaign for world peace, there are several factors which we must keep to the fore. The first of these is that war is unpopular with all peoples, including the German and Japanese populations, as evidenced by their protests against rearmament. The warmongers do not yet fully comprehend this opposition and do not gauge it accurately. Consequently, they will drive themselves and their forces into further impossible positions, both at home and abroad. We peace partisans must be prepared to use these errors to expose the warmongers and lead the people to struggle for peace. We must be prepared at these vital moments to unite all forces for peace to further check these bandits of destruction as they lash out in madness and desperation.

The second factor which we must take into account is the realization that the threats of warmongers cannot frighten us. The aroused Korean and Chinese peoples are demonstrating what we do with such threats. The courage which is daily being displayed on the ravaged soil of Korea is an example for the hundreds of millions all over the world who will fight for peace. It provides a mighty lesson. It teaches us that the decaying flower of imperialism is rotting on the vine of history, and in fresh bloom is a new flower with all the vitality of youth, a blend of national independence and internationalism. It explains that the strength of awakened people can meet and defeat any imperialist onslaught.

As to concrete measures, we must continue to spread the influence of the World Peace Council to every corner of the globe. We must make that influence part of the everyday life of the people, to wipe out any complacency or despondency in the fight for peace. They have lost faith in the United Nations because the warmongers have twisted it out of recognizable shape. We must revive the light and hope that the U.N. evoked upon its inception. We must show that war is not inevitable, that there is a powerful international organization which stands behind that idea —the World Peace Council.

We must connect the fight for peace with all other struggles on the national and local levels—for increased production in the people's countries; for civil liberties and against the oncoming fascism in capitalist countries; for independence in the colonial countries; for lifting the standard of living in every country. All of these questions are important and directly linked with world peace and peaceful coexistence.

Partisans of Peace! Our task is clear! Rally all those who declare themselves for peace behind the World Peace Council! Lead the struggle for peaceful coexistence! Lead the struggle to write in the annals of our time, "PEACE—what joys you unfold!"

INTERVIEW GIVEN TO THE CORRESPONDENT OF THE "RUDE PRAVO"

June 10, 1951

1. What is the importance of China in the struggle for world peace?

    In evaluating the forces for peace in the world, it can be said that since October 1, 1949, the founding day of the People's Republic of China, the possibility for securing world peace was greatly strengthened. On that day, 475 million people declared the New China. Since that day they have emerged as a united, organized and potent force, stepping to the side of the Soviet Union, the people's democracies and the other elements for peace, in the struggle to prevent imperialist aggression and world war. This was one of the most momentous shifts in behalf of humanity that has taken place in the history of the world.

2. What is the importance of the unity of the Chinese people and the construction of New China in the struggle for world peace?

    Warmongers would do well to recognize that their conception of China and the Chinese people is antiquated and erroneous. Never before in our entire history has China been as united as she is today under the leadership of Chairman Mao Tsetung, the Chinese Communist Party and the Central People's Government. Never before have our people been so filled with love for their motherland. Never before have they entered with such enthusiasm, such creativeness and such energy into the tasks of reconstructing our country. This indicates that our progress will be recorded in leaps and bounds, as there is already plenty of evidence to testify. A united China daily growing more powerful, daily reinforces the camp of peace.

3. What is the importance of the Stalin International Peace Prizes in the struggle for world peace?

The Stalin International Peace Prizes are important for many reasons. In the first place, they demonstrate that the mighty Soviet Union is in the forefront of the struggle to prevent war. These peace awards are in sharp contrast to the billions of dollars which are being awarded in war contracts to the armament-making "bosses" of the United States, Great Britain, France and other countries. In the second place, these prizes give the lie to the bleatings of the warmongers that their present race to rearm is a defensive measure against the Soviet Union. These prizes expose the true aggressors to the scrutiny of the world, by throwing a bright light into the dark hole of Wall Street wherein the plots are hatched to wage war on all the peoples. Thirdly, the Stalin International Peace Prizes are important because they come from a land where the projects of Communism are underway, and these are a vision of the future for all of mankind. Lastly, these prizes are important to the struggle for world peace because they bear the name of Stalin, leader of all working people and the very personification of peace.

THE INSPIRATION OF THE CHINESE PEOPLE

Statement Issued on the 30th Anniversary of
the Chinese Communist Party

July 1, 1951

Today, on its Thirtieth Anniversary, the Chinese Communist Party has risen to new heights in the minds and hearts of the people. This is the result of its strict adherence to the people's cause and its unwavering faith in the people's strength.

The Chinese Communist Party has evoked unparalleled respect from all sections of the population. As part of this, it has stimulated in us a love for our country and people such as China has never experienced before. I have but to cite one example.

During the Anti-Japanese War, there were constant campaigns and pleas to the medical personnel of our country to assist in the struggle against the invaders by servicing the soldiers at the front. The response to those calls was very poor indeed, the great majority of doctors, nurses and other technicians remaining in the cities to enjoy lucrative practices and forgetting the sufferings of the wounded. What a different picture we see today! With our land once again threatened by imperialist aggression, the doctors, nurses and others have immediately replied to the call, have followed closely on the heels of the courageous Chinese People's Volunteers to treat and heal them and their valiant Korean comrades-in-arms. This amazing difference in attitude and action is directly attributable to the deep feeling we have now for the party which leads our people's government. It is by far the prevalent feeling of our entire nation.

It is important to analyse why the Chinese Communist Party has awakened this sense of responsibility in all of us.

We notice first that the Chinese Communist Party is close to the masses of workers and peasants. In fact, it is part of them. It thoroughly understands them and when it acts it does so only in their behalf. Consequently, when the Communist Party takes a step, it has the sympathy and support of the overwhelming masses of the people.

A second cornerstone of the Chinese Communist Party's success is its united front policy. It is this distinguishing between friend and enemy on all levels —individual to individual, party to party and country to country—that has solidified all the democratic forces, those within the nation as well as the international friends of China. This policy has provided the base for unrelenting attacks against the enemies of the people. It has provided the base for sincere cooperation with the friends. This policy has in the past hewn out victory after victory. It will do likewise in the future.

Acting from these two basic concepts, the historic achievements of the Communist Party and its members set the example. From them we learn how to face unflinchingly our mistakes and resolutely set out to correct them. From them we learn the value of unceasing study and the necessity to lift our political levels as persons and as a nation. From them we learn what it means to love our country and make our maximum contribution to it.

In other words, the mainspring in the accomplishment of the Chinese revolution has been the policies and perseverance of the Chinese Communist Party under the leadership of Chairman Mao Tse-tung.

Now our nation faces tasks which are just as formidable as succeeding in revolution. Actually, they are a continuation of that struggle. First, we have to defend our motherland and our neighbors from imperialist invasion. Second, we have to consolidate and further develop people's rule over the entire land. Third, we must continue to make steady advances in our reconstruction. Once again, in determining the correct path to take, we will look to the leadership of the Chinese Communist Party. The breadth of its Thirtieth Anniversary celebration reveals what a great following the Communist Party has, how it inspires by its self-sacrifice and devotion to cause. This great unity predetermines that the New China will overcome all obstacles and achieve the utmost success in its national tasks. With these successes in hand, it will that much more strengthen the struggle for world peace.

Long live the Chinese Communist Party!

Long live Chairman Mao, leader of the Chinese people!

MESSAGE ON THE FOUNDING OF THE KAPURTHALA BRANCH OF THE INDIA-CHINA FRIENDSHIP ASSOCIATION

August 1951

Dear Friends:

It is indeed good news to learn that the people of Kapurthala are instituting a branch of the India-China Friendship Association. The Chinese people extend their hands in warm welcome and voice the ardent wish that the ties between our two great countries grow ever closer and stronger. Your action in starting this branch so soon after the founding of the Association proves that this is the path we are taking.

The Kapurthala district especially is much akin to China. Both of our peoples love the land, love to labor on it, to nurture the good earth so that it may return a bountiful life to the masses. Both of our peoples love knowledge, love to apply science to factory and field, to wrest the utmost from nature's products for the masses. Both of our peoples have a spirit of militancy, a determination to see justice done for and by the masses.

With such a broad area of similarity, the people of Kapurthala, jointly with all of India, and the people of China are sure to become firm and fast friends.

Such a friendship is a vital segment in the struggle against imperialist threats and aggression. It is a steel link in the great association of all peoples who want peace and peaceful construction in Asia and the whole world. Let us then dedicate ourselves and our energies to the development of India-China friendship.

Long live India-China friendship!

ACCEPTANCE SPEECH FOR THE INTER-
NATIONAL STALIN PEACE PRIZE

Peking

September 18, 1951

Mr. Chairman, Fellow Partisans of Peace:

This is no small moment in a person's life to be
awarded a prize for striving to fulfill one's obligation
to humanity, for struggling to achieve enduring peace.
It is an exceptional and profound honor to be associated
with the great name of Stalin in that struggle, to be
included in the company of men and women who have
carved an unusual niche in history by their fight for
peace. I am deeply moved and this is an occasion I
will long remember and cherish.

I will remember tonight and hold it dear not only
for what it means to me personally, but also for the
honor it accords the Chinese people. One does not work
for peace singlehanded, but rather expresses the desires
and hopes of the masses of people and acts jointly with
them. Thus, I accept this International Stalin Peace
Prize in the name of my countrymen, who in the past
100 years, and especially in the last thirty, have seen
their land and their neighbors' repeatedly ravaged by
war. I accept this prize in the name of a people who
since October 1, 1949, have tasted the joy of liberation,

national unity and unprecedented organization for peaceful construction. I accept this prize in the name of one-fourth of mankind, who, as a result of their experiences, have in firm determination joined the ranks of the partisans for world peace.

The Chinese people have given ample evidence of their stand. Over 223 million signatures were affixed to the Stockholm Appeal. This was exceeded by the 344,053,057 people, or over 72 per cent of the population, who have signified that they want a peace pact between the five great powers, and 339,903,092 people, or over 71 per cent, who voted against the U.S. rearmament of Japan. But even if this is not convincing enough, you have only to witness the herculean accomplishments of the Chinese people in reconstructing our nation. These symbolize without question how we treasure peace. If in a few short years we could emancipate the land for hundreds of millions of peasants, stimulate agricultural production to the point of self-sufficiency and beyond; if we could achieve in industry and trade the conditions for complete rehabilitation and further development; if we could simultaneously undertake gigantic, fundamental public construction projects, just imagine what we could do with a period of prolonged world tranquillity! Such a future would hold no limits for New China!

Because we wholeheartedly want such a future, the Chinese people have also given ample evidence of their courage in protecting peace. Along with their Korean comrades-in-arms, the Chinese Volunteers have shown that for this high purpose we are ready to shed our blood. No greater demonstration could be made in the name of peace. It is at the same time a demonstration of our unwilting perseverance in the face of imperialist aggression and our unequivocal intention to beat it back whenever it threatens our people's domain.

In the momentous struggle of building up our land, resisting American aggression, aiding Korea and protecting our homes, it is quite obvious to the Chinese people who stand constantly by our side and upon whose warm solicitude we can always count. It is with good reason that our farmers and workers call their Soviet friends "Big Brother", and look to Stalin as the greatest leader of all the peace forces. Throughout the long years of our revolutionary struggle, this bond between us was welded. Now today, our unity with the peace-loving Soviet people and our admiration for their brilliant leader are stronger than ever.

This unbreakable unity is based on our mutual appreciation for people's rule and peace. It is like a new star which has risen in the heavens and which shines with the brightness of the first magnitude. For this is an historical alignment that has changed the whole course of world relationships. The solidarity of the Soviet Union and People's China, in union with other progressive countries, represents a basic mass of land and peoples for peace such as never existed before. It combines the amazing accomplishments of the Soviet Union over the past thirty-three years with the recent rapid upsurge of China and other liberated nations. As the fundamental base in the struggle for peace, it has unparalleled might. It is the double assurance that the forces of peace will in the end prevail.

While this is the bright area of the world in which we live, there is another side from which emanates

gloom and cynicism, from which sounds forth a constant
barrage that war is inevitable. The unwanted and unreasonable leadership of the United States keeps this
group of lands in tow. There appropriations for the
people's welfare and culture are slashed to a pittance,
while those for war preparations reach unheard of
figures. This causes glee among the chiefs of a favored
few corporations as they have a feast of profits. But
it taxes the people until they are grim-faced and frustrat-
ed. There also a mockery is made of democracy. The
people's leaders are jailed merely for having an idea
in their heads, and those who sincerely utter the word
"peace" are treated as common criminals. At the same
time, the people are kept divided and impotent by
planned hate campaigns, especially in the United States
where they result in the legal murder of Willie McGees
because they are people of color.

But there is a limit to the people's patience and
even in this hysterical, foreboding sector, the penetrating
rays of peace and sanity valiantly struggle to throw
back the darkness. For all of their repression, in their
own bailiwicks, the warmongers are not having everything the way they want it. The U.S. banker-generals
may be able to snap their whips and have governments
jump, but when it comes to whipping the people into
line for their war plans, that is another question. The
people balk. The reason is that they oppose and abhor
war. They want peace.

The recent French and Italian elections indicate
that truth cannot be spelled with a dollar mark. The
U.S.-backed governments and their fascist cohorts used
gerry-mandering, vote rigging, threats and actual viol-

ence. But in spite of these, the electorate in those two countries cast large and most significant votes for the parties which stand for people's rule and peace. In Spain, over one million workers went out on strike against hunger caused by Franco oppression and unofficial inclusion in the Atlantic Pact for war. Once more the cities of heroic Spain have echoed with the cry, "Death to fascism!" In Japan and Western Germany, the people have evidenced their refusal to be the cannon-fodder in U.S. plans for world conquest. In England, the wave of protests mounts. The people voice their indignation at government officials displaying truckling subservience as junior partners to the United States. In the colonial and semi-colonial lands, there is a deep stirring. It signifies that the oppressed see the direct connection between their independence struggles and world peace, recognize that the threat to one is a threat to the other.

We can see that in the United States itself, although not fully organized, the people express their discontent with the Wall Street clique. We saw the joy expressed at the dismissal of the warmonger MacArthur. We witnessed the support they gave the calls for peace in Korea—Johnson's resolution in the Senate and Y. A. Malik's speech at the United Nations. This support developed spontaneously, despite news blackout and distortion in the so-called "free press". Radio commentators, news columnists, public opinion polls, notwithstanding their monopoly control, are forced to admit that the people want the war in Korea ended. Churchmen, professors, workers, the epic American Peace Congress with 5,000 delegates—all further report that the people in the

United States want overall peace, the same as do men and women throughout the entire world. As the casualty figure in Korea mounts, as more of their youngsters are pressed into uniform and spread all over Europe and Asia, American mothers, fathers and wives are frantic with anxiety. They are increasingly becoming cognizant of the need to struggle for world peace and are voicing their sentiments.

However, the agents of destruction have no ear for the word "peace" as they rush pell-mell to rearm. They have stepped up the instigation of fascism at home to stifle any resistance. They have twisted their youth into fascist beasts and unleashed them overseas. These few with the insatiate appetites, these would-be world rulers defy the wishes of their own and other peoples as they attempt to summon enough strength to start a war. They are out to pulverize the idea of people's rule, to ruthlessly censor from all minds the people's struggle to live as human beings can and should live, cooperatively and at peace. This is their morbid purpose, their fanatical frenzy.

But J. V. Stalin has told us that at this time war is not inevitable. We can still avert this terrible catastrophe if the people take the task of protecting peace into their own hands. When we see all around us how the people love and desire peace, we know this is the truth. But we must translate that truth into action. We must establish a broad endorsement for the concept of peaceful coexistence by cutting across all political, national and religious lines. If the world's common men and women, the ones who bear the sufferings of war, unite in demanding sincere negotiation in place of force to settle differences, then there will be no war. This endorsement and action can materialize by obtaining the widest consideration for the World Peace Council program, by obtaining universal recognition of the significance of a peace pact among the five great powers. The unified voice of the peoples can clear the way for a world existing in harmony between all nations. The entire human race will then exist only to build and enjoy the fruits of its labor. We must carry the struggle to that point of achievement.

CHINA'S GREAT MASS MOVEMENTS

Written for "People's China"

October 1, 1951

It has been two years since the founding of the People's Republic of China. This is a mere moment, but a whisk of time in history. Yet, in that short period, not only have the Chinese people asserted themselves within their own realm, but our Republic has become one of the most stable, progressive and powerful nations in the world.

There are several prime movers in this epic success. The first of these is the profound leadership of Chairman Mao Tse-tung, the Chinese Communist Party and the Central People's Government. The second is the patriotic fervor of the Chinese masses, their recognition of the necessity for struggle, their willingness to undergo hardship and sacrifice to achieve independence, people's democracy and the remoulding of our country.

During these two years, our leadership and our people, acting as one, have launched a series of mass movements which for size, scope and accomplishment are unprecedented in China's long history. Agrarian Reform, Suppression of Counter-revolutionary Elements, and the Resist American Aggression, Aid Korea, Protect

Home and Defend Country Movement—these have touched the lives of every person in the land, in every occupation and profession, of every shade of political and religious thought. The overwhelming participation of the Chinese people in these movements laid the foundation upon which our Republic proceeded from one success to the next, from one degree of strength to the next highest. It has been these three great mass movements which consolidated the victories of the Chinese revolution and provided the basis for future advances. As well, they have served notice that we will not allow our gains to be snatched from us.

The Agrarian Reform

The thorough and speedy implementation of agrarian reform has been a momentous victory. Already areas containing two-thirds of China's rural population, upwards of 310 million people, have experienced this elevating struggle. It is anticipated that by the spring of 1952, this movement will be heading toward completion on our mainland. The only exceptions will be special regions, many of them inhabited by minority races and groups, where the process will proceed more slowly and according to the local conditions. In the main, we can now say that in our nation the land belongs to the tillers. We can rejoice on this second anniversary of our People's Republic in all of the good things this means to us at present and for the future.

China's agrarian reform has been an intrinsic aspect of her revolution. The conditions of our peasants had to be among the first things changed in the old society if we were to have people's democracy, prosperity and the strength to defend ourselves. It was by the oppression of our farmers that feudalism held sway. And it was feudalism which opened the gap through which imperialism gained entry to our land and drove us to poverty and backwardness. Therefore, agrarian reform was provided for in our Gommon Program. The law defining the process of confiscation of landlord's land for distribution to the landless and land-poor peasants was derived from the vast experience of the Chinese Communist Party. This law has been enforced with signal success. In other words, the Chinese people knew what they had to do and they did it with certainty and firmness.

Agrarian reform has all of the characteristics of revolutionary struggle. We place our reliance on the masses of poor peasants and farm laborers. We promote unity with the middle peasants and effect the neutralization of the rich peasants. With the exception of those who committed criminal acts, we allow former landlords enough land so that they can maintain their lives and reform through labor. We do not liquidate them physically, but we definitely do away with what they represent— feudal exploitation and all of its manifestations. Through agrarian reform we put the final signature and seal on the death warrant of the feudal system. The landlords cease to exist as an economic and political class. Rural life comes completely under the control of the masses of peasants.

Because of its very complicated nature, agrarian reform is carefully prepared and executed. The actual work is implemented step by step. If an area is not immediately ready, the movement is withheld until the masses of farmers understand and demand it. Once started, the differentiation of the class nature of the various farmers, a most complex and extremely important work, has to be handled with skill and accuracy. This differentiation is based on the multiform relationships of the people to the means of production. All of the varied kinds of productive relationships between the exploited and the exploiters have to be considered and dealt with accordingly.

It is easy to roll off the tongue that 310 million people have gone through the land reform. But it is infinitely difficult to describe all of the hard work that went into that struggle. Behind the figure stands the indefatigable work of the land reform cadres, their ability to meet all sorts of problems, their patience with and understanding of our peasants, their coolheadedness and courage in the face of danger.

We must also note that the victory of agrarian reform would have been impossible without the ardent support of the peasants. This was expressed through their participation in the Peasants' Associations. It was through these organizations that the farmers themselves carried out the verification of available land and saw to it that the distribution was fair. It was in this work that the Peasants' Associations practically demonstrated the meaning of collective strength and the application of democratic procedure. From land reform the peasants move on to the administration of their own village affairs, then to districts, counties, up to the highest bodies in the land. This explains why there are over 84 million members in the associations, with some villages having as high as 50 per cent of their inhabitants enrolled. This total membership includes an impressive number of women, for whom the land reform has really meant emancipation by giving them their own land and economic independence.

From the Peasants' Associations stem the enlightened political outlook, the keen evaluation of science for the land and the vision of China's future farmers— the collective farmers.

Soaring production is the result of giving the farmers the land and heightening their political activity. This, in fact, is the aim of agrarian reform, to release the latent talents and creative forces which will lead to the attainment of self-sufficiency in agricultural products. This provides the basis for industrialization. Such was the dream of Sun Yat-sen. Such has been the fundamental platform of the Chinese Communist Party. Such is the working program of the Central People's Government. It is the correct and only solution to China's poverty.

Our Northeast and older liberated areas are demonstrative proof. There the great majority of the rural population have become middle peasants and very little difference separates the poor farmers from them. In general, their lives are daily improving. They have surplus grain in their bins. That means an increasing demand for manufactured goods. This demand is China's guarantee for our industrial reconstruction.

Thus, the great land reform mass movement affects the majority of China's population. It is the life-blood of our existence today and our foundation for tomorrow.

The Suppression of Counter-Revolutionary Elements

The second great mass movement—the suppression of counter-revolutionary elements—has accomplished several vital tasks with one stroke. It has effectually exposed those who would destroy our new life, apprehended and punished them. In the process it has given our people a deeper sense of unity and immeasurably fortified the belief in their own collective strength.

We people of advanced countries understand and practise the principle of leniency. But we have also learned that that principle has a limit. If we are too lenient, the bad elements take advantage of us and the nation suffers losses as a result. Revolutionary cadres are murdered; crops set afire; factories sabotaged; the people disturbed by wild rumors; friendly ties between our peoples threatened. This we cannot tolerate.

For the last thirty years, the Chinese people have been struggling for their revolution, fighting to create a people's domain. Many an uphill battle has been fought, many a revolutionary lost. Could we allow all of this tremendous effort, suffering and sacrifice to be expended in vain? Could we allow the success of our revolution to go unguarded? Of course not. Chairman Mao has taught us that unless we take steps to wipe out the activities of counter-revolutionary elements, the people's state is placed in jeopardy. Therefore, our people have demanded protection and preventive measures.

The government has answered the call, this as part of its responsibility to the people, to maintain their safety and the revolutionary order. In February of this

year, a law was promulgated which, in conjunction with
Article 7 of the Common Program and other directives,
sets up a thorough procedure to uncover those who
actively work against the people, to detail and verify
their guilt beyond question, to give them a fair trial
and to mete out deserved punishment. This law was
heartily applauded by all democratic parties and individuals and by the people's organizations. It was
widely supported by the general population, who en-
thusiastically joined with the public security forces in
bringing to book the unscrupulous elements.

Peasants and workers, students and professors, industrial and commercial circles, housewives, cultural
workers, the various religious circles—all took part in
this campaign. Participation on such a grand scale
attests to the fact that the Chinese people are becoming
politically awake. They recognize that the agents of
imperialism and reaction are a mortal danger to peace,
both within the country and throughout the world. Thus,
our people closed their ranks and mobilized their might
to strike these enemies down.

The people were active on every level of the movement to suppress counter-revolutionary elements. They
hunted down and turned over the criminals. They aided
in the painstaking certification of charges and evidence.
The people sat on panels and rendered judgment. Then
they joined by the millions in the public reviewing
meetings.

This was very involved work. It took time and
patience. But our alert public security cadres and the
people had that patience and took the necessary time
to track down every clue, some investigations covering

several provinces. Every effort was made to be absolutely certain that the correct person was brought to trial. No accusation was accepted which could not be backed by indisputable fact. Every fact was checked and checked again. This testifies as to the responsible attitude which the Chinese people have toward justice and to the seriousness with which they attacked the menace of counter-revolutionary elements.

The results of this campaign have visibly lifted the spirit of our whole population. In the cities, although many of them had been liberated for two years, some sections of the people were not experiencing the full joy of liberation. The criminals, an inheritance from the old society, continued brutally to oppress them. They were typical gangsters, operating in our streets, infiltrating into our factories and lording it over our workers on the wharves. But now these bad elements have been swept clean and our city people are truly emancipated. Now our workers go about their jobs with free minds. They launch into their problems with a new vigor, determined to keep their homes and places of work secure for all time, and to keep the production mounting.

The farmers too have been further liberated by this mass movement. They have rooted out the skulking, plotting feudal remnants, the ones who tried to burn the crops and those who thought they could reverse the revolution by the assassination of rural political workers. Now the land is secure and the peasants organized to protect it. Now they can throw their whole hearts into production. This is especially a new experience in the more recently liberated areas.

The Chinese people, while counting their gains, recognize that the suppression of counter-revolutionary elements is a long-term struggle. It will exist as long as imperialism exists, as long as there is a base from which these criminals can be supplied and sent to harass our people's land. Our policy then is as follows: be ever vigilant; to those agents who cut their imperialist and reactionary ties completely and sincerely repent for their misdeeds, the people will still be generous; but for those who persist in staining their hands with the blood of the people, we will relentlessly seek them out and destroy them.

In summary, this campaign has been another significant defeat for the imperialists and the feudal elements. The only persons they could enlist from our hundreds of millions to carry out their dirty work were a few scoundrels with long criminal records. But the people have control of the situation. By thus enhancing our inner strength, by guaranteeing that China remains in the hands of the people, we have contributed once again, in another wise and in increased measure, to our country's future and proportionately to the security of world peace.

Resist American Aggression, Aid Korea, Protect Home and Defend Country

The daily lives of the Chinese people are today immersed in the mass movement which resists American aggression, aids the Korean people, protects our homes and defends our country. This mobilization is carried out by the China Peace Committee, since it is impossible to separate the fight for peace from the actual threat of an imperialist aggressor. This great patriotic movement links the safety of our motherland with the protests against the rearming of Japan and Western Germany, with the demand that the five leading powers sign a peace pact. It puts the Chinese people, side by side with the Korean people, on the very first line defending peace.

It is quite natural that we go to the aid of Korea. In the first place the relationship between our two countries has a history of several thousand years. In the modern era, we were especially close during the Anti-Japanese War. Then, as now, our two peoples had a common imperialist enemy. Many Korean sons served in our famous Eighth Route Army. Many of them laid down their lives for China's emancipation. Therefore, our comradeship has deep roots.

In the second place, North Korea is a people's land. As such, it is part of the world peace camp. We could not sit by indifferently and watch the warmongers swallow it up.

Another consideration was that the Chinese people are thoroughly familiar with the tactic of "Grab Korea First". We recall with deepest wrath that the Japanese militarists used this same route to invade our Northeast.

Therefore, we had only one course open to us— to help our neighbor and thereby help ourselves and world peace at the same time. We organized the Resist American Aggression, Aid Korea mass movement and our nation has risen as one. We support the front with manpower, our volunteers with inspiring heroism notifying the aggressors that they are held accountable for

their mad destruction. We support the front with resources, both through increased production and a huge
donation campaign. Our people have never acted with
such despatch and force in their entire history. An
example of this is the increased production through
labor emulation, a mass movement in its own right
which has spread over the entire land through the
medium of patriotic pacts.

China's working class realizes that the fighter at
the front and the worker at his bench are intimately
connected, that the factories are a battlefield also. Therefore, they are fighting to raise production, lower the
cost per unit and lift the quality. This movement, at the
latest count, had 2,230,000 workers with signed patriotic
pacts, and 11,159 groups which are following the lead
of Ma Heng-chang's brigade. It has reached every
variety of factory and enterprise.

China's workers are simultaneously demonstrating
that they are the builders of a new epoch. Not only is
the labor emulation drive a primary force in the Resist
American Aggression, Aid Korea campaign, but it is also
preparing China's industry for the future. Workers
and technicians no longer accept old methods and
systems without critical examination. Now they reverse
the order of things and they become the masters of the
machines. They approach the problem of lifting the
production level with a scientific-revolutionary attitude,
to keep what is good of the old while unremittingly
searching for the new. In addition, the old way of keeping a good idea for one's own benefit has been discarded. Today a new idea must serve the people and the
more it is broadcast to other sections and plants, the

better. This outlook has led both to a greater unity of the whole working class, and to the development of a progressive type of worker, one who uses his brain as well as his brawn. It has also led to the swift promotion of workers to administrative posts. For example, in the mining industry last year nearly 7,000 miners became directors, technicians and administrative officers.

At the same time that production rises and more support goes to the front, the lives of the workers improve with heartening rapidity. There is no inflation to rob them of their wages, consequently they eat and dress better and advance their housing conditions. The medical and other benefits of labor insurance are gradually expanding to include more workers. Safety and sanitation on the job are constantly being lifted to higher levels. Also, not only can the workers' children have schooling, but the workers themselves can make up for lost time through the increasing educational and cultural facilities. All in all, the lives of our workers have completely changed, on the job and in their homes.

This circumstance is possible in China today because we are a nation where labor is honored, where those who work are the masters. This has nurtured our workers politically. Through labor emulation they demonstrate their comprehension of the spirit and principle of internationalism, how it is part of protecting our homes and defending our country.

The drive to contribute directly to the front through donations also shows the strength of New China. We can see that not only do we have the capacity to improve the living of the people, but we can also put cannon and shell, tanks and airplanes into the hands of our fighters who use them for the defence of peace. We have seen how the workers contribute. But the farmers contribute their share also through increased production. And non-productive workers—teachers, shop-keepers, relief-workers, cultural workers—all can do something extra or give funds to support the front. To date this drive has resulted in 2,481 airplanes being contributed, in addition to a number of field pieces, anti-aircraft guns and tanks.

The facts on the battlefield and the facts here at home in this great move to resist American aggression and aid Korea, illustrate what is meant by the phrase, "The new, aroused Asia". They prove that the mightiest of the imperialist powers, aided by a bevy of satellites, can be completely defeated. The struggle may be long and it may be hard, but there is no question as to the outcome. The Chinese and Korean peoples will win. This is a righteous war for our very existence and for the well-being of all mankind.

Conclusion

The Agrarian Reform, the Suppression of the Counter-revolutionary Elements, the Resist American Aggression, Aid Korea, Protect Home and Defend Country campaign —these three great mass movements have made the first two years of our People's Republic among the most glorious our nation has ever known. We have added our strength to the struggle for peace and dealt its chief enemy a hard blow. We have added our strength to the struggle of all Asian peoples as they surge forth toward independence. On this Second Anniversary of our People's Republic, let us take note of these significant accomplishments and prepare ourselves for the next step forward.

WELFARE WORK AND WORLD PEACE

Published in the First Issue of
"China Reconstructs"

October, 1951

There is a direct correlation between world peace
and welfare work. They run parallel to one another,
prosper under the same conditions and deteriorate
from the same causes. Build peace and you enhance
welfare. Destroy peace and you eliminate welfare. It
follows, therefore, that the attitude of a government
towards war and peace determines the welfare program
it plans and operates for its people.

The unprecedented progress of welfare work in
the new China this past year reflects our ardent desire
for peace. For example, labor insurance has become
the law of our land for the first time. Its many benefits
are gradually spreading, reaching millions of workers
and their families. In other sectors of our national
life, giant and fundamental solutions have been undertaken for age-old problems, such as the floods with
which the Huai River has plagued our people for thirty
centuries. Child-care, medical services, workers'
housing and modern facilities for workers' districts,
rural services of many varieties—all are growing and
raising the living standards of the people right before

our eyes. Such progress can only result from a policy which prizes peace and pursues the aim of peaceful relations among all nations.

We have such a policy. It arises directly from the needs of the Chinese people and the progress that it has brought is the result of their strength. The new welfare program of our country emphasizes the use of the people's might to overcome all problems, a basic approach clearly formulated at last year's All-China People's Relief Conference by Vice Premier Tung Pi-wu. In his detailed speech on that occasion, Vice Premier Tung described how welfare work is now in the hands of the people, how it has become part of a tremendous overall reconstruction effort and how it is founded on the principle of self-reliance.

Such policies, principles and progress are possible only in nations that are truly independent—nations that allow no infractions of their own right of self-determination while at the same time seeking coopera-tion with all who respect that right. In fact, the effort a government puts into people's welfare is not only an accurate measure of its devotion to peace;—it is also a reflection of its status among the nations of the world.

We know that in countries which are still in colonial or semi-colonial bondage, welfare work for the people is either nil or exists merely as a deceptive showcase, serving only a tiny percentage of those who need it. Vivid confirmation of this may be found even in the reports submitted by the colony-owning powers themselves to economic and trusteeship organs of the United Nations, although these obviously put the best possible face on a situation that is actually much worse than they admit.

History has shown too that when the rulers of any country seek to perpetuate colonial slavery or to dominate the entire world by force, their own people are among the first sufferers, as exploitation rises and welfare programs disappear to make way for arms budgets. Published facts on "wage-freezes", skyrocketing prices, speeding up of workers, material shortages and falling educational and health expenditures in the United States, Britain and Western Europe, provide many illustrations of this axiom right now, in 1951.

On the other hand, rising living standards and welfare provisions are evident in every country where the people rule, where state power serves the majority instead of small minorities either domestic or foreign. Whether we look at China, or the Soviet Union, or Central and Eastern Europe, we find that the damage of war has been repaired, new industries are growing, wages have risen and prices fallen in the last few years. Welfare and educational facilities, both in terms of total budget outlays and in terms of tangible improvements in the lives of working people, are increasing steadily and very fast. At the same time, mutual aid among these countries helps each one to accelerate its gains. All these facts are not only recorded in their own reports but admitted in serious studies by persons and groups who are not at all well disposed towards them. Here again the economic publications of the United Nations can be cited.

That China is on the side of peace, yet at the same time able both to defend herself and help her neighbors, is of special interest to the other peoples of Asia. They have seen how our peasants are now the masters of their own fields, how our workers have become masters in some of our factories and equal partners in others. They have seen how this has released the creative and productive forces of our people so that the output of material wealth in China grows both generally and in terms of each worker. They know that, in two years, we have not only solved our food problem but begun to export grain, something unheard of in the past. They have witnessed how our welfare work has grown to be an integral part of the nation's life, developing in the healthy atmosphere of a country that controls its own destiny.

Such is the status of welfare work in the People's Republic of China, which is one of the staunchest bulwarks of world peace. Our people have absolutely nothing to gain from war. Only peace is in our interest; so that we may further develop our services to the people and enlarge our contribution to the welfare of the world.

It should be clear too that the progress we have made is precious to us. Any aggressor will find that we will defend it with every ounce of our strength and courage. We will neither allow ourselves to be oppressed nor deny aid to others who suffer oppression. We stand for a peace among equals, with each people determining its own life.

We desire friendship and cooperation with all countries and peoples who are willing to live at peace and trade for mutual benefit, regardless of what their form of government may be or what views they may hold.

This outlook, uniting a country of 475,000,000 people, helps as never before to guarantee that peace will conquer war all over the world. It menaces no other nation and no honest person anywhere. It helps all who are working and fighting to make mankind's dearest dreams of peace and well-being come true in our own day.

FOR PEACE IN ASIA, THE PACIFIC REGIONS AND THE WORLD

July 31, 1952

The Peace Conference of the Asian and Pacific Regions to be held in Peking this September is taking place at a most vital time. Peace is far from being an academic question anywhere in the world today. It is most assuredly an urgent, practical problem in this part of the globe. Several wars are actually being waged here. Japan, against the expressed will of its people, is being remilitarized by the United States and prepared once again as a base for aggression; crude, ruthless economic and political pressure is being exerted by the American government on certain Latin American and Asian countries in an effort to force them into the war camp; American generals continue to pour salt into a nasty wound of their own making, further frustrating the Korean truce talks, stepping up their criminal bombing of the aged, the women and children in Korean cities already reduced to rubble, applying their so-called military pressure by bombing peacetime installations. This is in addition to their already mountain-high list of iniquities, topped by the most vicious—germ warfare.

The brutal, aggressive character of these policies in the Far East, plus the recklessness of recent acts of the Western powers in Europe, especially in regard to Germany, have caused a serious deterioration in the international situation. This is a circumstance which gravely disturbs many people all over the world. Each successive blow has increased the alarm and anxiety, the indignation with which they view the spectacle. Each person visualizes the mounting threat to himself: his home gutted or his loved ones lost. Each patriot visualizes the threat to his country: the chance of harnessing nature and building a happy life for the people instantaneously disappearing in a burst of fire. As a result, for an increasing number of people in East and West, a task has arisen: how to meet and stop this threat.

To give life, to build, to enhance—these are the main missions in man's life. For these, peace is the essential condition. But this peace, which we need and so ardently desire, has to be won. This we know. The small band of the war-minded are hard-headed and irresponsible. They do not easily give up their plots for profit. As we have seen on many occasions, they think nothing of defying the wishes of the people and are ready to fabricate their pretext for war or its extension at any moment. This means that the forces of peace, the ordinary men and women in their hundreds of millions, must be alert, must firmly resist being led along the road to oblivion. We must make our voices heard; our demand to live peacefully side by side with all peoples and all nations must be transformed into loud and strong words. We must be active; as the

ideals of peace and cooperation are sounded in the many
tongues of the many nations, there must be mobilization
on all sides, in every country.   This is to say, that if we
are not to be side-tracked, tricked or pushed around by
the few who would destroy us, then the majority has to
organize itself further to preserve progress and civilization.

The importance of the Peace Conference of the
Asian and Pacific Regions in this regard cannot be over·
stated. The 500 delegates, representing 1,600 million
people, have a tremendous task to shoulder, but they
also have an opportunity to create what will undoubtedly
prove to be a central factor in preserving world peace.
Supported by the World Peace Council, which is the
greatest movement of its kind in the history of man, as
well as by the already established and rapidly growing
peace organizations of various countries, the conference
is in a position to make an unparalleled move towards
achieving unity for peace over the earth's most populous
area.

There is a wide base upon which this unity can be
constructed; that is, the great similarity of conditions
in this part of the world which has had an important
influence on how we view peace.

Peace is a concept with many aspects for the peoples of Asia and the Pacific. It means more than the
absence of general war. Our long and bitter experience
has been that, even in times when there was no general
war, this by no means applied to those countries suffer·
ing the oppression of imperialism. There may have
been peace elsewhere, but in our countries imperialism
was threatening our very existence. Most of our na-

tions have a glorious past, great potentialities for a rich economy, a high level of cultural attainment. But imperialism attempted to grind our past into dust; it did reduce many of our economies into stifling monocultures or simply to suppliers of raw material and cheap labour; it vitiated our culture and tried to substitute its own. This has been the way of imperialism in a great many places in Asia and the Pacific. It brought us a vast misery and ignorance, a terrible toll in lives and a cruel retardation. It has incurred the wrath of all of us.

To Asian and Pacific peoples, therefore, peace and national independence are so closely linked as to be indistinguishable. Peace must be founded on equality of all peoples and mutually advantageous dealings between all nations. This is possible only when each people runs its country without outside intervention, according to its own wishes and to its greatest benefit. This, in turn, is closely linked with the question of a peace in which all nations co-operate to the greatest benefit of the whole world, no matter how differently they may govern themselves or operate their economies.

This concept of peace is accepted far and wide among the peoples of Asia and the Pacific. You will find important parts of this view or all of it in all ranks —among workers, farmers, intellectuals, officials, commercial and industrial circles. It has become our fundamental understanding of the way things stand in the world today. It can be said that this understanding, stimulated by previous examples, has been further and immeasurably heightened by the victories of the Chinese people.

China, at one time in her recent history, was referred to as the "sick man of Asia." This was the feeling many had towards us, some in pity, others with jeers. There should be no question in anyone's mind that today such pity is inappropriate, and jeers testify only to fatal underestimation. For in three short years, the Chinese people have elevated their nation to its rightful place, as one of the leaders of the world. We have regained our national dignity. We have forged a new might. These earth-shaking accomplishments are due to our successful struggle for independence, to the fact that we have proclaimed and implemented a people's democracy. By these victories, by our giant strides in the reconstruction of our country, we have set a new standard for the peoples of Asia and the Pacific. We have given them a new outlook on their own problems.

The enhanced prestige that the Chinese people now enjoy has yet another cause—our unwavering stand for peace. Peace is part of our tradition as a nation and as a people. Throughout the thousands of years in which we Chinese have had relations with the peoples of Asia and the Pacific, we have never acted in a warlike manner. In this present period, peace is the basic tenet of the foreign policy of our People's Republic of China. We have demonstrated in every way that with us the seeking of peace is a serious pursuit. In carrying out the policies of our country, in the defence of our land, as organizations and individuals, it is always the quest for peace which guides and dominates our actions.

That the peoples of Asia and the Pacific regions recognize this fact is attested to by their sending representatives to our capital to take a new and historic step for peace. Peking, the blending of the old and the new, is a city born of the unity of the Chinese people. Now it serves as the birthplace of the new unity of the Asian and Pacific peoples in their struggle for harmony among the nations.

Thus, the Peace Conference of the Asian and Pacific Regions is the result of the general upsurge for peace throughout the world. The peoples represented will have a solid base for unity, since peace is what they demand and peace is part of the solution of their own national problems. And finally, the conference is to take place in a country, in a city and among a people dedicated to the preservation and protection of world tranquillity and cooperation. The results are bound to be grand and magnificent.

We can be sure that these results will be far different from those of another conference which has just taken place in this part of the world. I refer to the meetings which have been called by the United States government to form the so-called "Pacific Council." In these meetings they also talked peace, but in fact planned further aggression. In these meetings they also talked cooperation with "backward" nations, but in fact they set in motion more schemes to further enslave certain Asian and Pacific countries. In these meetings they also talked about equality of peoples, but in fact the terms of this "council" will be dictated by one power, its United States government.

It must be pointed out that the politicians of the United States who will lead this council of war do not in any way represent the people of that country. The people of the United States, in fact, could not even get

in at the door of that meeting. This is in sharp contrast to the way the Peace Conference of the Asian and
Pacific Regions will provide a platform from which can
be heard the true voice of the American people.

We sincerely hope that a large delegation can be
present to represent the people of the United States.
As members of a Pacific nation, Americans will have
a definite interest in what we decide, and they will be
able to make a definite contribution. The conference
will also give them an opportunity to learn what this
part of the world is thinking. Many terrible things
have been done in their name. They should learn the
truth about these acts. They should also learn, and I
am sure that we can impress them with the facts, that
the peoples of Asia and the Pacific make a clear distinction between them and the real perpetrators of those
acts.

We hope that representatives of the American
people can come to see us in the flesh, to gain first-hand
knowledge of the new developments which are taking
place. We want to assure them that there is no threat
to them or their way of life from us or from any of the
lands where the people rule. We think we can prove to
them that the threat is in their own midst, that their
enemy and ours is one and the same. We want the
American people to know that there are many reasons
why we should cooperate as peoples and as nations, but
that there is not one single reason why we should be
fighting each other.

Together with the American people, we of Asia and
the Pacific want to answer the question: "Who benefits
by the fighting in Korea, Viet-Nam and Malaya, by the

unilateral treaties which keep other countries as colonies, by rearmament, by restriction of trade and cultural intercourse?" Together with them, we want to work out the real correlation between the fact that U.S. corporations registered a profit of 44.8 billion dollars in 1951, eight times the peace-time figure before World War II, and the fact that one-third of their average personal income is gobbled up by taxes. We know the direct relationship between all these things, and we think the representatives of the American people will agree with us.

In other words, we and they, and all peace-loving people face a common enemy, the handful of wilful men who profit from war. In the struggle against this enemy, for our existence and for peace, the peoples of Asia and the Pacific look upon the people of the United States as an ally, as a crucial ally. We hope they will join us in all their strength. We hope they will join us in working out the peace, and then in making this world a place of fruitful labour and joy, a safe and sound place for their children and ours. We will grasp their hands in this greatest of crusades, to make this our time one of the finest ages in the world's history.

Working together at the Peace Conference of the Asian and Pacific Regions, the representatives of many nations will forge the unity of all races, colours, creeds and religions for peace! Together we will lay the ground-work for the participation of Asian and Pacific peoples in the extraordinary Congress of the Peoples for Peace next December! Together we will make immense strides towards winning the world for the people!